ADVANCE PRAISE

"The description of Jerry's struggles to combine his inner work with outer environmentalist work makes this memoir a unique, readable, and ultimately valuable guide for others."

ED BEGLEY JR., actor, author, committed enviromentalist

"Absorbing, engaging, informative and inspiring, I loved Jerry's memoir, from the first page to the last. I am left feeling encouraged and enriched."

CATHERINE PARRISH, Chair, Pachamama Alliance, Founder, NextLevel Consulting

"...an engaging memoir, giving us a model of how to integrate spiritual growth and environmental activism into life, with the intention of shaping a career that can be of service to the well-being of humanity and the planet. As a neuroscientist who is also trying to advocate a broader view of consciousness with my fellow scientists, I appreciate his thoughtful efforts."

MARJORIE WOOLLACOTT, PhD, Professor, Institute of Neuroscience, University of Oregon, author of *Infinite Awareness: The Awakening of a Scientific Mind*

"...a delightful dive into the birth of the environmental, green building and sustainability movements. With wit, humor and beautiful insights he shares the challenges and gifts that arise from balancing our inner and outer lives."

ANDRÉS R EDWARDS, author of *Renewal* and *The Heart of Sustainability*

"An intrepid engineer learns how to take scientific principles and apply them to real world problems ... and a skeptic learns how to take spiritual principles and apply them to real world solutions. Becoming flexible. Overcoming obstacles. Pressing on to show others the way. This book is a journey full of joy."

SHAR MCBEE, author of *Leadership with a Twist of Yoga and To Lead is to Serve*

"Jerry Yudelson precisely connects the existential environmental crises we face with concrete action. He takes on the big questions like—*what is my purpose? And, how can I use my life to do good?* Jerry's memoir takes us on an environmental and spiritual journey through the radical 1960's that shaped him as a young man, to his quest to make a positive impact on the world through a career as an environmentalist that spanned government, private-sector entrepreneurship, and thought leadership. Jerry's story is a virtual history of the environmental movement and serves as an important totem for future environmental leaders who will follow the trail he blazed."

DREW SHULA, CEO, Verdical Group, Founder of the world's largest Net Zero event

"*The Godfather of Green* is a fitting title for this memoir (and a perfect nickname for Jerry Yudelson) because this story will show you what it means to walk the talk. The green building movement wouldn't be where it is today without Jerry and this journey of personal, spiritual and professional accomplishments shows how much of an impact he has made. You'll read 100 pages before you know it, drawn into the history of the green building movement, told by a true pioneer."

KELSEY MULLEN, Real Estate Investor

"Jerry Yudelson invites us along as he explores coming of age in the modern environmental movement. The story is amplified throughout by his search for spiritual meaning in a world challenged by ecological crisis. He offers a deeply personal account of the achievements and trials of that journey, beginning at a time when eco-activists and spiritual seekers were striking out on their own, without mileposts or even maps. Yudelson gifts us with a reassurance of what is possible at a time of pure discovery of both self and science, sharing those moments where logic and heart conspire but sometimes also clash."

DAVID SCHALLER, Retired EPA Environmental Scientist

"Jerry Yudelson has written a powerful, engrossing, and endearingly self-aware personal memoir. It is also an historically significant chronicle of the environmental movement by one of its chief leaders."

VICTORIA BETANCOURT, Lifetime Achievement Award Winner, National Association of Women Business Owners

"By taking us on his journey, Jerry Yudelson gives us a primer on how to effect positive change in our world. This is a generous open-hearted invitation to take on the challenge of our climate crisis."

JULIET MORAN, Founder, Open Eye Art, artist, writer, teacher and former Nike VP

"Jerry's integration of the classic and romantic elements to his being remind me of reading *Zen and the Art of Motorcycle Maintenance* in 1974. Unlike that book, Jerry's tale is not fictitious, it's a candid real-life reflection of his role in the evolution of sustainable design and development. The Godfather of Green may come across as an over-the-top title for anyone. However, read the book yourself and see if you don't agree with me that it's a fitting title for an individual who has done as much, if not more, than anyone to advance the proliferation of green buildings throughout the US and our precious Earth."

NATHAN GOOD, FAIA, Award-winning green architect

"Many of Jerry's revelations will startle you. Some, in my opinion, unveil secrets of the universe. His honesty, the richness of political and cultural context, and his plunges into the unknown blend in a flow that is easy to read. These elements made his memoir hard to put down, even when I wanted to dwell on what he said. Jerry Yudelson provides calming guidance in this climate-changing world through this compelling work: a book to savor."

SONJA PERSRAM, MBA, sustainability consultant

"Jerry is always ahead of his time paving the way on the road less traveled. I loved reading about his eco journey which also coincided with the development of a deep spiritual practice. Jerry's memoir is a must read for anyone looking to lead a purpose filled and passionate life."

DEVIN SAYLOR, Former Director of Sustainability, Skanska Europe

"An inspiring 'eco-spiritual odyssey' of his inner and outer journey, as he is touched by deep forces through his relationship with nature and his studies of eastern thought that began under Baba Muktananda. Jerry helps us understand how the climate crisis is not only a crisis of the environment but also of our souls when the health of the entire planet is as stake. He urges us to step up and face our biggest challenge."

RENIE KELLY, Real Estate Consultant, Encinitas, CA

"It is a rare occurrence when rock-solid engineering know-how, combined with charm and charisma, meet a social sensibility and vision—this is the case with Jerry Yudelson."

DIPL.-ING. ULF MEYER, Berlin, Germany's leading architectural critic

"*The Godfather of Green* will make you 'an offer you can't refuse' (to paraphrase a famous movie!)—invest a couple of hours to read the absorbing personal journey of an amazing visionary leader and awaken your own inner activist, teacher, mentor, and high-achiever, all in service to a planet in peril. Knowing that people like Jerry Yudelson are inspiring and designing our communities gives me hope that we can create a truly sustainable future for generations to come."

TERRY TAMMINEN, Secretary of the California EPA for Governor Arnold Schwarzenegger

THE
GODFATHER
OF GREEN

BOOKS BY JERRY YUDELSON

Reinventing Green Building: Why Certification Systems Aren't Working and What We Can Do About It (2016)

The World's Greenest Buildings: Promise vs. Performance in Sustainable Design (2013)

Dry Run: Preventing the Next Urban Water Crisis (2011)

Sustainable Retail Development: New Success Strategies (2009)

Greening Existing Buildings (2009)

Green Building Trends: Europe (2009)

Green Building through Integrated Design (2008)

Choosing Green: The Home Buyer's Guide to Good Green Homes (2008)

The Green Building Revolution (2007)

Green Building A to Z: Understanding the Language of Green Building (2007)

Marketing Green Building Services (2007)

Marketing Green Buildings: Guide for Engineering, Construction & Architecture (2006)

THE
GODFATHER
OF GREEN

An Eco-Spiritual Memoir

JERRY YUDELSON

Wyatt-MacKenzie Publishing
DEADWOOD, OREGON

THE GODFATHER OF GREEN
An Eco-Spiritual Memoir

Jerry Yudelson

ISBN: 978-1-948018-72-2
Library of Congress Control Number: 2019956859

Cover Illustration © Tetiana Ustik
Cover Illustration © Benjavisa Ruangvaree

Wyatt-MacKenzie Publishing
DEADWOOD, OREGON

Wyatt-MacKenzie Publishing, Inc.
www.WyattMacKenzie.com
Contact us: info@wyattmackenzie.com

To My Beloved Teachers

Baba Muktananda and Gurumayi Chidvilasananda

and

My Life's Companion

Jessica

With Great Respect

Heartfelt Love

and

Soulful Gratitude

Notes on Sources and People

Spiritual Teachers and Teachings

Throughout this book, I refer to my encounters and studentship with two perfected spiritual Masters, Baba Muktananda and Gurumayi Chidvilasananda, Gurus of the Siddha Yoga path. I italicize those teachings I remember or heard, especially those with a major effect on my life. In some cases, I quote remarks directed specifically to me, as I remember them or recorded them in my journal at the time. When I quote from their books or talks, it's with permission of the copyright holder, SYDA Foundation.

People's Names

No one asks to be in another person's memoir. In a few cases, I used only a first name to protect people's right to privacy. In other cases, where even using first names might compromise privacy, I used pseudonyms.

For politicians, public figures, and people whose work in the environmental, renewable energy, and green building movements is well known, I've used their actual names.

For my first wife, I use a pseudonym. For my wife Jessica, I use her actual name. For everyone else, I describe real people and historical events as I remembered them.

TABLE OF CONTENTS

"The past has a future we never expect."

JAVIER MARÍAS, *Thus Bad Begins*

FOREWORD

I BECAME AN ENVIRONMENTALIST AFTER THE FIRST EARTH DAY IN 1970. It wasn't hard. Los Angeles was ground-zero for air pollution and people were literally dying from smog. Half of the year was smoggy, air too dangerous to breathe. Beaches in Santa Monica Bay polluted and unsafe for swimming—the evidence for environmental damage was everywhere.

I decided to do something personal. For $950 I bought my first electric vehicle, a three-wheeler so slow that kids on scooters would pass me, laughing. I started recycling and composting, changed my diet and became a vegan.

By the time I bought my first house in Studio City in 1988, I was committed to environmentalism. By then I had an electric car with four wheels that I'd take over the hills to go into Hollywood for work or auditions. I was doing everything I could personally to reduce my environmental footprint. At times, I'm sure people thought I was nuts, but as I learned how much I could do, I kept doing it. Early in my career, I was the typical struggling actor, so I also figured out the practical side of my obsession—I saved money while protecting the environment.

I know that personal actions alone won't save the planet, but I also think it's essential for leaders to walk the talk. We need to have integrity in our actions if we want people to want to listen to us.

That first Earth Day galvanized people to act, both in our personal lives and more importantly in our political and economic life, so that we could clean up the messes we'd made and help people live healthier, longer lives. The environmental movement that grew out of Earth Day made many things better. The population of Los Angeles County more than tripled, the number of cars grew fourfold, but over forty years we cut air pollution in half! That was then, but now we need a new movement that will tackle the most critical issue we've faced in my lifetime—global climate change.

I've been talking about the climate crisis for nearly twenty years. During that time, the scientific evidence has become overwhelming, the roar of global warming even louder. Now it's Earth Day 2020—the 50th anniversary of that first celebration. We know that we face huge challenges in the decades ahead, that we will have to reform our economy and politics to tackle them, and that if we don't succeed, our kids and grandkids will face a far more difficult future, with floods, droughts, heat waves, and species losses at unprecedented levels.

I first met Jerry in 1988 when he ran for Congress in Orange County on a strong environmental platform. I supported him then, admiring that Governor Jerry Brown ten years earlier had put him in charge of developing a strong solar energy industry in California. I also learned from this memoir that like me, he became an environmentalist because of that first Earth Day and that he's stayed with it ever since, the last twenty years as a global advocate for green building.

I liked that Jerry felt obliged to walk the talk by building a low-energy passive solar home in northern California while still in his early thirties, building it out of adobe, the very earth itself. Thirty years later, he took an older home in Tucson and got it certified by the city for its ecological operations as well as its solar and energy efficiency measures, becoming the first home-based business in that city so recognized.

I also like that Jerry's been a vegetarian for ethical and environmental reasons since he was thirty. I'm still a vegan, so we're half-brothers. But he brings something else to the party: a strong commitment to his practices of meditation and mindfulness. It's the description of his struggles to combine this inner work with his outer environmentalist work that makes this memoir a unique, readable, and ultimately valuable guide for others.

I especially like that Jerry's still active in the fight against climate change, well past the age when most men focus on improving their golf game or enjoying the simple pleasures of playing with grandkids. At the close of his memoir, he writes a moving letter to today's young Climate Strike activists, urging them to move forward with challenging the political and business establishment, much as we did during that very first Earth Day, assuring them their elders have their backs.

But he also encourages them to take time for themselves, to build strength for the struggles ahead with their own inner work, letting the political become personal and the personal, political. It's a message of making lasting change through peaceful protest and thoughtful, nonviolent actions, with an understanding that over the long run we're all in this together.

ED BEGLEY JR.
September 2019

I
THE ODYSSEY BEGINS

I STOOD BEFORE THE CASKET LOOKING AT THE LIFELESS FORM OF MY FATHER, dead at 58 from his fifth heart attack, exactly twice my age. He'd had heart disease since I was twelve, so his early demise wasn't exactly a surprise. Through my tears, I reflected on all I had learned from him, all I had accepted and made part of me, all I had appreciated about him and how he had lived, and (more importantly now) all I had rejected.

On my wrist I wore a watch with a golden rim and a brown leather band that I'd received at graduation from Caltech, an award as the student who'd contributed the most to "student life" during his four years. It meant I'd done almost everything—sports, activities, clubs, and organizations—I found interesting and worth doing, except studying as hard as most of my classmates. It belonged as much to my father, to his example, as to me.

I took off the watch and, when no one was looking, carefully placed it alongside him in the casket. I was no longer the overachieving son he'd so carefully nurtured and encouraged. Along with him, I wanted to bury the persona represented by the watch. I was looking for another kind of fulfillment, one centered in the heart, not in the intellect or in outer achievements.

The past three years I'd become a seeker. I was looking for a master who could open my heart and guide me toward a more meaningful life. As it turned out, I was looking for Baba.

INITIATION

SILENCE. Early morning. Still dark outside. Awakened from deep sleep, I dress quickly and head to the meditation hall, the main room of this conference center and retreat deep in the Santa Cruz Mountains. Now I'm sitting cross-legged on a thin woolen *asana*, a meditation seat I've placed atop a folded blanket. Even so, I can feel the hard wooden floor. A hundred other seekers have quietly entered the hall and placed their asanas on the same uncomfortable floor. We're ready to begin the first morning meditation of this four-day retreat with Baba Muktananda.

Today we all expect to receive initiation, an awakening into awareness of the profound state of the inner Self, a state I've heard Baba lives in all the time. A quiet, profound anticipation suffuses the room. We're near the ocean; there's some early morning dampness. People wrap shawls, coats, or blankets around them to ward off the chill. I'm wearing a burgundy wool V-neck sweater over my tie-dyed, rainbow-hued T-shirt. Not much cover, but enough to stay warm.

My legs already hurt from sitting for only a few minutes, but regardless of the pain, I'm determined to sit for as long as it takes to meditate deeply, something I haven't ever done. Shortly after five, Baba enters the dark hall. He trails an exotic scent, reminiscent of the patchouli oil I remember from my hippie days. I sense something coming my way: delicious, deeply moving, yet unknown. My anticipation grows as Baba moves slowly among the rows, walking softly and purposefully from one person to the next. I open my eyes to peek, see him approaching the row where I'm sitting, softly close them again.

In his left hand, Baba swiftly but gently swings a peacock-feather wand onto people's heads, making a *whack!* sound, mingling and blending with the scent of the oils, creating a majestic sensory portrait. Sometimes Baba also brushes the feathers against each person's head before pinching them between the eyebrows or touching the top of their head with the right hand.

Now he's standing in front of me. He smacks me on the head with the wand, brushes the feathers lightly across my face, as if dusting away eons of impurities, and gently puts his hand on top of my head for a few seconds. His hand is soft and warm, the touch loving. I experience energy flowing from him into me. Immediately my attention moves inward and upward toward the crown of the head. Sparkling blue lights hold my gaze; pulsating, scintillating blue dots move around inside the space at the top of the head. Wherever I look, blue lights shine in the inner space. Mesmerized, enchanted, I eagerly watch these coruscating, iridescent blue specks as they move in and out of view.

As Baba's energy moves around inside my head, my mind becomes still, perhaps for the first time. I am both inside my body and, in my awareness, floating freely, somewhere outside. The energy invokes feelings: blissful, unexpected, intensely familiar. I am present in each moment, without any thoughts pulling at my attention or luring me away from this bliss.

From somewhere far away, I hear a resonant gong ringing one, two, three times to end the meditation session. I slowly open my eyes and glance at my watch. It's six o'clock. Nearly an hour has passed. An awareness stirs, a recognition something extraordinary has happened.

Suffused with unexpected gratitude, I feel something new, something I can't name, something special, elevated, extraordinarily rich. As I look outside, I see the sun creeping over the top of the mountains to the east. Early morning daylight shines through the treetops, softly lighting the hall. Touched by the sun, the day begins warming, awakening the world to a new beginning.

After meditation ends, we eat a light breakfast: chai tea, granola, and a banana. People eat in silence, indrawn, taking in and processing what has happened. After eating, I walk around the grounds, still trying to understand what transpired. Was this instant enlightenment or only the beginning of a long journey? Was it merely a blissful moment of transcendence, a view of snowy mountain peaks soon to be shrouded again by clouds of endless thoughts, desires, memories, dreams?

~

Baba had a unique art: he could deliver a spiritual awakening to hundreds at one sitting, with no prior preparation (or prerequisite) on their part. To receive this life-transforming gift, you only had to be in his presence, watch him as he talked and moved around, and get his touch. Some received the awakening if they merely saw his picture on the cover of a book, repeated the mantra Baba gave, or heard his voice chanting on a recording. In person, he delighted my senses with his radiance and inimitable presence. When he spoke, his voice was resonant and joyful. He came to where I lived—my great good fortune. I doubt I'd have had the courage to drop everything and go to India to find him.

What a blessed auspicious day; how lucky I was! What other people wait a lifetime for, travel halfway around the world to get, I only had to drive an hour from my home to receive. July Fourth, 1974 became my personal Independence Day. One special touch from a great master changed my life forever and gave me the energy and insight I needed to accelerate my spiritual journey and pushed me forward on an eco-spiritual odyssey.

WHAT'S AN ENVIRONMENTALIST?

I WAS NEVER A TREE HUGGER. I was a student, a would-be scientist, a kid growing up in Southern California during a time of choking smog and polluted beaches. I was against pollution mainly because it affected me personally.

Raised in a conventional suburban household in Los Angeles in the mid-twentieth century, I didn't intend to get involved with movements. When I was a teenager, Sputnik and the Space Race dominated the era; I wanted to be a physicist or astronomer. Like many young people, I wanted to make a difference with my life's work. Ultimately, this longing led me to the environmental movement.

If you'd asked me when I was a kid if I wanted to be an environmentalist, I would have said, "no way." Nature was "out there," something mostly to avoid, like the times my mom got upset when I came back from playing outdoors with too many grass stains on my jeans. Other than hanging out with other kids for hours some days in a nearby vacant lot, chewing on the green grass of spring, playing "hold the fort," or simply lying on my back and looking at the sky, I was a city kid through and through. I never went fishing, camping, or hunting: my dad relaxed mainly by reading a book or throwing a ball to his boys in our back yard.

Many summer weekends, to escape the heat of L.A.'s San Fernando Valley, all seven of us—five kids plus Mom and Dad—would pile into the family car (a white 1958 Pontiac Chieftain when I was a teen) and drive west of Malibu to Zuma Beach, the closest uncrowded beach. We didn't get any closer to nature than going to the ocean. My mother put zinc oxide on our noses and shoulders and slathered on Coppertone ("Tan. Don't Burn.") to protect our backs and chests, but even on overcast days we often got sunburned.

As a young teen, I got to go for a week to a YMCA summer camp in the forested San Bernardino Mountains. I loved being outdoors, inhaling the country smells, all pine resin and needles. Still, I had to learn the hard way about being in nature: don't pee uphill at night in the woods and don't pee upwind at any time. (You'd think most boys wouldn't have to "learn" such things, but I did.) Right after I figured out how to pee in the right direction, I had to go home.

In 1963, during my second year in college, President Kennedy's assassination changed me. I cried while watching his funeral on TV, the black riderless horse slowly following the casket, two backward-turned boots in the stirrups, the rider gone, never to mount again. After this, I became more political. I thought real change could come only from collective action. We were in a battle, our standard bearer had fallen, and we foot-soldiers had to rush in, pick up the banner, raise it again, and move forward. The civil rights movement inspired me to get involved in politics. In 1964, I walked precincts for the Democratic Party in African-American neighborhoods of northwest Pasadena, seeking votes for Lyndon Johnson's election after Kennedy's assassination. I started a Young Democrats club at Caltech and invited a local politician, Tom Bradley, to Caltech, the only black speaker on campus I remember from my undergraduate years. A Los Angeles City Councilman at the time, a decade later he became L.A.'s first African-American mayor.

After I returned in 1967 from a fellowship year studying water engineering in West Germany, I participated in antiwar rallies, teach-ins, and candlelight vigils, first in Cambridge while at Harvard, later in Pasadena after I returned to Caltech.

The antiwar movement touched a nerve. The draft snared some high-school classmates and sent them into the military. A few died in Vietnam. The draft didn't touch me so long as I stayed in school.

Vietnam was not my father's war. In 1942, soon after Pearl Harbor, my father joined the U.S. Army. Because of his college ROTC, he received an officer's commission. He soon was sent first to England, then to French Algeria, taking part in the campaign to defeat Rommel's army. Once there, he served on General Eisenhower's staff, interrogating German prisoners of war.

I admired his commitment to military service when the country called and his spending two weeks each year afterward on duty as a colonel in the Army Reserve. Perhaps implicitly trying to win his respect or follow his example, I considered applying to West Point. I might have received an appointment through our local Congressman, my father's close friend, but I opted for science instead of soldiering. Had I chosen West Point, right after graduation in 1966, as a junior officer I would have headed right to the front lines in Vietnam.

As I got older, I became even angrier as I gradually learned about the extent of rampant pollution and environmental destruction. Our civilization had treated the environment as an infinite waste dump for too long—we had to stop the destruction. Many activists demanded radical solutions, novel approaches striking at the root of the problem: corporate greed. The 1960s put capitalism on trial again, as it had been in the 1930s during the Great Depression.

In an interview late in life, the author Philip Roth claimed, "Radical change is the nature of American life. That's the only permanent thing we have."

Students engaged in the civil rights movement, antiwar teach-ins, and environmental protests demanding radical change unknowingly participated in a ritual of cleansing and renewal dating back to the country's founding.

Working in the early environmental movement, I came to view the ecological crisis not as an economic struggle of polluters versus the people, but more as a spiritual crisis in the larger society. After meeting Baba, as I became more aware of my spiritual self, I knew if I was going to be effective at protecting the environment, I'd have to translate contemplative practices into useful action.

More importantly, I saw how environmentalism could help us recover our lost kinship with the earth; help us create a society that could exist sustainably and harmoniously with the planet into the far future.

How does anyone's story become a memoir? What you get is an arbitrary selection of moments set in a cultural context. The novelist Julian Barnes wrote, "Art is the whisper of history against the noise of time." It is the same with my story: I've amplified a few whispers, some pivotal, some ordinary; some external, some internal; diverse recollections set against the cacophony of our time.

My past, your past, our past exists for us in the present moment as fragments of recollected events, fantasies, muscle memories, meaningful conversations, and ossified emotions, modifications of our essential mind-stuff, ordered and reordered to suit our needs. The contemporary physicist Carlo Rovelli wrote:

"The destruction of the notion of time in fundamental physics [leads to] the realization of the ubiquity of imper-manence...the difference between things and events is that things [stones] persist in time; events [kisses] have a limited duration...the world is made up of networks of kisses, not of stones."

My story, your story, our shared stories are ultimately sweet kisses: warm, soft, moist, intense, heartfelt, passionately touching a deeper reality, internally and externally, for brief moments. What we bring to those encounters, what we make of them, what we do with them, how we recount them, ultimately provides a kaleido-scope of colors, a palette for painting our own life's portrait, for assembling an elastic collage of revelations plucked from the flot-sam of time's onrushing river.

II
EARTH DAY

CHILDREN INTUITIVELY KNOW AND LOVE THE EARTH. From the time their mother puts them on the ground to crawl, the earth is a constant companion. My earliest childhood memories are of running barefoot on tall green grass, feeling the coolness, the tickling texture underfoot. As a young teen, I spent many evenings gazing through a small telescope. I could see Jupiter's four large moons, Saturn's tilted rings, dozens of moon craters, the deep red face of Mars—everything Galileo saw three hundred years earlier.

When I was fourteen, the first visible tendrils of air pollution began to creep into the San Fernando Valley from downtown Los Angeles. Over the next four years, choking smog increased, filling the entire valley and the L.A. basin fully half the year. In 1962, the year I went to college, the publication of Silent Spring, *Rachel Carson's searing indictment of the chemical industry, awakened the environmental movement.*

I wrote a senior research thesis opposing building more dams in the Grand Canyon, motivated by a Sierra Club ad campaign opposing them, headlined "Should We Also Flood the Sistine Chapel So That Tourists Can Get Closer to the Ceiling?" I decided to study environmental engineering in graduate school.

In Santa Barbara in 1969, a massive oil spill (at the time the largest ever), galvanized the environmental movement in California into full-fledged resistance to offshore drilling. Still, industry and autos continued to pollute our air.

With millions of others, for years I'd demonstrated against the Vietnam War. But saving the environment required more than opposing pollution; it required entirely new ways of thinking. In response to this dilemma, Earth Day provided a lifeboat in a sea of troubles. Earth Day made me an environmentalist.

GROWING UP

THE 1950s FEATURED OZONE-DEPLETING AEROSOL HAIRSPRAYS FOR BOUFFANT hairdos; Hollywood westerns with strong, silent, masculine heroes like John Wayne; Barbie dolls and hula hoops; stay-at-home moms with their coffee klatches; sitcoms like *Ozzie and Harriet* where married couples slept in separate beds; Elvis, Chuck Berry and rock 'n' roll; pick-up sandlot baseball games after school; and backyard barbeques with friends and relatives.

Americans enjoyed peace, prosperity, and a growing economy following two decades of economic depression and world war. When I was six, we moved into a conventional ranch-style house in the San Fernando Valley, busily transforming then from a semi-rural area with walnut groves, citrus orchards, and smallholdings into a vast suburb with nearly a million people. The Santa Monica Mountains encircled the Valley, rising at the top to almost 3,000 feet, culturally and geographically isolating the Valley from the rest of Los Angeles.

Here and there you could still see vestiges of the Valley's agricultural and ranching past. Across the street from us lived an older couple, Jack and Ethel, who operated a small chicken and egg ranch. I was fascinated by seeing rattlesnake skins stretched along the ceiling beams inside the chicken coop. They caught snakes trying to eat their chickens and killed them. When they told us snake meat "tasted like chicken," we believed them. In the late 1950s, construction of the San Diego Freeway, which opened in 1962 directly across the street from our house, buried their property and hundreds like it under thousands of tons of dirt.

We got two newspapers a day, morning and afternoon, and left our dairy order (milk, butter, cream, and cheese) out on the back porch every night for the milkman to deliver early the next morning, the milk always in recycled glass bottles. The Helms Bakery truck came by five afternoons a week with white bread, hamburger buns, and—best of all—a pull-out drawer with lemon and cherry jelly doughnuts. The idyllic 50s!

The house had three bedrooms and two bathrooms for the seven of us. The three boys slept in a converted garage at one end of the L-shaped house and the two girls, Mom and Dad, slept at the other end. Geographically removed from parental oversight, the boys often carried on at night, but Dad always heard us and came back to open the bedroom door and yell at us, "Be quiet!" or sometimes if we were too loud or it was late, simply "Shut up!" But how did he always know? As I got older, I figured it out, in one of those *aha!* moments peculiar to childhood: the heating vents carried our voices directly to their bedroom.

Every Christmas, we decorated a tree, the one religious concession my Jewish Dad allowed to my Catholic mother. On Christmas Eve they set out cookies and milk for Santa Claus in the kitchen. On Christmas morning, as the kids woke up before seven and raced into the living room to see what Santa had brought, I noticed the cookies would be gone and the milk glass empty. So, Santa had come after all! When I was seven, I did the math: So many presents + so many chimneys to climb down + so few hours before dawn = impossible! I asked my mom about it; she made me promise not to tell the younger kids. "Let them believe in Santa a while longer."

I loved to read, anything I could get my hands on. Dad would take me to the Van Nuys library to get two new books almost every week. We had a deal: I would choose one book and he'd pick the other, ensuring I'd read at least one book a week with redeeming educational value. I read incessantly, ruined my eyesight early on by lying flat, head propped up by a pillow, book on my chest, in a semi-darkened bedroom many afternoons after school, devouring a hundred pages or more before dinner.

Dad thought kids should learn American history (at the time it meant mostly the history of white men), so he subscribed to a series written for kids, and I got a new biography every month: Davy Crockett, Daniel Boone, Abraham Lincoln, Thomas Jefferson, etc. Seeing a brown cardboard mailer in the day's mail on the dining room table, I'd open it, remove the book, go to my room and often finish the book—170 pages—that afternoon. I recall reading only two books that departed from the dominant patriarchal narrative: one on Betsy Ross and the origins of the American flag; and one on George Washington Carver, the black Tuskegee scientist who found a thousand uses for the humble peanut (indirectly enabling a Georgia peanut farmer to become President).

Because my father thought that education was the high road to success in life, he made sure to encourage his kids to study hard. As the oldest and his oldest son, he put lofty expectations on me. From the beginning, I always got top marks in school. In most nuclear families those days, the father was the head of the family and the breadwinner; he sat at the head of the table at dinner and his wife served him. Seeing this "natural order" of things, boys naturally wanted to please their fathers, to make them "proud," whatever meant most to their Dad. In my case it meant getting the best report cards. That desire to please and to stand out in the family drove me to do whatever I could to win my father's approval.

But childhood is not all sunshine, ball games, good grades, and moonlit nights; there are times of darkness. The night was full of nameless terrors, not only monsters lurking in the closet. Isolated from the rest of the house, three boys alone in a converted garage, sometimes the sound of branches from a large walnut tree scraping against the window screen scared me. I worried someone was trying to break in, though we lived in a peaceful suburb. Petrified with fright those nights, I couldn't move, get up and go over to the window to look, hiding instead under the covers. After a few years, once I got brave enough to get up and find out what made the noise, I could see the sound happened whenever a strong wind swayed those branches.

How does a young boy become brave enough to face his fears? I couldn't talk about it with anyone; I could only endure those agonizing moments. I admired my best friend Stewart for being more confident, if not fearless. His tall, skinny father had trained him at the age of ten to stand up for himself through two-handed slap-fighting, hitting him lightly across the face with an open hand until he learned how to block a blow and strike back. My dad didn't train us that way; he was a lawyer, more comfortable with words than physical activity. I never learned how to punch back until I got to high school, played basketball on the varsity squad, and learned from the guys around me when and how to fight back.

About 2200 square feet, our house stood on a quarter-acre lot with 19 fruit tree varieties planted in back, side and front yards: walnut and almond; peach, plum, persimmon, and pomegranate; fig, orange, and lemon. One by one, my Dad removed most of them, once to build a patio extension, more often to give us a larger, more open yard to play in. He took out the fig tree because the fallen fruit attracted bees; no one ever thought to dispose of rotten figs on the ground or eat them right from the tree, as we did with soft deep-red Santa Rosa plums and ripe yellow peaches. Like most suburbanites, I was disconnected from the earth and the source of our food. Food came from the grocery store; everyone knew that—only farmers grew their own.

We walked to elementary school about six blocks away. Though we usually didn't, we could walk or bike to junior high and high school. During puberty, who wanted to get tired, sweaty, and smelly riding a bike to school? Living in an almost exclusively white suburb, I had a monocultural upbringing, particularly during grade school. Housing segregation was widespread. Restrictive covenants on new homes in the Valley prohibited homeowners from selling to minorities, a practice that lasted until the late 1960s. Restrictive covenants effectively segregated schools.

When I went to junior high school for the seventh grade, for the first time I encountered Chicano boys and girls from nearby Pacoima. The boys mostly wore white T-shirts with rolled up sleeves and khaki pants. In my imagination, they looked tough, always ready for a fist fight: threatening to the mind of a skinny 13-year-old Anglo boy, so I avoided them.

In middle school, our male teachers were mostly former soldiers who had gone to college on the GI Bill after the war to get a degree in education. Corporal punishment was still in vogue in the 1950s. If you acted up in class, teachers sent you to Mr. Schachter, the boys' vice-principal, who worked weekends as an NFL referee for L.A. Rams' games in the Coliseum. After watching grown men engage in legally sanctioned mayhem on Sundays, he must not have seen anything wrong with taking out his flat wooden paddle and telling misbehaving boys to "assume the position," hands on knees, for a painful swat on their butt. You didn't want a teacher to send you to his office.

Girls took home economics, learning skills like cooking and sewing useful for their expected future roles as housewives and mothers. My sisters learned to make frilly aprons and dresses from patterns. Boys took shop classes, preparing for a factory job. I took wood shop, electric shop, metal shop, gardening, and drafting. In electric shop, I carefully wound copper wire around a thin piece of wood to build a crystal radio, a useless exercise as cheap Japanese transistor radios soon became widespread. The shop teachers also gave swats, some more sadistic than Mr. Schachter: their paddles had small round holes drilled in them to provide an eerie whistling sound as they delivered the blow. Beyond the soreness, your butt would resemble Swiss cheese for a week. For extra credit, wood-shop teachers invited some boys to fashion new paddles, applying shellac for a more finished look and sanding the edges so they'd be more aerodynamic in use. All in the name of advanced vocational education, I suppose.

After a while, getting swatted without crying became a badge of honor, a symbol of incipient manhood for boys already dealing with wispy mustaches, hairy underarms, and unruly crotches. I feared the pain of the paddle, but I feared even more having other boys consider me a sissy, so one day in drafting class I acted up so I could get swatted. It didn't hurt as much as I expected, but once was enough.

I hated shop class; I was a real klutz, having learned no practical skills from my father. By way of compensation, I was good at academics. I especially loved science class. Our eighth-grade teacher was Mr. Samuels, a nice middle-aged man. He knew how to hold the attention of 13-year-olds. When he demonstrated electromagnetism, he'd invite a girl to come to the lab table at the front of the classroom and ask her to pull one electromagnet away from another. Easy peasy. He'd then invite a boy to come forward and try it, secretly flipping a switch behind the counter to turn on the electricity. Each boy strutted to the front, grunted and groaned while trying to lift the magnet—no dice. One after another, girls had no problem: Mr. Samuels secretly flipped the switch off again. Boys' faces got red until he explained the scientific principle at work. I thought: now, THAT was cool!

I was always skinny, without any defined muscles, and a bit nerdy looking. Even though I had poor vision, 20/400 in the left eye, 20/40 in the other, I refused to wear glasses, fearing I'd look even nerdier. I couldn't hit a baseball during those pickup games because I couldn't see the pitched ball until it was right on top of me. I never told my friends, who thought I was uncoordinated but otherwise okay.

When I entered high school, I got the first generation of hard contact lenses from Dr. Otto Jungschaeffer, a balding Viennese eye doctor with a gap-toothed smile who practiced in downtown Van Nuys after the war, where, with a heavy Germanic accent, he dispensed vision upgrades to middle-class kids. After the war, many Germans and Austrians immigrated to the U.S., indirectly paying reparations by bringing us rocket science and advanced ophthalmology.

When I wanted to play basketball in high school, the coach told my dad I'd have to learn to use my left hand and to put some muscle on my upper body if I wanted to make the team. I envied my buddy Bill, who worked with his dad on construction sites each summer beginning at fourteen and came to school in the fall with well-defined biceps. I began working out with barbells, inspired by the Charles Atlas bodybuilding ad in the back of comic books ("I was a 98-pound weakling...").

My mother sought to relieve my anxieties, reassuring me that I'd be OK when I grew up, that *some* girls would surely like me for my brain, but I was insecure about being skinny. She tried her best to sooth my concerns, tackling them with the same calm assurance that she brought to the wrinkles in my father's dress shirts, which she starched and ironed to crisp, smooth perfection.

In tenth grade, I was sure I was the smartest kid in the class until I got my first (and only) B in English. I quickly figured out I had to up my game to stay on top, so I began studying more diligently. As the oldest and the first one who shined academically, I got star treatment, but Dad made it clear: any grade lower than a regular A wouldn't do. The same standard held for my two sisters, also talented students. By the time my brother Jim, the fourth child, got to high school, I suspect Dad stopped caring so much about grades, figuring kids number four and five would most likely turn out OK. I'm sure that, like most fathers, Dad wanted his kids to do well, perhaps surpass him academically, so he could brag about them to his brothers and friends.

MOM WENT OFF TO WAR

My mother joined the Army as a nurse during 1942. Sent to Algiers as part of Operation Torch to liberate North Africa, soon after arriving she met my father, an Army Lieutenant Colonel on General Eisenhower's staff, at an officer's tea: it was love at first sight. During the courtship, my parents got to know each other while huddling in her hospital's basement bomb shelter, as German bombers coming from Egypt and Italy must have mistaken the red cross on the hospital roof for a red "X" and used it for target practice. Later, he contracted double pneumonia; after her regular shift at the hospital, she'd visit his sickbed in the officer's billet in old Algiers, climbing 37 steps from the street to bring him some hot soup and cold compresses for his forehead. Most people don't die from double pneumonia, but he always said she saved his life.

Once he recovered, not wanting to let a "good one" get away and as concerned as any soldier to leave behind a legacy no matter what might happen, my father proposed. The mayor of Algiers married them in May 1943, a brief ceremony conducted in French, a language they could neither speak nor understand, except to say *Oui* at the right moment. Mom quickly became pregnant with me and, leaving Dad behind, flew home to New York, their parting reminiscent I'm sure of the final scene with Bogie and Bergman in 1942's *Casablanca*.

On the way home, her plane made stops in Dakar, Recife, Trinidad, and Miami, a prenatal journey from which I must have got my lifelong love of travel. Nine months and 15 days after the wedding, I popped out. To ensure a legacy, my parents wasted no time. Pregnancy ended Mom's war, but Dad had to stay behind. The next year, as a new father, he persuaded the Army to transfer him back to the States to fight the war from within the friendlier confines of the Pentagon. Mom joined him in Washington, where my older sister was born, a mere fifty weeks after me. As a good Catholic, my Mom produced two more babies in the next four years.

FAMILY LIFE

My parents were always romantic with each other. Mom liked yellow roses; Dad always gave them to her in a bouquet on special occasions. They loved each other for thirty years, until my father died. Yet they had diverse backgrounds. His Jewish parents immigrated to Chicago in 1893 from the *shtetls* of Latvia and Lithuania, fleeing repeated pogroms in Imperial Russia. Her Catholic mother emigrated from Ireland to New England in 1893, two generations after the potato famine. Dad affected cool rationality. Mom was more warm-hearted and emotional, but their roles reversed more frequently than I'm sure either would have admitted.

I recall vividly how he would dismiss her (supposed) intellectual lack with some remark often ill-disguised as humor, since he had both a college degree and a law degree, rare in the 1940s, while she had only gone to nursing school. From him I took a cue about a man's supposed intellectual superiority, an attitude which both affected and afflicted me for many years.

My mother went to Catholic schools in Norwalk, Connecticut, through high school. She demonstrated Christian love through serving others, first as a nurse, then as a mother, and in other ways. In summertime she took glasses of ice-cold lemonade to the men collecting garbage. In those days, garbagemen lifted heavy cans of wet garbage by hand into the back of the truck. The San Fernando Valley can easily heat up to the 90s and even mid-100s on summer afternoons; garbage men loved the cold drink. From this example and similar acts of serving others beyond her immediate family, I got an early glimpse of true humanity, practicing love in action, serving God by serving others.

My parents tried their best to civilize five kids. My older sister and I had to take violin lessons at about ten, as soon as we could easily hold a bow in one hand and a violin under our chin with the other. Our violin teacher, Mrs. Lehmann, a tall, thin, older woman had tinted blue hair and wore purple velvet dresses. For two years, she taught us rudiments of playing violin. Sometimes during class she'd rap her bow on the music stand for emphasis or in exasperation. When our parents came to the annual class recital, they could easily hear they were wasting their money: I didn't have the music gene. Besides, I wanted to play sports with my friends in the afternoon and not be in violin class. Soon the lessons stopped, a mercy killing for us and, I'm sure, a relief for Mrs. Lehmann.

During the first half of the twentieth century, most of America marginalized Jews. Many professions, including law, politics, and academia, had explicit or implicit quotas on the number of Jews they would hire or admit to exclusive schools, and I'm sure Dad had to soft-pedal his faith to be accepted in the larger Christian, WASP-y world of the San Fernando Valley. After he established his own law practice in the 1950s, he unexpectedly benefitted from this prejudice: many gentiles preferred to hire a Jewish lawyer because they imagined he'd innately know how to "play the angles" better than other lawyers. The truth was more prosaic than genetic.

At that time, because of religious discrimination, Jews had a harder time getting into college, then going on to law school and becoming lawyers, so those who made it through were smarter than most. My father always worked hard; to pay his way through college he waited tables at a fraternity house.

My Irish Catholic mother came from another group long discriminated against and marginalized. When the Catholic John F. Kennedy ran for president in 1960, many Protestants openly expressed concern he'd be taking directions from the Pope in Rome instead of the American people. The WASPs who still ran the country didn't want to see the son of a 1920s bootlegger from the Boston Irish elected President.

In school in the 1950s, I encountered prejudice not only against Jews and Catholics, but also against blacks and Chicanos. Hard to avoid: in junior high and high school everyone told ethnic jokes, stereotyping anyone not a WASP. For a while, we heard lots of Polack jokes—none of us knew who or what a Polack was, but it didn't matter—the joke made them the butt, and I laughed along with everyone else. If someone wanted to know where the name *Yudelson* came from, which to an educated person might sound like, "son of a Jew," to make light of it, I'd say Scandinavia. It was almost true. My Jewish grandfather was from Latvia, a brief ferry ride away from Sweden.

For important religious occasions, each year my father would read prayers in Hebrew and recite passages explaining their significance. (Every year at Passover, we'd hear him intone the *four questions* beginning with "How is this night different from all other nights?") I had no other Jewish religious education. Unlike his three brothers, my father never sent his sons to *shul* to study Hebrew, to visit Israel as a teenager, or to have a bar mitzvah. As a concession to secular times or a way to accommodate my mother's Catholicism, each year we had the Christmas tree, which he sometimes jokingly called a "Hanukkah bush." As kids, we were a little jealous that our Jewish cousins got presents for eight days instead of only one.

My mother went to mass occasionally on Sundays, again at

Easter and Christmas, but less often as the family grew to five kids. At ten, I went with her sometimes to have a look at what went on in the pews, but nothing clicked. I'd ask myself, why did she tap her heart (or maybe it was her stomach) three times when the priest rang a bell? *Stand, then kneel*, over and over, on the padded wooden railing? It made no sense, and I lost interest in going to church with her.

If God existed, He didn't make house calls where we lived.

LOSING MYSELF

In high school, I came to terms with these prejudices, abandoning any overt interest in religion or religious identity. Only once do I remember reflecting on the broader subject of who I was.

One day I told a friend, "I have the feeling I've always been here." I had an inkling of my continuity as a *soul*, as a living entity, although I'd had no experience of a previous life. What did it mean, to have "always been here"? I didn't pursue this insight into the eternality of the soul. Contemplating life beyond surface appearances didn't interest me.

Fitting in became a mania in high school. I dove into academics, sports, and student government. Not popular enough to win any significant office, I discovered an obscure position called Commissioner of Halls and Grounds. I couldn't tell you today what it did, but it got me elected to the student council.

Even though I got all "A"s (except for that one B in tenth-grade English), I tried to downplay my academic prowess, learning instead how to handle myself amidst the daily verbal combat in the quad during recess and lunch periods. I learned all the dumb jokes and quick comebacks that make adolescence so memorable and so stressful. I became like a chameleon, taking on the background color of whoever I was with. With jocks, I shared teenage crudities and sexual innuendoes. With diligent students, I had passionate discussions about English, science, and math. With student government types, we talked about "improving" the school. With socialites, I'd talk rock 'n' roll and the latest movies. As a junior and senior, to be sociable I'd join the vacuous Wednesday night car cruise along Van Nuys Boulevard, from Bob's Big Boy restaurant ("Home of the Double-Deck Hamburger") on the north end of town to Bob's on the south end.

I became so adept at fitting in, I surrendered my sense of self to the overall high-school culture. Sometimes I overdid it. As a junior, I walked around the high school quad affecting a strut, a swagger I picked up watching football players parade around campus in their distinctive maroon and gray lettermen's jackets with the school's "Wolves" mascot emblazoned on the front.

My friend Jim was 6'5" and as a senior starred at center for our basketball team. We'd been pals since junior high, when I'd join him some days after school as he paced the sidewalk across the street from a girl's house, hoping that Kathy, his cute blond crush, would notice him and wave or, better yet, come out and talk to us.

One day he saw me strutting and asked, "Why are you walking around like you have a stick up your ass?" His ridicule cured me of walking with a jock's swagger but not the habit of imitating others instead of simply being myself.

I would pretend to be culturally Jewish if I happened to be hanging out with other Jewish students, the ones who became doctors, lawyers, and accountants, sprinkling Yiddish words like *schmuck, putz, meshugganah,* or *tuchus* into conversations, but I never felt personally connected with Jewish culture.

This dual upbringing had a benefit and a drawback. The benefit: I learned to respect both the Old and New Testaments. The drawback: I didn't get much instruction in either. Because my mother wasn't Jewish, I technically couldn't be Jewish, but because I had my father's name and some of his looks, I'm sure my friends and their parents assumed it.

A SENSE OF SEPARATION

In the summer of 1952, my mother took her four children, ranging in age from three to eight, to visit her father in Connecticut. Airlines still used prop planes, the trip took longer, and planes flew at lower altitudes. My first plane flight scared me as we bounced along through heavy thunderstorms on the way to New York.

Then 77 and a widower for the past five years, Grandpa Moore still lived in the family's hilltop two-story house at number six Kellogg Street in Norwalk. Tall for his time at 6'4", Big Jim spent his working life as a skilled craftsman and machinist. Now retired, he was a quiet man with glasses and a kind expression. Surrounded by his only four grandchildren, most warm days he'd wear a workingman's sleeveless white undershirt, baggy blue denims, and suspenders.

Built in 1895, after more than fifty years of family life the house and everything in it smelled old and musty, especially the large double bed with a wooden headboard where my older sister and I slept. In the backyard an old cherry tree creaked and groaned as we swung on a tire hung by ropes from a sturdy branch. An old-style washer tub with a manual clothes wringer on top stood on a screen porch off the kitchen.

Most days we went to a nearby beach on Long Island Sound where my mother often had gone as a kid, racing other kids along the beach until, as she told us, her calves cramped from running on sand.

That summer, my father stayed in Washington, DC. For many years, he spent two weeks there each summer completing his annual Army reserve requirement and reuniting with friends from wartime service. The Army arranged an annual desk job for him at the Pentagon, some assignment he could complete in two weeks. He had specialized in personnel matters during the war, and he'd handle similar issues during that annual tour of duty. Usually my mother and the kids stayed behind in Los Angeles, but this year we were all old enough to travel, so we'd come east to see Grandpa Moore.

One Sunday Mom took us to New York City, where she had worked as a nurse before the war. We walked on Forty-Second Street near Times Square. The streets were quiet, nearly devoid of people. As the oldest child I confidently ventured well ahead of my mom and the other three kids.

Suddenly, theater doors flew open as a matinee ended, and a crowd rushed out toward the curb, anxious to catch a cab. Engulfed and separated from the family, alone in a strange city, I panicked. Like a small boulder in a fast-moving stream, people flowed around me as I tried to hold my ground and looked for my Mom. Petrified by more people than I'd ever encountered at once, I held tight to a light pole, fright no doubt visible on my eight-year-old face.

After the initial rush subsided, I called out, "Mom!"

My mother saw me and shouted "I see you! Don't move," dragged the other kids over, and rescued me from the swarm.

About twenty years ago I attended a meditation retreat in Palm Springs. One day in meditation I vividly remembered this incident and along with it the same panicky sensation I had experienced not only as a child, but in my mid-twenties, separated from my own essential self by life's confusing onrush. I was so grateful Baba had appeared in my life, answering my unarticulated prayer, rescuing me from my sense of isolation and my overwrought feeling of cleverness. Offering protection and support on the spiritual journey, his grace was like a gentle wind at my back.

DREAMS OF MY MOTHER

My mother's brother John died from scarlet fever when he was ten and she was eight. They were very close; that loss motivated her to go to nursing school, then to serve as a public health nurse in New York City's Lower East Side in the late 1930s. In 1942, my 28-year-old mother, the youngest of four children, enlisted in the Women's Army Corps (WACs), got an officer's commission, and sailed across the Atlantic, first to England and in December onward toward Oran, Algeria, aboard the *Strathallan*, a passenger liner pressed into wartime duty.

After they passed uneventfully through the Straits of Gibraltar, a German U-boat torpedoed her ship the next night in the Mediterranean, but Mom survived. The heavily damaged ship took twelve more hours to sink, exploding before going under the following afternoon. Of more than 5,000 troops and crew on the ship, only a few dozen perished.

A decade ago, nearly ten years after she died, I had a vivid dream of her, in which she relived that night's trial. This poem arose spontaneously as I woke.

Dreams of My Mother

Late afternoon. She sleeps now.
Exhausted, drained from the long trip home,
at her side the baby wrapped in swaddling.
She dreams of her husband, still at war.
The weak March sun fills the room;
her fitful dreams return—
can it be only eighteen months
since she herself set off to war,
sailed across the great ocean?

The longest night of the year,
a beautiful full moon.
Out on deck,
salt spray in her face, seagulls flocking,
her ship sails on—a clear target for U-562.

Two hours after midnight,
safely through the narrow Straits—sighs of relief.
Now on a long run to port—
had they really made it?
Suddenly two explosions,
the big ship shudders, sirens, everything happening at once—

The dream remembers only confusion,
the ship listing,
climbing to the railing,
going over the side,
the welcome netting below her feet.
Hanging on, watching, dismayed,
as each lifeboat pulls away without her.

Long hours clinging,
fingers white and numb,
the chilly winter night,
hearing the wetness sloshing, the sea,
the sea waiting to claim her.

With stiff fingers, she tells the rosary in her pocket.
Now is the time to pray—she calls on the Virgin:
Hail Mary, full of Grace, the Lord is with thee...
Pray for us now in our time of trouble.
What the nuns had taught her
comes back unbidden, from deep within.

Suddenly it's over—
In the dawning light, she's in a lifeboat,
safely aboard the British destroyer.
She turns, watches as the crippled ship heaves
and silently lists some more.

IN TUMULTUOUS TIMES

I CAME OF AGE DURING TUMULTUOUS TIMES. In the summer of 1963, I was 19 when the Reverend Martin Luther King Jr. gave his "I Have a Dream" speech to a quarter-million people at the March on Washington for Jobs and Freedom. Three months later, President Kennedy was assassinated. As I turned 21, President Lyndon Johnson, the "peace" candidate in the 1964 election, escalated the Vietnam War. Two years later, large-scale opposition to the war emerged as millions of people demonstrated against it. In my twenty-second year, only thirty miles from home, over a six-day period in August 1965, more than 30,000 rioters in the black ghetto burned and looted Watts in south-central Los Angeles. Chaos continued everywhere throughout the sixties, fueled by urban decay, the civil rights movement, and antiwar protests.

If you're under sixty today, you may have trouble understanding this hugely unsettled and culturally divisive period. One year stood out: 1968. In the spring, assassins shot and killed both the presidential candidate Senator Robert F. Kennedy and the Reverend King. In August, during the Democratic Party's national convention, without provocation the Chicago police force attacked crowds of peaceful antiwar demonstrators. Like many young people, I lost hope: we saw things falling apart and no one trying to put them back together. After Kennedy's killing, students despaired at ever changing the system. After King's death, race riots took place in 120 cities, including Chicago and Washington, DC. One well-known commentator described it as "the year the country came apart" over cultural divisions.

EARTHRISE

But the wheel of change continued to revolve. At the end of 1968, on Christmas Eve, a remarkable event briefly brought people together. Three American astronauts in *Apollo 8* orbited the moon ten times; for the first time, human beings saw the back side. They took hundreds of pictures of Earth from space. On one of the orbits, a hastily shot photo showed an "Earthrise," an image of the waxing Earth appearing isolated against the blackness of space, rising indelibly blue and green above the desolate surface of the moon below. Though everyone had seen earlier spacecraft photos showing the whole Earth, for the first time we saw the contrast between the moon, lifeless and unchanging for eons, and the dynamic beautiful cloud-covered Earth, nurturing and abundant, our only home in the universe. For the first time, people experienced viscerally we were all in this together as a singular humanity, that the fate of the human experiment was inevitably, inextricably, and eternally intertwined with the fate of Earth's life-support systems. By providing an emotional connection to our home planet and its fragile beauty, Earthrise led many to become environmentalists, more determined than ever to protect it. Even after six moon landings and many similar photos, Earthrise is still *sui generis*, one of a kind in its impact on the human psyche.

THE CHAOS CONTINUES

During 1969, the newly elected President, Richard Nixon, expanded the Vietnam War; nearly 12,000 American soldiers died that year. On the West Coast and on college campuses, the counterculture dominated, with Timothy Leary and others telling young people not only to oppose the war, but to *tune in, turn on, and drop out*, using mind-altering drugs such as marijuana and LSD. I had smoked dope occasionally, but I didn't delve much deeper into drugs or mind-altered states, fearing I would lose my sense of "self."

I had returned to Caltech in the fall of 1968 after getting a master's degree in environmental engineering at Harvard. In contrast with the chaos of the times, I found a calm oasis in life as a graduate student. Most of my fellow students worried only about completing their studies, defending a thesis, and getting out of school with their PhD. Beyond getting his degree, my officemate Joe most looked forward to regular shipments of his favorite food—heavily salted baked hams—from his mother in North Carolina. Unlike other students, I couldn't ignore the world outside. At 25, I wanted to get on with my adult life and stop being in school. I had a lot of inner tension (what to do, when to do it, how to grow up at last) amid growing conflicts with the heavy demands of graduate studies and my own desire to "get going" with life.

BECOMING AN ENVIRONMENTAL ENGINEER

Why did I become an engineer? Growing up, I knew nothing about engineering. My father was a lawyer, his friends were lawyers, but I was never interested in law. When I enrolled at Caltech, I wanted to be a physicist, but two years of struggling through six required, fast-paced physics courses curbed that ambition. I'd been the best student in a small graduating class of 200 at an undistinguished public high school. I thought I was smart until I took chemistry and physics from Nobel Prize winners like Linus Pauling and Richard Feynman. The truth hurt: I wasn't as talented as many classmates; and I was unprepared for Caltech's rigor.

I met with my academic advisor to choose a major near the end of the second year.

"I've been looking at your grades," he began gently.

I could sense where he was headed; I had done average work in physics and chemistry, reasonably well in math, and excellent in English and history, representing Caltech's required curriculum for the first two years.

After asking about my goals and interests he offered, "Have you thought about engineering?"

"What's that?" I responded, interested but cautious, my pride still wounded from the bruising two-year encounter with Caltech's academic demands.

"It's when you take scientific principles and apply them to real-world problems. You might like it. Why don't you take some basic engineering courses—heat transfer, fluid flow, structures—your junior year and see what appeals to you?"

I agreed to try it; I wasn't going to quit. I was still confident I could do the work.

I soon got interested in studying water and the amazing phenomena of how it flows in pipes, channels and culverts, in rivers and streams. I found the physical reality of water far easier to understand and way more interesting than the metaphysical probabilities of quantum physics. Water studies seemed to fit my innate personality: I was born in early March under Pisces, a water sign.

I got a new advisor, Norman Brooks, a professor of civil engineering, a pioneer in water pollution control, and one of the few engineering professors with an outwardly expressed social conscience. He guided me to study how we could end the era of large dam-building, already thirty years old, that had destroyed many of the country's wild and scenic rivers. During my senior year, I wrote a long research paper opposing proposed dams at Marble Canyon and Bridge Canyon on the Colorado River in the Grand Canyon, which Brooks sent to our local Congressman.

Did other engineering students follow similar paths? Were mechanical and chemical engineers born under fire signs, aeronautical and electrical engineers under air signs, and environmental and structural engineers under earth signs? After Brooks opened my eyes to how civil engineers could help solve environmental problems like water pollution in Santa Monica Bay (where I sometimes went to Will Rogers State Beach), I got hooked. I focused on pollution engineering for graduate studies. Gradually, I became an environmentally oriented engineer, which satisfied a desire to do intellectual work while still addressing my growing social concerns.

A PERSONAL AWAKENING

My political awakening came from recognizing the extent and pace of environmental destruction and from the futility of my anger over Vietnam, pushing me to put my energy in a positive direction, instead of merely opposing things like the war.

But what about an inner awakening? During this time, I still had to deal with life. It resembled a 500-piece jigsaw puzzle where someone had thrown away the box with the picture on it. I tried assembling life's jagged and jumbled pieces into a coherent whole, without any clue as to what the completed puzzle might look like.

What changed me from someone strong and purposeful, with academic success and a clear life path ahead? Many small things, I guess, like a series of short rocket bursts that change a space satellite's course, but one incident stood out. In the spring of 1968, I worked in the Cambridge offices of Abt Associates where I had a part-time gig as a junior consultant. As a typically impoverished grad student, I appreciated the small paycheck. Abt exemplified a new breed of applied social science consulting firms doing work to support President Johnson's Great Society programs. I worked with others on a report for the federal government on how cities abused their waterways during urban development and what we could do about it. For the project, I took field trips to Seattle, San Antonio and Pittsburgh.

During a lull in the office chatter one day, I listened as a Harvard grad student, a rising star in the economics program, considered tops in the country, gloated to anyone who would listen about a major conceptual error he'd found in a paper by one of his professors. I'd had enough graduate economics courses to comprehend this guy's basic point. Yet in the telling I heard a distinct *Schadenfreude*, taking pleasure in someone else's misfortune. He spoke like a young warrior who, having set out to defeat the tribal chief and usurp his position, now stood over the prostrate form, blood-soaked sword raised, glorying in victory.

I was competitive, but this type of intellectual combat seemed too ruthless for comfort. Did it represent the life I wanted to lead? If such extreme intellectual arrogance characterized the milieu of Harvard academics, should I pursue this career? For the first time, I became uneasy with the life choices I had made. I was like a moth dancing around a flame: prestige, money, and career success drew me closer, but I could clearly sense danger, a risk of losing myself in the ceaseless striving to become (and stay) a world-class expert. I needed a catalyst to change direction and give my life a larger purpose. I found it in Earth Day.

EARTH DAY

I N SEPTEMBER 1969, a year after leaving Harvard, as I began my second year as a PhD student at Caltech, Wisconsin Senator Gaylord Nelson announced that a national *Earth Day* would take place the following April. The environmental movement already existed, but it was small, fragmented, and regional, far from a national crusade. Earth Day aimed to nationalize the movement and shift it into overdrive. Nelson's announcement electrified me, gave me a cause I could readily support: a clean environment, with action focused on passing laws to reduce air and water pollution.

When Senator Nelson first proclaimed "Earth Day," I knew a lot about pollution from a technical perspective, but I still had an academic's outlook, considering pollution an interesting "problem" to "study," not something I should take a public stand against. Earth Day challenged this detached mindset.

Earth Day organizers envisioned holding events on college campuses and in schools around the country. Young people would create educational teach-ins for other students, their parents, and the community. Earth Day was a wake-up call, speaking to my political conscience and experience of demonstrating against the Vietnam War. As a student of environmental engineering, I had to be involved.

Even before Earth Day, the public wanted to do something to reduce pollution. Almost weekly, we heard or read of another environmental horror story. In 1969, the evening news reported how the Cuyahoga River in Cleveland was burning from a toxic coating of oil and industrial wastes. That same year, only 90 miles away from me in Santa Barbara, a blowout of Union Oil's offshore oil drilling platform fouled local beaches with crude oil, killing thousands of marine mammals, fish, and birds.

ORGANIZING EARTH DAY

I decided to organize an Earth Day event on the Caltech campus. With only 700 undergrads, Caltech was small. It made identifying people to work simpler than at a larger university. My graduate advisor, Norman Brooks, introduced me to Paul Wegener, a senior who hung out in the same lab where I had my office. After we met and talked about it, Paul agreed to co-chair the event.

Paul was tall, lanky, and artistic, a "Caltech brat;" his stepfather taught aeronautical engineering. Paul lived off-campus in an old house in Pasadena, in one of the many narrow canyons at the foot of the San Gabriel Mountains. He majored in environmental engineering, but his passion was folk dancing. Once on board, Paul recruited a few other students.

We formed the Caltech Environmental Action Council, which met twice a month in a small, partially empty, older building he had located. A few scientists used a research greenhouse in the basement. We got permission to meet in the building's ground-floor office. It had everything we needed for Earth Day: desks and chairs, phones we could use, and meeting space. We got a half-dozen people involved, a few undergrads and a couple of women from the community: a single mom concerned about her kids' futures and a friend of Paul's from his folk-dancing group. As an all-male school, we wanted to include women to broaden our outlook to the effects of pollution on people's health and their hopes for the future.

Initially we had no clear idea about how to organize for Earth Day, but I had learned something during my undergrad days about managing events; I once promoted a big concert in the campus auditorium featuring the folk singer Judy Collins. To recruit other students, we printed flyers announcing our meetings and stuck them on bulletin boards around campus. We got few responses. Paul and I did most of the work, with several other students helping as needed. As I got more involved, I wanted our Earth Day events to focus on what we could do politically to stop pollution. Paul wanted to focus on community issues and ground-level environmental actions like recycling. We were a good match.

In our meetings, we discussed how to navigate the Caltech bureaucracy, which speakers to invite and how to get publicity: standard event stuff. Excited by the prospect of educating students and others about environmental issues, we didn't know how a small and conservative place like Caltech would perceive and respond to the event. During the second quarter, we invited faculty speakers to give subject-matter talks during what grew into a larger "Earth Week" observance. We persuaded the Caltech Faculty Council to allow students to skip classes without penalty to attend Earth Week presentations.

To generate more interest, we decided to get a keynote speaker who could attract the media and help us connect with the larger Pasadena community. I called the office of George E. Brown Jr., a liberal local Congressman, and worked my way through a series of aides locally and in Washington until we got his commitment. Meanwhile, Senator Nelson and other Earth Day supporters raised enough money to put eighty-five young people in a Washington office, creating a national Earth Day organization headed by a Harvard graduate student, Denis Hayes. The event rapidly gained credibility in the national media. Politicians lined up to get involved with a popular event like Earth Day.

All this organizing activity took place in the paper-and-pencil era: no mobile phones, no Internet, no personal computers, no social media, no cheap copiers or printers; it took a lot of time, mostly face-to-face meetings, to organize a large event. Still, good things happened; it simply took longer.

At first, I connected with students at nearby campuses like USC, UCLA, and Pasadena City College. A few months later, I helped to organize a Student Environmental Coalition of California with Earth Day coordinators from ten campuses throughout the state. I took several days away from my studies to attend statewide organizing sessions. Among its organizers, the Coalition had nine Democrats and one lone Republican, a ratio among environmentalists mostly unchanged over the years.

In planning Caltech's events, we focused on the teach-in aspects of the celebration, but we also wanted exhibits to attract people: information on how to recycle, conserve water, protect natural areas, and similar activities. As we organized our events over the next six months, I knew I wanted to be far more active in the fight against environmental pollution than I could be as a graduate student or researcher. As "ground zero" in the U.S. for air pollution, Los Angeles had the worst smog in the country, with 180 days a year of Stage 1("severe") alerts. This polluted environment affected me personally.

Pasadena had some of the worst smog in the L.A. air basin. As an undergrad at Caltech in the early sixties, many days after I got up, I would look north and see the 5,000-foot peaks of the nearby San Gabriel Mountains. After morning classes, when I came back to my dorm for lunch, they had disappeared, hidden above a thick blanket of smog.

My eyes stung from air pollution those days. Playing four years on the Caltech basketball squad, I suffered: some days, air pollution was so bad I could see a smoggy haze *inside* the gym where we practiced. My lungs would ache for hours after a workout or a game. Scientifically, we already knew smog came mostly from auto and industrial emissions, which then combined with L.A.'s unique inversion layers of stagnant air to form ozone on most sunny days. But what could we do about it? We couldn't study it forever—we needed action.

As *Earth Day* approached, I passed my PhD oral exams and completed coursework for a doctorate in environmental engineering science. I was making academic progress, but I doubted whether my PhD thesis analyzing water supply alternatives for two nearby desert cities would make a difference to anyone. I wanted to be more active, so I devoted even more time to Earth Day preparations.

Subliminally, I wanted something to force me to leave school, to venture out into the real world; Earth Day came along at exactly the right time. During the final quarter of the school year I abandoned any pretense of going to class or doing any further work on my thesis, working instead on something I considered more meaningful.

Hanging around younger students, listening to their concerns, I became more emotionally connected with environmental issues than most grad students or professors. Paul thought even more deeply than I did about social justice issues. We discussed the need to deal with human aspects of pollution and not focus solely on technological solutions. I spent time with people from the community who clearly wanted experts to tell them what they could do to clean up the mess. Some days, indecision tormented me. Should I remain a disinterested observer, an impartial expert like most students and professors, or should I get more personally involved?

ROMEO AND JULIET

I was so busy with my studies and with organizing Earth Day, I didn't invest much time in relationships. I wasn't ready for anything permanent; I was so self-centered I only wanted a girlfriend to sleep with and occasionally to take out to a movie or go to a party. At my age, twenty-six, most women wanted more than a sex partner. They appeared to want a "real" relationship where people cared for each other, did things together, even talked about the relationship, something I assiduously avoided, fearing I'd have to commit myself to someone. I found it easier to date younger women who weren't as demanding. I was a nice enough guy but wasn't that caring or giving; I mainly looked after my own needs. I was estranged from my own heart and confused about life's purpose. I freely offered my confusion to anyone I got involved with. This condition usually manifests as immaturity, and it still held me in full sway.

After Paul and I started working together to organize Earth Day, we hung out together, which is where I met Karen, one of his friends. She was twenty-one, with long brown hair and a sweet smile. We started going out and on the third date, obeying an unwritten rule of the times, we wound up in bed at my house.

She lived in a room at a girlfriend's family home in South Pasadena, not far from Caltech. It was a nice setup, but she couldn't have visitors. South Pasadena is an upscale suburban community with large, five-bedroom, two-story older Mediterranean-style homes on expansive tree-shaded lots. Though not as upscale as neighboring San Marino, it was desirable for families with money and an even closer commute to offices in downtown L.A.

Karen had her own phone; one night I called around eight. "Would you like to get together? We could go out and listen to some music at a bar I know."

"It's too late for that, but you could come over here."

"I thought you couldn't have visitors."

"There's a way, if you're interested." She laid out a plan.

It was audacious. Would I do it? What was I thinking? The answer was simple—I wasn't. Like in a lot of young men, the reptilian brain had kicked in; there was only one thought: MUST. HAVE. SEX. Casting aside any caution or mature common sense, I drove a short distance to the house, parked down the block, approached the entrance to the yard, and walked slowly and quietly along the driveway. (She'd already told me there was no dog.) The night was cool, clear skies, pitch-dark; I was sure no one would see me.

Karen had a second-floor bedroom with old-style, glass-paned metal French doors opening onto a large balcony on top of a *porte cochere*. The house had a hotel-like entrance; cars could drive up to the front door under the balcony, so you wouldn't get wet if it was raining. Sturdy large vines grew on trellises on either side of pillars supporting the balcony.

Inside the living room on the first floor, set back from the entrance, I could see lights and hear music playing, so I assessed the situation. Remaining below, with Karen upstairs inside the balcony, so close, with me playing Romeo to her Juliet, was out of the question. I put our plan into action. The music would hide any sounds.

Taking care to move quietly, I quickly climbed up a trellis and stepped onto the balcony, tiptoed across the deck, and tapped on the glass doors outside Karen's room. She let me in; we embraced and lay down. We laughed softly about how, like a skilled burglar,

I got into the house without alerting anyone. She was ready, wearing only a long T-shirt. Without further ado, taking care not to make a sound, we fucked urgently but quietly, not that easy to pull off.

I left the same way. Descending the trellis carefully, not wanting to stumble or fall, I walked back to the street, got into my car and went on my merry way, quite pleased with myself. Our affair didn't last much longer; Karen wanted more than a boyfriend interested primarily in sex. It was OK with me. As I got busier with Earth Day preparations, I stopped dating for a while and threw myself into the work.

EARTH DAY ARRIVES

Earth Day—April 22, 1970—finally arrived. We'd prepared for six months. The day was warm and clear in Pasadena, surprisingly not smoggy. Bright sunny weather with a blue sky; clearly, the gods had smiled.

The Caltech campus was compact: seven undergrad dorms bordered one end of a long brick walkway flanked by olive trees and stained black by years of fallen olives, leading at the other end to an old, three-story administration building in the middle of campus, beyond which stood classroom and lab buildings. We timed and situated the event to draw students, with speakers featured from 11 to 1 on a plaza near the student union and exhibit tables placed along the Olive Walk near the dorms. Local volunteers from the Sierra Club, Planned Parenthood, Zero Population Growth, Planning and Conservation League, and Get Oil Out (GOO) staffed exhibits. For balance, we also invited two oil companies to exhibit.

Delighted to see hundreds of people from the community and the campus milling about and looking at exhibits, I listened to the main speakers: Congressman Brown and some Caltech professors with pollution control expertise. At one forum, two Caltech engineering professors debated air pollution's origins and proposed solutions with scientists from two oil companies, Atlantic Richfield and Union Oil.

Congressman Brown spoke about what Congress had done to address environmental issues. As students, we were angry about pollution and environmental decay. We wanted action *now*. I hated the tremendous effort it took to get politicians to address this issue. But I knew we needed an informed public to help move things forward; hence Earth Day's focus on the teach-in.

We presented an Ecology Faire for the community, bringing together children and their grandparents, serving organically grown food under lines of black balloons (representing air pollution) floating skyward. At the Ecology Faire, people built two open-air, Buckminster Fuller-inspired, geodesic-type domes on the lawn near the faculty club, simple structures costing under $100.

Pleased with what we saw and with ourselves, Paul and I walked along the rows of exhibit tables and booths and listened to talks. We had pulled off a successful anti-pollution event on a conservative campus, one that had been mostly quiescent during the tumultuous events of the past five years. We saw something unexpected: students and professors demanding action for a clean environment.

In the evening I joined a group of students who built a small campfire on the lawn inside one dome. We sat around sharing a bottle of cheap wine, smoking a little weed, and talking about what to do next, how to seize the momentum of Earth Day for further environmental action. At Caltech, it was a day of celebration, of talking about a better future, not a day of protests.

In an article for the Caltech magazine a month after the event Paul wrote,

> "The Teach-In and Ecology Faire were designed around people and laughter, not numbers and fear. Numbers are vital to an understanding of what is to be done and how to do it, but there is a point at which they should be left behind."

He expressed the sentiment of Earth Day succinctly: we should celebrate what is good and work to change what is not, never forgetting we're doing this for both ourselves and future generations.

THE ENVIRONMENTAL MOVEMENT BEGINS

At the first Earth Day, about 2,000 college campuses and almost 10,000 schools held "teach-ins" about the environment and pollution. Twenty million people attended events throughout the country, ten percent of the U.S. population at the time, a mass movement bigger than any demonstrations against the Vietnam War during five previous years.

As a one-day event, Earth Day came and went. Nothing changed right away, but it spurred national political action and gave birth to an enduring environmental movement. With people pressing for major changes at both national and state levels, Earth Day quickened the process. In 1970, Congress created the Environmental Protection Agency. The California Legislature passed the California Environmental Quality Act in 1970. President Nixon and Governor Ronald Reagan, both Republicans, signed these laws. By channeling public outrage, Earth Day created momentum to bypass "politics as usual" and get things done in a hurry.

The environmental movement became powerful, with the political system adjusting rapidly to accommodate its interests and issues. Because everyone breathes polluted air and everyone wants a cleaner world for themselves and their families, we could galvanize millions of people. It was the right movement, at the right time, for the right reasons.

What made Earth Day so significant? The historian Adam Rome observed,

"Earth Day was an educational experience as well as a political demonstration. That rare combination enabled Earth Day to have both a long-term and short-term impact."

In a sense, Earth Day activities created a new tribe of young activists. The events were our new home, organizing meetings served as our family life, and our tribe's members became more like our real family than our own siblings. We didn't need parents in this family, because everyone was equal; we tolerated leaders only if they stayed true to our values.

Earth Day activists were political neophytes, but more seasoned political operatives quickly seized the opportunity for change presented by Earth Day's massive public support. In June, along with a hundred campus activists from around the country, I flew to the Black Lake Training Center of the United Auto Workers (UAW), the most progressive trade union in the U.S. Located in the woods of northern Michigan, the Center existed as an organizing college for political and social change. The UAW saw the potential for marrying the labor movement with the environmental movement to pressure large corporations and the federal government into massive changes.

Feeling solidarity with student activists from all over the country, I welcomed the union's involvement. Collectively, we were sure we could force politicians to act on our demands. The UAW introduced us to "movement" philosophy and tactics. At the end of each day, we joined in singing "Solidarity Forever" and "Joe Hill," classic labor movement songs. Presided over by Victor Reuther, brother of the late Walter Reuther, UAW's founders in the 1930s, the meeting lasted only two days. But like many student organizers, I was convinced our efforts counted in the larger political context.

I could see the road ahead for environmental change would be long. How could I carve out a proper role for myself? I didn't want to relinquish my hard-won technical expertise to become yet another political operative. I knew at some point the movement would need this expertise to make effective changes. Emotionally, I resisted the "solidarity" the UAW laid on us. I wasn't looking for a union to stand up for me; most likely I never would.

I paid a cost for all this activity. Organizing Earth Day consumed most of my time. As the academic year progressed and the burden of arranging Earth Day events increased, I doubted I would ever complete my thesis. I had to make a choice I'd avoided for the past year. Should I stay with my graduate studies in engineering at Caltech or move away from a purely academic focus on the environment to a more active engagement? I couldn't put off a decision much longer.

LEAVING SCHOOL

I hadn't developed a plan or purpose for a career, for what I wanted to do after finishing school. I was waiting for someone or something to push me in the right direction. I had to make a real-life decision and live with the consequences.

What did I want to become? How could I discover my true calling? I wasn't ready to take an engineering job with a large consulting firm or with the government, offers I had received earlier. At 26, enmeshed in confusion, what should I do next?

There weren't many environmental jobs. Some groups offered a few poorly paid positions (even the Sierra Club had only a small staff). Consulting firms helping companies and government agencies meet environmental laws didn't exist because the legal and regulatory framework was not yet in place. I couldn't see a clear path for taking my environmental concerns into a real-world job.

After I left graduate school in 1970, I never looked back. I wanted to take what I had learned and put it to some beneficial social use. But I had little money, and I was out of sorts emotionally, with unresolved conflicts in relationships, how I wanted to live, and what I wanted to do with my engineering education. In my heart, I knew I had to enter a new phase in my life.

I crumpled what I considered a poorly written first draft of my life story and threw it in the wastebasket, as if it no longer pleased me, agreed with me, or even represented me. I discarded it hoping no one would read it, but its essence still lingered in my father's example, in memory, fantasy, and the ego's subtle clutches.

In *Rules of Civility*, the novelist Amor Towles wrote,
"To have even one year when you're presented with choices that can alter your circumstances, your character, your course—that's by the grace of God alone. And it shouldn't come without a price."

Without much money, facing the prospect of never finishing graduate school, without knowing where I could go or what I should do, still I thought I had options, though I don't know where I got that optimism. Maybe I was avoiding a look over the precipice, fearing what I might see below. I discovered that dramatic actions often deliver unexpected consequences. I had to pay a big price, as I stepped away from almost everything I had learned growing up.

My personal odyssey began much in the same way as the original *Odyssey*, the inspiration for everyone's life's journey, the archetypal story of all calamities that may visit us, with a shipwreck and life on a distant shore far from home. Crashing out of graduate school and winding up nearly broke was my shipwreck. It took some time for me to land on that distant shore, to be in a place from which I could once again return home, be at peace and engage in useful work.

DROPPING OUT

DROPPED OUT OF GRADUATE SCHOOL TWO MONTHS AFTER EARTH DAY, taking the first significant risk of my life, turning my back on what I had considered a purposeful life. Where was I headed? I didn't know. What was I going to do? I didn't know. I knew only one thing: I had to move on. As birth had expelled me from the womb, an equally strong impulse propelled me into life. I took my first breath of freedom. Not knowing what would happen, I had faith in myself: something would surely turn up.

I called my childhood friend Stewart Lenox to discuss the situation. He invited me to live in a cabin on his property in Felton, a former logging town along the San Lorenzo River in the Santa Cruz Mountains. He was a grad student at the University of California campus in Santa Cruz, ten miles away. I left Pasadena that summer and went north to live in the woods like Thoreau. My friends and family must have questioned what had become of the young man who excelled in school and showed such "promise," sometimes looking askance when I showed up looking like a hippie, sometimes asking pointed questions about my behavior and intentions.

I recall a sunny Monday morning in August 1970. Earth Day was only four months in the past, but it already seemed like ages ago that I'd left Los Angeles to move three hundred miles north. The early morning air was cool and a little damp in the coastal redwoods, but it would get warmer that afternoon, to about 80 degrees. With no electricity and no refrigerator for milk, I drank a cup of black coffee made on my coal-fired stove, laced with white sugar, leaning back in a rickety old chair on the porch of this one-room, cold-water cabin on Stewart's land. Originally situated in an old-growth redwood forest, logged more than a hundred years earlier first to build San Francisco during the Gold Rush and again to rebuild it after the 1906 earthquake, the site still had lots of tall trees along with tree stumps, fallen trees, bracken ferns, and poison oak, the harbinger of disturbed soils in the West.

Behind the cabin stood an outhouse (for my personal use!) where I sprinkled lime from a can after each dump. I had no electricity, no phone, only well water from one faucet at the kitchen sink. Two kerosene lamps provided light at night that allowed me to read, and I could use the phone in Stewart's house if I needed to. It was primitive, but after leaving graduate school in a funk, I was grateful for any place to call home.

If I timed it right, I could use the showers and toilet a hundred yards uphill at the main house, once Stewart and his German wife Angela left, he to the university for a graduate seminar some days and she to her regular job at the university library. Angela trained in Germany for a career as an interpreter. She spoke and read five languages, a skill she'd parlayed into a permanent job as a librarian.

Angela and I already knew each other. While I was studying in West Germany four years earlier, and she was Stewart's long-distance German girlfriend, she invited me to spend a white Christmas with her family in Bavaria. I had a car, and for two weeks we drove around in my green MGB roadster while she showed me the Bavarian countryside, the medieval treasures of Augsburg, and the magic castle of Neuschwanstein. On Christmas Eve in 1966, we'd gone to the local Catholic Church and sung *O Tannenbaum* and *Stille Nacht, Heilige Nacht*.

Stewart had enrolled in a new graduate program called, in typical modest university fashion, "History of Consciousness." It was essentially a philosophy PhD program, but decked out with a new name to appeal to the era's consciousness-raising ethos. He was writing a PhD thesis on Nietzsche. I became convinced he thought he was the model for the Übermensch (Superman) in Nietzsche's *magnum opus, Also Sprach Zarathustra*.

On days when he wasn't at school and on some weekends, he often pressed me into duty helping him renovate the old house. He'd walk the hundred yards to my cabin after breakfast and ask, "Can you give me a hand?"

"Sure, no problem," I'd say. That meant working the rest of the morning, having a ham-and-Swiss sandwich and a coffee with him for lunch, afterward stopping for the day so he could study.

His father taught him to use power tools: table saw, drill press, and belt sanders; using them first to renovate an old cabin in the mountains near Lake Arrowhead and later to build a sailboat in their garage. Now in his own garage he had a circular saw, jig saw, two sawhorses, a few hammers, a carpenter's T-square, screwdrivers, pliers, wrenches, several files, and a chisel. With these tools and his carpentry skills, he could build or fix almost anything.

I had access to Stewart's library, heavy on modern Western philosophy, and I indulged my reading habit. I read all he had by Nietzsche: *Ecce Homo*, *Nietzsche Contra Wagner*, *Zarathustra*, *Beyond Good and Evil,* and the like; also books by twentieth-century philosophers such as Martin Heidegger. I became more learned, but no wiser. Working alongside him as a carpenter's helper, I learned practical building skills, which I considered far more valuable than abstruse philosophy.

Born two weeks apart, Stewart and I had been friends and friendly rivals since the second grade. I'm a Pisces and he's an Aries. He was a good athlete (I was barely OK) and I was better at academics. Stewart exuded self-confidence, even arrogance, as a kid. Our fifth-grade teacher Mr. Simon once called him an *egotist*. We got excited to learn a new word until we read the definition in a dictionary. As their first child, his family pampered him; he had his own tennis court.

He could swim well; I couldn't manage much more than a simple Australian crawl for a few laps of the pool. At 12, he saved me possibly from drowning when I got leg cramps while swimming away from shore in the chilly waters of Lake Gregory, near Crestline in the San Bernardino Mountains. Spurred on by our parents, we motivated each other to get better in areas where the other was stronger. We grew to be about the same height and build. We captained the Van Nuys High varsity basketball team together. Many weekends during high-school summers we sailed the 16-foot Snipe-class boat he and his father had built. He was bold where I was cautious, smooth with girls where I was awkward.

But it had been eight years since high school. We'd grown up and hadn't recently spent much time together. As an old friend, he stepped up to offer me a place to chill out after I burned all my bridges at Caltech. I felt he owed me this much, because I'd paid for the plane ticket to bring Angela from Germany two years earlier so they could get married. I had money then from my part-time consulting gig at Abt Associates. As an impoverished grad student at Wisconsin, he needed $500 for her airfare, and I gladly wrote the check.

Stewart and I took walks almost daily in the woods around his property with his young brown-and-white basset hound, Boudu, named after the title character in Jean Renoir's classic 1932 movie, *Boudu Saved from Drowning*. In the movie, a despairing tramp jumps into the River Seine to end his life. A kindly bookseller rescues him and takes him into his home. Boudu soon creates such a nuisance that everyone regrets saving him. Stewart returned from a year in Europe with a full load of such existentialist and nihilistic baggage. Boudu the dog emulated his namesake: stubborn, untrainable, and inclined toward getting into the underbrush, forcing Stewart to carefully remove ticks after each walk. I didn't share Stewart's mental pain, his anguish that life was pointless, but his despair influenced me; I was still sorting things out.

Living in the woods as a hippie represented a dramatic change. Barely eighteen months earlier, before I moved to the woods, I had a decent job with Abt, first in Cambridge and later at its office in Santa Monica while I pursued my PhD. For the first time, I had spending money. I bought trendy clothes, favoring open-necked ruffled blue shirts, plaid dark brown and tan bell-bottoms, and brown leather boots, all in a faux late-Beatles, Peter Max-influenced style. I bought pieces of fine art—several paintings and a kinetic sculpture—at the Kanegis Gallery in Boston, sipping Scotch some afternoons with Sid, the owner. But I wasn't happy; I had constructed a thin façade of prosperity and sophistication, but it didn't represent me. I was already 25, still in school with no idea what I wanted to do.

Relationships were a problem. I was an inconstant lover. By my mid-twenties, as sex became a persistent itch, the more I scratched it, the more it itched. I had many brief relationships, a few weeks or a couple of months here and there. If one ended, I wasn't worried: surely there'd be another right around the corner. I treated women as if I was shopping in a dating department store with unlimited free returns, a personal Nordstrom. Take it home, try it on, and if it doesn't fit or accessorize well, return it, no questions asked. It was a two-way street those days, as many women I met shared the same outlook. Our attitudes reflected the sexual revolution, kindled by the contraceptive pill and fueled by the social chaos engendered by the Vietnam War.

I hadn't had a good relationship since I coldly left my sweet young German girlfriend back in Cologne three years ago, coming home to try to reconnect with my college girlfriend. After failing at that, I became more insensitive in relationships, looking only to satisfy my immediate sexual needs. I lost touch with my sense of love or respect for others, very much opposite to my upbringing in a loving family.

The year before, I had a brief relationship with Carol, a single mom about eight years older. She had three preteen daughters and worked the graveyard shift as an operator at my answering service, so she could be at home with them most evenings until they went to bed. I lived in a one-bedroom furnished apartment on south Sepulveda near Pico in west Los Angeles. Most nights I would stay up late, working to complete everything I had to do for both school and work. Shortly after midnight one night, I called for my messages and struck up a conversation with the woman on the other end of the line. Each night after that, I called right after midnight to get my messages, so I'd have an excuse to talk with her. Within a few days, we got more personal. She'd break off the conversation to take a message for someone else, and we'd resume. This went on for a couple of weeks. We kept having friendlier conversations. Soon I invited her to stop by for a visit in the evening on her way to work. An attractive blonde, she surprised me with her openness. After we talked a little and got past the awkwardness of this unusual "blind date," she decided I would do as a lover, overlooking the bare apartment, the lumpy mattress with threadbare sheets borrowed from my mother, the plastic couch, and my heavy smoking habit.

We were lovers for about six weeks during the summer of 1969. The night of the moon landing by *Apollo 11*, she came over at nine, earlier than usual, to watch the live TV feed. We sat in bed watching as Neil Armstrong took "one small step for man" and, with Buzz Aldrin, cavorted on the lunar surface, planting the American flag in the airless, dusty soil. As I got to know her better, I found out she practiced Wicca, a newly revived pagan religious movement. That made me uneasy; I wasn't ready for anything spiritual, especially something smacking of witchcraft. After six weeks, she figured out I wasn't good husband or even boyfriend material— we never went out—and stopped coming over before the midnight shift. Used to such casual relationships, I moved on without regret, certain I could find someone else.

Over the next year, after I had quit the consulting job and moved to Pasadena to be closer to Caltech, I had other short-term relationships: a Montessori teacher, one of Paul's friends, another graduate student. Like a neophyte hunter, if something moved, I shot. If I missed, I'd go looking for another deer. I was unfocused and increasingly anxious about what to do with my life.

Shortly after Earth Day, leaving school behind, I sold my old car to get some cash, hitchhiked around the country and eventually landed in Boston. I stayed for a few days with Peter, a guy I knew from two years earlier as a consultant in Cambridge. The last time we'd seen each other, we were both well-dressed young professionals working part-time at Abt. Now he found he'd offered his apartment as a crash pad for a longhaired, disheveled, quasi-hippie sleeping on a mattress on the floor, sweating through the sheets during hot, humid Boston summer in a place with no air-conditioning. Shocked to see me this way, he was visibly relieved when I left after a few days.

I found a ride all the way back to California with a young couple I met through a classified ad in the *Phoenix*, Boston's alternative weekly. I paid for half the gas and rode in the back of their station wagon next to a panting, drooling Saint Bernard. During the drive, the weather was hot, and the car's A/C didn't work well. Misery loves company, and there I was, sitting or lying in back, sweating profusely even in a T-shirt, all the while dodging the dog's copious drool.

Once I got to Stewart's place in Santa Cruz, nearly broke and still conflicted, I grew a beard, bought a Pendleton wool shirt and a couple of tie-dyed T-shirts, and adopted a hippie look. By 1970 Santa Cruz had become a mecca for young people, with a cultural scene far mellower than in San Francisco or Berkeley.

State Highway 9 ran a few hundred feet downhill from my cabin. Many days, I'd stand by the roadside to hitchhike a ride into town, flash the peace sign, jump quickly into the back of any pickup truck that stopped, and bump along seven miles into Santa Cruz. I'd nurse a cheap beer at the Catalyst bar while trolling for women.

I tried to get it on with women but what could I offer? A roll in the hay on a lumpy mattress in a hard-to-find, cold-water cabin they had to drive to, then afterward drive themselves back home in the dark? I got my hands on a couple of tabs of psilocybin, magic mushrooms, and offered to share them with Debbie, a single mom I met at the Catalyst, a sweet twenty-something with dark hair, a raspy voice, and two kids. I convinced her to come by one evening for the psychedelic experience; after she didn't show, I took a dose myself. It was such a downer that I tossed the other tab. When I ran into her again at the bar, she claimed she'd had car trouble and there wasn't any way to reach me. We never did get together.

I rolled my own cigarettes with pouch tobacco and ZigZag papers, hung out with other drifters and the local working class. For the weekly alternative newspaper, *Free Spaghetti Dinner*, I wrote bad poetry and occasional essays on personal philosophy. In one,

"Restoration of Kinship," I traced environmental disasters to a contemporary loss of kinship, a feeling of oneness with the Earth and all life that had disappeared during four centuries of conquest and industrialization.

On sunny warm summer days, I sometimes went skinny-dipping with fellow hippies in a secluded section of the nearby San Lorenzo River. It may sound idyllic but hanging out this way only added to my uncertainty: after Earth Day, what did I want to do with my life?

I was depressed. By leaving my graduate studies without getting a PhD, for the first time in my life I had failed at something I valued. I hadn't finished what I wanted most. I'd never get a doctorate, something I had always expected would be a crowning academic and personal achievement.

I tried to make sense of things, reading books to discover life's meaning, works I had overlooked while pursuing my technical education. Beyond German philosophy, I read much of Herman Hesse: *Siddhartha*, of course. I also studied poetry and psychology; subjects I hadn't taken in college on my way to becoming a technical specialist in water engineering. I was most drawn to poetry that connected me emotionally with my deepest longings. I went to readings at the Santa Cruz campus, especially to hear Gary Snyder's poetry, with its Buddhist environmental consciousness that showed how to combine intellectual work with outer activism.

I read voraciously, had intense discussions about life with Stewart and other friends, and in general worked to broaden my education. The more I read, the more I became like a talking parrot, spouting philosophical truths without having any direct inner experience.

A few lines from a poem by the 15th-century Muslim poet-saint Kabir described my situation:
"The truth is that you turned away yourself
      and decided to go into the dark alone.
Now you are tangled up in others and forgot what you once
      knew,
And that's why everything you do has some weird failure in it."

I may have turned away from the light, I may have failed at getting a PhD, but I hadn't quit. After chilling out at Stewart's place and hanging out at the Catalyst with other dropouts and hippies for several months, one day I woke up.

I thought, "This is not who I am; this is not the person I want to be."

Barely a year earlier, I was a doctoral candidate at a top school, passed my oral exams, and only had to finish a thesis to get a PhD. Now one step away from being a washed-up bum, I knew I could do better with my life than waste away in Santa Cruz, flashing the peace sign at everyone but not feeling at all peaceful inside.

This period of depression or melancholy may have had a deeper purpose, one in which I could find a different, perhaps better, more creative version of myself. I read widely and allowed myself to explore intellectual, emotional and spiritual terrain I had never noticed.

Like someone awakening abruptly from a deep sleep, I staggered for a while. Much like a drunk after a night of carousing, I had a sour taste in my mouth and a hangover from a decade of striving to be the best at schoolwork. I still nursed a persistent headache brought on by poverty and lack of direction. But once awake, I wasn't going back to sleep.

DROPPING BACK IN

After four months living an austere and celibate life in the cabin, I was still wallowing in a self-dug hole. First, I knew I needed to stop digging. Second, I had to find someone to pull me out. With these two realizations, I recovered a more optimistic outlook and searched for a way to get back to doing something useful for the environment. I needed to find work; my savings were running out despite my ultra-low-consumption lifestyle.

During the fall of 1970, some days I'd ride to school with Stewart on the back of his BMW motorcycle and hang out at the university, getting a sense of how things worked at UC Santa Cruz. Eventually I met Professor Richard (Dick) Cooley, an expert on polar bears, who'd written two highly regarded books on natural resource conservation. The university had recently hired Dick to create an environmental studies program. We hit it off immediately, and he pulled me out of the hole.

My Caltech and Harvard degrees impressed Dick. Since I was only 26 and he was 45, he also saw me as a bridge to the student generation. Dick had the quiet demeanor of someone who had spent years in the Alaskan bush and the Arctic, talking with native people and, through binoculars, watching polar bears mate.

Hawk-nosed, with black horn-rimmed glasses and thinning hair, Dick smoked a lot, as did I. I got the habit from a girlfriend in my senior year at Caltech (she smoked Newports, heavy on the menthol) and I developed a pack-a-day routine (unfiltered Camels or Galois) while studying in Germany, which I had continued at Harvard and Caltech. Dick and I often discussed environmental issues while sharing a smoke in his office (you could still do that.) Wanting to force myself to quit the habit I'd had for six years, I bummed cigarettes from him whenever we met. Occasionally, I'd buy a pack of his brand and bring it with me, dropping it ceremoniously on his desk to even our accounts, saying, "I owe you this."

Mark Twain wrote, "Giving up smoking is easy; I've done it hundreds of times." One day in the spring of 1972, I saw how ridiculous this looked and quit smoking, "cold turkey." I soon lost the urge and never smoked again.

After we got to know each other, Dick offered me a contract part-time as a Lecturer in Environmental Studies. I designed and taught courses, one or two per semester, at the academic ladder's lowest rung. Teaching became my lifeline, a new way to participate in the environmental movement and to return to what I considered a more normal life, where I could work, make money, and be productive.

TAKING ON THE POLLUTERS

Beyond oil spills, dying lakes, and rivers on fire, a sense of urgency pervaded the environmental movement after Earth Day. People were dying prematurely from air pollution caused mostly by auto exhaust and industrial emissions. They got sick from drinking contaminated water: along most major rivers in the country, your drinking water, while treated, came from someone else's contaminated discharge a short distance upstream.

Silent Spring raised the technical issue of indiscriminate chemical pollution to a national political concern. We couldn't stop all forms of pollution overnight, but the movement mobilized public opinion against egregious use of toxic chemicals.

Within a few years, these concerns led to regulations banning or heavily regulating such chemicals. Lawsuits and growing consumer backlash led to companies reformulating many products or removing them from the market. The chaotic environmental movement, as a hotbed of citizen concern, had a noticeable impact on government and business faster than activists thought would happen.

As I continued to study water issues and environmental science, my outlook broadened to other issues, especially the role of phosphate-laden detergents in causing eutrophication in lakes. With a growing U.S. population, increasing amounts of phosphates from household detergents passed through sewage treatment plants and entered water bodies such as lakes. More phosphorus led to the rapid growth of algae (blooms), consuming all the oxygen in the water when the algae died, in turn killing fish dependent on high oxygen levels.

The largest detergent producer was Proctor & Gamble (P&G, makers of Tide). Environmental science clearly established the connection between excessive amounts of phosphates and fish kills. The right action to save lakes from algae blooms and prevent fish kills was to ban phosphates from detergents.

After its publication, chemical companies attacked *Silent Spring* using classic corporate PR strategies: deny any connection between their products and environmental harm, denigrate critics as ill-informed and unscientific, preach the need to wait for a "scientific consensus," delay government action through lobbying, and continue to profit from selling polluting products.

One of my father's friends since World War II days, someone he always praised as a man of integrity, served in a high position at the White House during the Eisenhower Administration in the 1950s. I got angry when I learned this man was the chief lobbyist for P&G, orchestrating their strategy of delaying necessary regulations to eliminate phosphates from detergents. I criticized him personally in a major newspaper. My father didn't like it, but I wanted to take a stand against corporate polluters, even if it caused discomfort in our family.

Eventually bowing to their critics and to the growing demand for regulation, soap companies figured out how to get clothes "whiter than white" without using phosphates in their detergents. Tide stayed the best-selling detergent, and damaged lakes soon recovered. Realizing I had to temper my anger with tact, I decided to be less personal in my environmental activism and to focus more on systemic causes.

ENVIRONMENTAL STUDIES

As I grappled with understanding the science behind eutrophication in lakes, I could see my environmental engineering education lacked not only the human element, but also basic biology and ecology.

As I developed into an ardent environmentalist, I came to regard ecology as the core of environmental work. This was an eye-opener, pushing me away from relying solely on an engineering approach to pollution control, instead taking a more holistic view of how to tackle these problems.

The truth of John Muir's understanding finally dawned on me, viscerally more than intellectually: "When we try to pick out anything by itself, we find it hitched to everything else in the Universe." If I was going to be effective as an environmentalist, beyond science and engineering I had to learn politics and economics, everything that created these issues.

I went "back to school" on my own initiative, studying ecology and environmental economics so I could teach, using a broader knowledge base. In this way, I hoped to galvanize students into activism, showing them how to connect their personal concerns with scientific and economic facts.

In the wake of Earth Day, the early 1970s marked the beginnings of Environmental Studies as a separate and recognized academic field. By teaching ten courses over two years as a university lecturer, I helped Dick Cooley pioneer this field at UC Santa Cruz.

More importantly, I met Elle.

ELLE

RELIEVED TO BE WORKING AGAIN, I spent a few days each week hanging out at the Environmental Studies Program's student center, preparing my courses. One day, a student wandered in, looking for a friend. January 1971, and there she was: tall, slim, long blonde hair, rimless granny glasses, a lovely smile, sweet energy.

I noticed her immediately, using a special radar young guys have when an attractive and (apparently) available woman comes into view. We introduced ourselves casually: I found out she was a junior, making her about 20, and her name was Elle: that was it. After that first meeting, I'd see her at the center occasionally, we'd talk some, sometimes have coffee or lunch, and I'd learn more about her background.

An only child, unplanned by parents nearing forty when she came along, Elle grew up in a middle-class San Jose suburb thirty miles away. Her dad drove a delivery truck for a bakery. When Elle was nine, her mom returned to college to become credentialed as an elementary school teacher. For several years, they studied together most evenings at the dining room table while her dad watched TV in the living room.

Until she was ten, Elle said she talked mostly to horses. Later, I found out that at sixteen, she'd had an unsettling experience with her first sexual encounters, seduced several times by a youth worker in his mid-twenties who was counseling her. Freaked out by it, for the next four years she swore off sex. But now at twenty, she was ready to try again. What better choice (I thought) than a bearded, longhaired faux hippie teaching courses in her field: environmental studies?

She was obviously intelligent. In one end-of-course written evaluation, the practice then at the no-grades Santa Cruz campus, a professor wrote, "This is the best undergraduate economics paper I have ever read." We talked about environmental issues regularly over lunch and at coffee. This shared intellectual interest underpinned our blossoming relationship.

But we both wanted something more intimate. Elle shared a two-story large old Victorian with ten other women on High Street, a steep road leading from Santa Cruz town up to the university. She had a double bed, a small dresser and an old wooden desk in an unheated room, a converted outdoor sitting porch. One evening, we ate dinner at the house and talked for a few hours. When it became too late to hitchhike safely back to my cabin in the woods, by accident (or intent) we wound up in bed. We soon became inseparable.

After a month, I left my mountain cabin and moved into the house on High Street. When the semester ended, we moved into a rented house on a bluff overlooking Santa Cruz and the mouth of the San Lorenzo. Neither Elle nor I had ever lived with anyone. This was a big step for both of us, but we never discussed any further commitment; it seemed like the most natural thing to do. Even though Elle's parents didn't accept it right away, she went ahead.

After I moved in with Elle, gradually Stewart and I stopped spending much time together. I taught summer school classes at Santa Cruz and he was busy with his thesis research. He didn't like Elle, thought she was young and naïve. Over the past few years, he'd also become estranged from his parents; perhaps it wasn't only Elle he disliked. He took a lot of LSD those days; maybe that also affected his attitude. We grew distant.

Whenever we'd get together, sometimes at the Catalyst, Stewart acted openly dismissive of Elle to her face. I couldn't persuade him to change, so I had to choose between a once good friend and the woman I was living with. It wasn't hard. I turned away from Stewart, ending our twenty-year friendship.

Sometimes friendships end when there's nothing more to say,

or when one person has no interest in changing or growing. Maybe it was a guy thing; neither of us wanted to discuss intensely personal issues, to be open or appear vulnerable with each other; maybe it was a combination of things. Still, I was sad; good friends are rare. My casual attitude might have disguised the hurt of separation; at an emotional level I found it disturbing. Parting with Stewart created a stronger connection with Elle. She knew I'd chosen to be with her; she opened more to our relationship.

We connected not only through environmental issues, but through Elle's strong interest in spirituality. I could talk about it philosophically, but she wanted direct experience. Getting closer to nature provided a bridge for us into that realm. As committed environmentalists, we both wanted to learn more about California native plants and took field trips in the redwoods bordering the campus with an older woman named Brysis. An amazingly spry 65-year-old, she knew local Native American lore and could tell you precisely which plants and herbs to use for which illnesses, how to make herbal teas from native plants, ways to divine forest spirits.

I was skeptical about spiritual matters after spending eight years pursuing a rigorous technical education at a time when many academics, especially in science, actively dismissed religious belief. Still, I went along with Elle's interests. At our new house, we met Tom, a neighbor and merchant seaman, also a spiritual seeker. He had a large library of transcendentalist texts, many of which I borrowed and read. He was a *Tai Chi* adept, something he'd studied during long layovers in the Far East. Whenever he stayed in town, Tom led classes on his front lawn. I tried to slow my mind enough to perform such common movements as "carrying the tiger back to the mountain." I struggled with the slow pace but eventually got into the flow of this graceful ballet.

After two years in Santa Cruz, we moved to Foster City on the San Francisco Peninsula to be close to our work as environmental consultants and avoid the awful daily commute. We lived in an apartment close to San Francisco Bay; after work, I often walked during summer afternoons along the levees, getting away from the city's hustle and noise, moving past quiet marshes with teeming birdlife: long-billed curlews and marbled godwits, white herons, and Clapper Rails. Most afternoons, a fast-moving white wall of fog spilled through the Golden Gate. I'd watch as it advanced toward me, blanketing everything in a dusky mist, placing a cool damp shroud over the calm body of the Bay. By mid-morning the fog dissipated, vanishing into the warmer air of the advancing day until returning in the late afternoon.

Once we moved to Foster City, we went to programs at a spiritual community in San Francisco. At each step of this journey, I resisted, but Elle's inner longing overcame my hesitation. Following her lead, we kept snacking at the ever-expanding smorgasbord of Bay Area spiritual offerings.

Spiritual seeking kept us going as a couple, because I didn't always treat her well. During her senior year, right before graduation, as we drove one day in the redwoods toward Felton, I asked, "What do you want to do with your degree?"

"I'd like to be an environmental consultant, something like that."

Without reflecting on what she might have meant, immediately I responded, "You can't be a consultant—you don't know anything."

She shrank back and leaned away from me. "That was really nasty!"

I tried to soften the impact. "I'm sorry, I didn't mean it that way." Still, she was pissed. Instead of being supportive, I was as dismissive as Stewart had been. I had conveniently forgotten my own ignorance when I began a consulting career as a graduate student only four years ago.

During our first two years, we fought a lot over many trivial things and one important thing: respect. Was I unwittingly repeating my father's behavior toward my mother? Elle and I separated a few times for a day or two but always reconciled after I apologized. I was sure of my superior intellect, with degrees in technical subjects from the best schools; besides, I was six years older. I had too much ego for a relationship between equals. Selfishly, I wanted only a compliant lover and a companion for adventures.

Despite such conflicts, we shared many likes and dislikes. Elle liked my brothers and sisters. Having come from a family of seven, I never thought much about how lonely she might have been after graduating, with few close girlfriends and usually only me to talk to. Now she had acquired two sisters and two brothers and went to family gatherings like birthdays and holidays. They liked her, too; I was the boring older brother, but she was their new, more interesting younger sister.

We hiked and camped in the Sierra Nevada, took road trips around northern California and rode horses on the Santa Cruz campus. After two years, misfortune struck. One spring day in 1973, Elle's mare reared suddenly. She fell off backwards, landing awkwardly on a paved road. She hurt her back badly. To relieve her pain, we visited chiropractors for the next two years, some as far away as Monterey, forty miles distant. Gradually the severe pain vanished, but nothing helped to strengthen her back. A year later, a car rear-ended us on the 101 Freeway in San Francisco. Elle got whiplash, her neck and back pain returned, and we resumed therapy. Because of her back problems, we gave up hiking and camping in the mountains for less strenuous urban recreations like walking, visiting friends, and traveling.

LAND OF ENCHANTMENT

In late September 1973, Elle and I took a two-week vacation and set out to explore northern New Mexico, wanting to get to know the place, with the vague thought of possibly moving there. We shared a romantic fantasy of leaving the big city and finding a place for ourselves to live and work among the three cultures of the area: Anglo, Spanish, and Native American. With the "back to the land" movement in full force, we bought into the ideal of living closer to nature, each month eagerly reading the *Mother Earth News*, with intriguing stories of young couples like us raising goats and tending vegetables in rural paradises.

We searched for something to help us open our hearts, some place we would find more spiritual; we thought that to get closer to our real selves we had to live closer to nature, somewhere in the country far away from the crowds, noise, and traffic of the big city. With that goal in mind, we set out for New Mexico, full of the spirit of exploration, committed to changing our lives.

We drove through the mountains to Santa Fe, where we fell in love with the indigenous adobe architecture. We wandered through the marketplace in the plaza, with local Indian women selling silver and turquoise jewelry to tourists from blankets spread out along a covered sidewalk. At 7,000 feet, nestled at the foot of the southern end of the Sangre de Christo range, with peaks rising above 14,000 feet, for the past half-century Santa Fe had inspired artists and dreamers, poets and urban refugees. At a shop off the plaza, we bought two *retablos*, images of Saint Francis hand-painted on an eight-inch tile, surrounded by a hammered-tin filigree. We later hung them in our kitchen.

Santa Fe was a magical place, especially the old town surrounding the plaza, as close to visiting another country as one could find in the United States. We loved the eclectic mashup of art, architecture, blinding light, deep greens and browns, in a place still retaining a slower-paced, 19th-century urban sensibility. Santa Fe was unique, not only in the sense of a historically preserved place, but as a small city, human-scale, walkable, close to nature and vibrant with culture, like similar places I remembered from my student days in Germany. Elle and I took a long look around. Was this our place? We didn't know if it was the right time for such a big move.

Over the course of this trip, we reconsidered our dream of taking part in the "back to the land" movement, whether in New Mexico or in northern California. We accepted the truth: we were thoroughly city people. We recognized we'd have to find another way to "make a difference" with our lives and careers, and we'd most likely do it while living in the Bay Area. We began to grasp intuitively, however inarticulately, that spirituality had little to do with *where* we lived, but everything to do with *how* we lived.

I wanted to live a different life from what I'd known growing up. My father had died less than two months earlier, and I didn't want to live the way he had lived, pinned down at a desk working as a lawyer, with a large family to support. At 29, I valued personal freedom more than the burdens (and joys) of family life. Only 23, Elle wanted to explore the wider world after having led a comfortable but utterly conventional middle-class life.

On the way back, we made a side trip to the Hopi Reservation in northern Arizona, to take in the magic and mystery of that place, often described by Hopis and early anthropologists as a gateway between heaven and earth. After staying overnight at the new motel on the Second Mesa, seeing only what Hopis allowed tourists to see, we drove back to the Bay Area. We received something valuable and unexpected from this trip to New Mexico, insights that destroyed certain fantasies but opened new avenues for personal exploration. Instead of driving all over, looking for somewhere else to live, we decided to stay in the Bay Area.

THE FIRST OIL EMBARGO

Our interests in environmental protection soon migrated into an infatuation with alternative energy resources. The week after we returned from New Mexico, war erupted between Israel and the adjacent Arab states. To punish America for supporting Israel, OPEC shut off oil supplies to the United States. This unexpected Arab oil embargo alerted Americans to the fragility of our energy supplies. For the next six months, we had to plan our driving carefully as gasoline prices quadrupled. To fill the tank, I often waited in hour-long lines at gas stations.

Government agencies searched for alternatives. Elle and I both became convinced solar energy represented the best long-term solution to energy supply problems; sunshine flowed freely, and no one could embargo it. The trick became figuring how to use solar economically. We studied the technology, joined the Northern California Solar Energy Association, went to their monthly meetings, and learned how solar technologies worked.

By engaging with the alternative energy movement in the Bay Area, we met the visionary architect and UC Berkeley architecture professor, Sim van der Ryn, an expert in ecological design and solar use in homes. We first encountered Sim at the Integral Urban

House in west Berkeley, a pioneering urban ecology demonstration project operated by the Farallones Institute, which he co-founded. The renovated old two-story house had a vegetable garden, chickens, a solar water heater, and a Swedish Clivus Multrum composting toilet. Exotic stuff at the time!

Our visits to the Integral Urban House planted a seed with Elle, which grew into a longing to build her own eco-friendly house. We thought we could make a difference with our work by influencing people in cities to live with lower environmental impacts. At the same time, we could explore deeper mysteries by absorbing the spiritual qualities of each place we visited. Integrating our spiritual longings with our work as environmentalists led us to become "eco-warriors."

ECO-WARRIORS

AT THE BEGINNING OF THE ENVIRONMENTAL MOVEMENT, state and national politicians vied with each other to pass new laws protecting the environment. Written often in haste, the laws weren't always clear; this was unfamiliar terrain. Courts often had to step in and interpret the statutes, sometimes momentously.

In October 1972, the California Supreme Court issued a decision in a landmark case called *Friends of Mammoth vs. Board of Supervisors of Mono County*. The court ruled that the California Environmental Quality Act, CEQA (passed in 1970 soon after Earth Day) required an environmental review for *any* government action approving a *private* project, including land use approvals, rezoning requests, etc. Before *Friends of Mammoth*, most people assumed CEQA applied only to government-sponsored projects.

Overnight a new industry arose in California: the environmental consulting business. Every private development required an Environmental Impact Report (EIR). At a small Bay Area research firm, Environmental Science Associates (ESA), the president, Paul Zigman, saw the potential for growing his five-person team into a much larger company, with environmental consulting as its core business.

After teaching ten courses over two years, my gig at Santa Cruz ended in 1972 after the summer session. Teaching had been fun, but I wanted to have a more immediate impact on protecting the environment. After a few months of looking around, in the late fall of 1972 I hired on as a project manager with ESA. After Paul hired me, I convinced him to interview Elle. With her newly minted degree in environmental studies from Santa Cruz, she soon got her dream job as an environmental consultant.

A few months before, I'd created and led a spring semester course at UC Santa Cruz, a student seminar in environmental activism. As an activist, I'd already questioned a convention center proposed for a location on the Monterey Bay headlands at a popular surfing spot known as Lighthouse Point. After reading the economic justification report the previous year, I became convinced it would both destroy scarce oceanfront open space and represent a bad public investment.

In the early 1970s, the mindset of most public officials favored unlimited economic growth, but I knew we could do better. The twelve students in my seminar dug into the proponent's reports and other background material and produced a report slamming the project on both environmental and economic grounds. We released the report at the end of the spring term, and it tipped a hornet's nest. A citizens' opposition group soon formed, the Save Lighthouse Point Association. Within a month we gathered 4,000 signatures on a petition opposing the project, in a town with only 32,000 people, and presented them to the City Council. Our vocal opposition stopped the project's momentum. Two years later, the city and county abandoned the project. (In the 1980s, Lighthouse Point became a state beach.)

After our success at Lighthouse Point, I thought we could use the new EIR process to rein in other poorly-thought-out development projects. Since our clients, local government agencies, generally sided with developers, we had to appear professional in our reports and be circumspect with our analysis, but we still had mostly anti-development attitudes and intentions.

ESA's president Paul Zigman did the marketing. He was the smooth talker, the schmoozer, the one who brought in the work, reminding me in that way of my former boss at Abt. In his late 40s, soft-spoken and short, Paul still had the physique and swagger of the younger body builder he once was. He also had terrible eyesight, wore thick glasses to see, and bent his head close to the page when reading reports. He had an unusual hobby: collecting fortunes from fortune cookies at Chinese restaurants. He ate a lot of

Chinese food, saved the fortunes, and assembled these little paper slips into a notebook. He'd review the collection when he had a business problem to solve. Sometimes I'd go into his office and see him, head bent low over the fortune-cookie notebook, trying to figure out how to apply "your happiness is just around the corner" or a similar pithy saying to a business problem.

Preparing EIRs for public agencies required us to deal with developers and their architects. We had to meet the legal requirements for the contents of an EIR, as defined by the courts and the CEQA law. That meant we had to present the unvarnished facts and describe potential alternatives to a project, something public agencies often glossed over or ignored in the rush to approve new developments. We had to review each EIR with developers before we could submit it to the client, the city or country. We often had contentious meetings about our findings and recommendations.

One summer afternoon in 1974, I found myself sitting in an architect's conference room in San Jose. Sun streamed in though unshaded windows, the room was stuffy, and the architect was yelling at me and my two colleagues, Bill and Tom, overall a decidedly unpleasant meeting. We'd written a draft environmental impact report on his project in Marin County, a medical office building in Greenbrae, located on a former tidal wetland adjacent to Corte Madera Creek near San Francisco Bay. He was angry because in the report we wrote that "Alternatives to the Proposed Project" (a required section) should include reopening the wetland to tidal action, letting it function again as a tidal marsh.

"That's not a reasonable option—no other project has to do this," he argued. He wanted this alternative deleted from the report, but we wouldn't budge.

"It has to be in the report, or Marin County may reject it as not meeting legal requirements," I replied. "If the report is incomplete, people may sue your client and delay the project, so we need to keep this alternative." After more discussion, the architect relented and agreed that we could leave this section in the EIR. This EIR was one of the first in California to recommend preserving and restoring wetlands, saving them from development.

The Greenbrae project offered us a chance to stake out an even more radical claim than preserving wetlands: we should restore historical marshes, the most productive ecosystems on Earth. Twenty years earlier, the US Army Corps of Engineers straightened Corte Madera Creek and lined it with concrete, severely disturbing the Greenbrae marsh. Even so, some wetlands remained and still harbored wildlife.

During his fieldwork, our staff biologist, Tom, had identified a listed endangered species living in the marsh, the red-bellied, saltwater harvest mouse, a small rodent that survived by eating marsh plants and drinking saltwater. The little fellow led a precarious existence: at low tide, it could feed and breed in the pickleweed and salt grass, but at high tide, it had to climb atop plants to stay out of the water, exposing itself to raptors circling over the marsh. Imagine twice a day your home floods and you cling to the roof while a gang of thuggish birds flies above, looking to eat you. Sounds a bit like Alfred Hitchcock's movie, *The Birds*, right?

That little mouse turned the tide. After we convinced the architect, we added preserving the existing marsh as a reasonable alternative in our EIR. Both the developers and our team knew Marin County would make the final decision, no matter what the report revealed.

The controversy alerted people in the area to the ongoing destruction of marsh habitats from filling in for development projects, a practice eventually halted around the Bay by the 1980s. After they watched a growing public protest over putting a building in the marsh, the developers abandoned the project. (Later restored to full tidal flushing, it's now called Creekside Marsh, a natural ecosystem protected as a Marin County park.) Our work stopped this development, which pleased us immensely. The medical office building might have been a valuable project for the community, but it belonged in another place.

Chalk up another win for the environment!

Over three years at ESA, I led teams that wrote three dozen EIRs on development projects in the Bay Area. We didn't block most poorly planned developments; sometimes we couldn't even improve them, as I'd hoped after our success with the Greenbrae project. At best a speed bump or a yield sign on the development roundabout, an EIR slowed the process but usually didn't change the outcome. Most local governments continued to champion commercial development.

Working together, sharing friends, my relationship with Elle blossomed. I came to appreciate her intelligence and innate wisdom, and she learned to work around my moods and occasional flare-ups. Outside of work, she wanted to learn meditation, so we took TM (Transcendental Meditation) training from her friend Kristy and set aside a small meditation corner in our apartment. I couldn't get the hang of TM. Even using my "personalized" mantra, I couldn't sit still or quiet my mind for the required twenty minutes. Still, my early attempts to learn meditation opened a door. They made me more interested in, and receptive to, genuine spiritual experiences, but I still needed a teacher who could guide me. I didn't have to wait long.

III

ENCOUNTERING THE MASTER

BABA LOVED CHANTING. From the day I first met him, I chanted, sometimes spiritual texts, sometimes the mantra Baba gave, sometimes in a large group singing spirited fast chants called namasankirtana. *I loved these chants: the blending of voices into a devotional chorus, the deep inner resonance of the syllables, the ecstatic crescendo, the still mind resting in the heart after the chant ended.*

But why? Why did I have such a strong connection with this ancient practice? I wasn't at all musical; I couldn't carry a tune or play an instrument. One day I got a clue. Not long after meeting Baba, I read a book called Saints of India *by a traveling teacher of bhakti (devotional) yoga, Sant Keshavadas, which included various chants sacred to those saints. As I read, I came across a well-known chant that begins, "Ramakrishna Hari." I burst into tears, sobbing heavily, as an ancient memory of singing this hymn of devotion to God in a previous life flooded into my awareness. Over the years, I learned dozens of these devotional chants, but I never again experienced such a strong emotional reaction to a chant upon first reading the words.*

It's a modern conceit that we live only once: this life we are living now. Ancient wisdom cultures maintain otherwise - they teach we are spiritual beings, souls, who assume physical bodies on this earth to learn certain lessons. We take birth repeatedly until we master them, evolving during each lifetime toward complete Self-knowledge. Perhaps I had been chanting the divine name for many lifetimes, beseeching God to open my heart fully. Now this primal yearning for grace was about to find fulfillment.

"HE HAS GOOD ENERGY"

AS ELLE AND I CONTINUED SEARCHING FOR SPIRITUAL GUIDANCE, we attended programs (*satsangs*) at a small ashram in San Francisco with a resident Indian guru. I read the guru's two books and met him but never experienced any strong connection. We liked the ashram's quiet atmosphere and gentle people and often went to their satsangs. We became friends with some people, including one of the leaders, Mary, a tall, slender, graying middle-aged woman with a PhD in psychology who wore flowing all-white clothes and was always kind and gracious to us.

One day in April 1974, she returned from meeting Swami Muktananda (known to all as Baba, or "Father"), a renowned Indian Master, a Siddha ("perfect being"), who had recently arrived on his second American tour. We asked her what he was like.

Her response was mysterious: "You should go see him. He has good energy."

What a colossal understatement!

With her recommendation, we found out where this Baba stayed and decided to check him out. One afternoon we left work early and drove to a home in Piedmont, a small upscale city in the foothills east of Oakland. People welcomed us and directed us to sit on the floor and wait.

A short while later, Baba came downstairs. He blew away my concept of a master; I had only seen photos of old men with flowing white beards and kindly expressions. Baba was dark-skinned, with a scraggly salt-and-pepper beard. He wore orange silks, dark glasses and an orange knit ski cap. He radiated peace, but was constantly in motion, talking with the people around him, twiddling between thumb and forefinger a rose someone had given him, leaning over to listen to a question from someone seated or kneeling on the floor before him.

Because Baba spoke no English, his assistant had to translate everything. To me, it seemed that what someone asked didn't always matter, because Baba could size up the questioner without waiting to have the entire question translated. He'd look intently at the person, lean toward them and respond, sometimes with a few words, sometimes at length. He seemed always to know *the question behind the question.*

As soon as he sat on his chair in the living room with 50 or 60 people sitting on the floor around him, I sensed this incredible magnetism radiating from him. Mesmerized, immobilized, I couldn't take my eyes away from him. Baba was incredibly relaxed and natural, vibrant with energy, shining with an inner radiance. Watching him, my active mind stopped—for a moment.

After half an hour, Baba left the room and Elle motioned for us to leave, but, indrawn, I didn't move fast enough. Abruptly, everyone stood. Dozens of people blocked the path to the door; we couldn't leave without pushing through them. Someone handed me a song sheet showing the words to the evening *arati*, in India the traditional chanting and waving of lights toward day's end. I followed along with the text, not knowing how to pronounce a single word. After twenty minutes, the chant ended, and we left.

Over the next three months, we attended Baba's public lectures, where he spoke about the *Kundalini Shakti*, a subtle dormant spiritual energy embedded in all of us, something a Guru had to awaken before real spiritual development could take place. Existing in the subtle body, once awakened the Kundalini energy would move up the chakras from the base of the spine to the crown of the head, leading to higher states of awareness and spiritual development.

Baba's message was new, replete with mysterious terms and ideas I had never encountered. I took it all in. Baba's mastery was visible, all encompassing. I drank eagerly from his fountain of wisdom. Baba delivered these esoteric teachings with an infectious and attractive mix of enthusiasm, humor, and joy.

After we met Baba, my reading habit intensified. I wanted to read everything he had written or whatever someone had written about him, anything I could find that explained this yoga. Initially, I found only one book written by Baba, his spiritual autobiography *Play of Consciousness*, but I soon bought a five-volume set from the early 1970s, in which a devotee had recorded questions-and-answers with students at his ashram. I eagerly read every word.

By reading his books, I convinced myself I could eventually understand Baba's teachings and grasp what he had to offer. I figured becoming a student meant simply to engage your mind in learning the Master's teachings. I understood only much later that I had to open my heart to receive what he truly wanted to give me.

The early-twentieth-century Indian saint Sai Baba of Shirdi often said, "I give people what they want, so that they may want what I have to give them." I wanted scriptural knowledge, but I soon found out Baba had so much more to offer, a natural way of living each moment from the highest perspective.

Baba's teachings blended learning, love, and discipline. I treasured learning but didn't yet care much for discipline or grasp what he meant by loving God and seeing God in each person I met. The next three months, we went back often to the Piedmont house to bathe in his radiance. Sometimes I would approach his chair, bow, as was customary, put an offering in the basket by his feet, and glance at him. I never asked a question. Occasionally he wouldn't wear his dark glasses and I could look into his eyes for a moment. When I did, I saw only an ecstatic inner focus.

Baba's gaze mirrored my own state. When I felt his love, when I experienced my own love, I saw love everywhere. When I feared having to change, to give up my small ego and embrace the higher Self he talked about, I saw him as a fierce warrior, ready to strike at my limited sense of myself, my identification with the body, mind and personality. When I had concerns about how he regarded me, I remembered my sometimes stern but loving father who had passed the previous year. Baba became like a substitute father, spurring me on to a more genuine approach to life.

During Baba's tour in northern California in 1974, he lectured at local theaters and concert halls. On stage, Baba was captivating and energetic, with a deep-throated chuckle whenever he told a funny story. His delight in these stories generated laughter and engendered moments of recognition. A picture of his own Master always hung behind his chair or sat on a table at his side. In his presence I became still and peaceful, yet joyful and energized at the same time.

I knew little of this world before I met Baba. By attending satsangs at the meditation center in San Francisco, we knew about yogic masters, but Baba operated at a much higher level: dynamic, loving, wise in both worldly and spiritual realms. To call his presence *esoteric* could hardly describe the full flavor and vast scope of Baba's teachings and personality. Although he referred mostly to Indian scriptures and teaching stories, Baba's outreach had universal appeal.

I was transfixed. In front of me lay a clear path and a teacher rich with spiritual knowledge, holding open a gate leading into an unknown but alluring realm. What should I do with this blessing? I didn't know yet what I wanted from Baba. I was drawn to him but couldn't articulate why. Without hesitation, I walked through that gate, eager to learn, determined to immerse myself in his love and the experience of inner bliss. I might have had trouble expressing what I was doing, but I was confident it was the right thing; whatever changes I needed to make in my life would happen naturally on the other side of the gate.

AWAKENING TO THE INNER WORLD

ELLE AND I SOON GOT TO KNOW SOME AMERICAN DEVOTEES WHO'D SPENT time with Baba in India. We occasionally received whispered asides from these "old hands."

They'd ask, *sotto voce*, "Have you got Baba's touch yet?" Sometimes simply: "Have you received the touch?"

We tried to get them to explain what happens with *the touch*. They called it *shaktipat*, the descent of the master's spiritual energy into the seeker. Sometimes they called it "Baba's grace." People couldn't tell me clearly what happened with the transmission of Baba's energy, except that for them it changed everything. They called it initiation, the inner awakening, the end to everything that had come before, the beginning of the spiritual journey.

I wasn't ready for a Master. I'd never followed any spiritual teacher. I was as green as green could be. I'd read spiritual books for the past five years but hadn't learned much I could use. I wasn't sure what "it" I was looking for. To become wise? To get rid of doubt? To drop my pretentious anger? To become "conscious"? Even after two years of TM, I couldn't sit quietly for ten minutes of meditation. Instead, my mind usually spun: planning what should I eat for dinner, remembering my last sexual encounter or anticipating the next one, composing my to-do list for tomorrow, anything but inner peace.

To experience peace, nothing had worked: not hatha yoga, or focusing on an object, gazing at the tip of my nose; nothing. My legs always ached after a few minutes' sitting in a half-lotus or *easy posture*. I couldn't focus my mind on anything for long. I found it hard mentally, and physically agonizing, to sit long enough for meditation to happen, for my mind to quiet enough to experience the sweet stillness promised by so many teachers and texts.

When Baba offered a four-day meditation retreat over the July Fourth weekend, Elle and I decided to go. On July Fourth at five in the morning, an hour before sunrise, Elle and I found ourselves sitting on the floor of the retreat center, awaiting Baba's touch. We'd driven there the previous afternoon from our apartment in Foster City, forty miles away.

That first morning, I received the "touch," awakening the inner meditation energy, the Shakti. After meditating each day, I could sense some inner peace and love, but still I struggled to sit quietly and indrawn for a half-hour or longer. One day I would have strong experiences of Baba's spiritual energy coursing through my body, the next day I would sit for an hour and experience nothing except incessant mental activity.

I told myself, "This is just a process; I'm sure I'll get the hang of it soon."

No matter how "spiritual" I had tried to make my actions, history, or disguises, I still hadn't had what Baba described as the core spiritual experience: simple unaffected love for all. Something had to happen to change my bad habits and tendencies. Now I had the chance to change myself, this time with a true Master.

Baba's touch was like Alexander the Great's sword, which cut through the legendary Gordian knot, fulfilling the prophecy that whoever could undo it would rule all of Asia. Alexander recognized he couldn't unravel the knot; there were no visible ends. He decided to change the terms of engagement, drew his sword, and with one blow sliced the knot in two.

Baba didn't try to untie the knots of the psyche, regress your past lives or delve deeply into childhood traumas, aiming to make you a less damaged and more functional human being. Instead, he bypassed such modest goals and aimed directly at the main issue: I didn't believe I *deserved* God's love. Somewhere deep in my psyche, I was convinced I would *never* be worthy of such perfect love.

By receiving Baba's touch, my world changed in ways I couldn't articulate. At the time, none of these "explanations" of what he had done mattered, made sense, or even registered in my aware- ness. I knew something truly mystical had happened but had no idea what to do with it. Baba gave his touch early each morning during meditation. Each day during the retreat we meditated twice. Each day I could more easily slip into deep meditation, even if for only a few minutes. Each afternoon we listened to Baba talk and had *darshan*, a time when we could approach Baba, bow at his feet (if we chose), ask questions, receive a card printed with the mantra he gave, or silently thank him.

Accompanied by a harmonium and tamboura, slowly and melodiously we chanted the mantra he gave. We chanted fast de- votional hymns in Sanskrit to the beat of a *mridanga*, an Indian drum, and the clash of finger cymbals. At the end of the retreat, men and women danced slowly in a circle facing the flame of an oil lamp, stepping in rhythm to the simple, ancient, and uplifting chant, *Hare Rama Hare Krishna*. After four days, I was refreshed, renewed, fully energized. I had learned how to meditate, and I had fallen deeply in love with Baba.

Like receiving an unexpected inheritance or winning the Powerball lottery, you're told the money is coming, but—wait a minute!—there are still some formalities, a little paperwork before you get the reward. Initiation comes once in a lifetime, but I found out I'd have to do more work before I could claim the grand prize: the experience of enlightenment, reveling in sweet, light-filled inner bliss.

In high spirits, Elle and I drove home from the retreat in our yellow VW bus, unprepared for what might happen over the next few weeks and months. For four years since Earth Day, I had lived through a whirlwind of constant change, but that was nothing compared to what happened next.

In deciding to follow Baba I took the second big risk of my life, far bigger than leaving graduate school without a plan. I had no way of judging a spiritual master, no way of knowing if this was the right path. I had only faith to guide me: faith in myself; faith that what I had experienced with Baba was real and overwhelmingly important; faith in Elle's spiritual discernment, in her willingness, her eagerness to walk the path with me; and an unarticulated faith in the ultimate benevolence of the universe. I had faith the way someone at a leadership training course might jump backwards off a ledge, sure that the crowd of hands below will catch and hold him, confident if he leaps into the unknown no harm will come; instead, he will be buoyed by the support of others, which will forever banish fear from his life.

THE SPARK

What did Baba *do* during this initiation? He seemed to be sharing his fully enlightened state with each of us. But how? According to people who knew more about Baba, he awakened the dormant *Kundalini Shakti* or spiritual energy of a seeker. They described the awakened energy as intelligent, all-knowing, and infinitely loving. They told us this energy gives each of us *exactly* the experiences we need to expand our awareness and allow us to drink from the fountain of Baba's unconditional love.

The best analogy I heard: the awakening is like one lit candle lighting an unlit candle. While growing up, each night during Hanukkah I watched my father light candles the same way: first ignite the "master" candle and use it to light the others. If I watch closely as I light a candle, I see how there's a leap, when the intense and focused flame from the match causes the unlit candle to burst into flame. The unlit candle already has the innate potential to blaze fully, but it needs the spark, the leap, to experience its own light, its own glory.

This teaching, that we all have the same potential as Baba, needing only to put in the same devoted work as he had done to enter this enlightened state, was at once both deeply empowering—asserting that Baba and I shared the same Self—and incredibly intimidating. A few months earlier, I had read (devoured is a better word) Baba's spiritual autobiography, *Play of Consciousness*, describing his experiences, including 25 years as a wandering monk before meeting his Master and receiving the spark. Despite his already evolved state, Baba performed intense meditation practices for another nine years before achieving perfect Self-realization.

Would I have as much dedication and stamina to find a state even remotely close to Baba's? As excited as I was to be in his presence, I had many doubts that I could do what he had done. Still, Baba's wisdom and spiritual power enchanted me; I wanted to learn as much as I could. In the presence of his greatness, I sensed an unaccustomed humility. I knew I had a long way to go. At the same time, I had immense gratitude to Baba for showing the path, giving me the push I needed to walk it.

In my earlier life, it seems I had circled back again and again to a few themes guiding, and yet confining, my life into predictable patterns: pride in my intellect and intellectual attainments; my ego's aversion to confrontation and inner experiences; lust for women; fear of being open with others about my feelings; and anger at my father's generation for the Vietnam War, endemic racism, and environmental destruction. Even when I did new things, these inner forces constantly pulled me back into making the same choices. Now I had a countervailing force—Baba's touch, his energy, his incredible love—giving me options I hadn't considered, opening new vistas, tearing me away from ingrained habits and attitudes.

As I meditated at home each day, I experienced these new inner forces at work, subtle impulses leading to inner delight and expansion, forces of revelation pushing me deeper into examining my own motives, beliefs, practices, and habits; challenges to my self-image; insights that I had to face and change deeply ingrained patterns of thought and behavior. Reflecting on my incredibly good fortune in meeting such a divine master, I wrote this poem.

The Divine Glance

Time has two metrics:
Common to everyone, the first begins at birth
and ends at the time already appointed
for leaving this life.

The second, particular to the devotee,
begins with the descent of grace from the Master
and continues, cycles, until all fear dissolves
into the permanent experience of Oneness.

The divine glance of the Master
Creates a new time for the devotee.
It marks, remarks the beginning,
offers a new birth, and this insight:
We have been together many times before.

The divine glance of the Master
changed my perception completely.
What I saw only as outside, I could now see within.
What once I thought lost, kinship with everyone,
I now find wherever I go.
The veil of fear that hides the true Self
evaporated with one touch,
and I saw wholeness, tasted tears of joy,
enjoyed spontaneous meditation.

The divine glance of the Master creates all time,
turns me inward toward my true Self
offers a continuous beginning,
starting always with the present moment:
Whenever I remember the Master,
no matter how fleetingly,
I am in the eternal present.

The Master's great mission,
bestowing grace,
resets the clock continually
so that there is
            no beginning to sorrow,
            no end to ecstatic delight.

FOLLOWING BABA

LATE ONE AFTERNOON, two weeks after initiation, Elle and I sat in a café in San Mateo and discussed what to do next. We'd heard Baba's tour would travel in a few weeks to Aspen, Colorado, for the month of August and onward to the East Coast for the fall and winter. We might not see him for many months and didn't want to lose the contact we had made or let this great gift, the inner awakening, slip away from us. Even though we now meditated daily and had sometimes subtle, sometimes notable inner experiences, most of all we wanted to be in Baba's physical presence. In a few months, he'd become our pole star. Spending more time with him seemed like the most important thing we could do. We both had jobs, but we had vacation time coming and could ask the boss for two weeks' more of unpaid leave.

As Elle and I discussed the situation, we decided to follow Baba's tour to Aspen. As soon as we made the commitment, Elle flushed beet-red, a deep blush that I first saw on her forehead and which, over the next few minutes, descended all the way to her feet. With her blond hair and fair skin, the blush was remarkably visible. We took this as a sign: Baba's Shakti energy approved our decision. The message appeared unmistakable: we should spend more time with Baba.

As I continued to meditate, I received more inner guidance through physical and mental movements of the Shakti energy. I understood I needed considerable practice before I could consistently achieve even a few thought-free moments in meditation. I yearned to experience the inner states Baba eloquently described; that desire kept me going. Each time I had an insight, I took it as coming directly from Baba. As experiences continued, I developed tremendous enthusiasm for this path and respect for my meditation practice.

A few weeks later, we drove to Aspen with our young Siamese cat Kokopelli. We named her after Native American's humpbacked trickster figure we first heard about during our travels the previous year in Arizona and New Mexico. Each night, we camped in our van; each day we attended satsang with Baba.

Sometimes we recognized celebrities such as the folk singer John Denver and the dolphin researcher John Lilly, but we were like most people there: ordinary people touched by Baba's love, who had received his grace and wanted more experience of his state. After dinner some evenings, when the crowds had left, we'd sit quietly with Baba, everyone bathing in his love. Sometimes he'd have his false teeth out and sit there with us in stillness like an old grandfather. At other times, he'd ask people about practical matters. Those evenings with Baba were magical, intensely moving, unforgettable.

AN INTENSIVE MEDITATION RETREAT

In Aspen, Baba offered a new program, a more structured four-day meditation program he called an "Intensive," held in a large white geodesic dome. We were excited to be there, relishing the opportunity to dive deeper into meditation twice a day, something we hadn't done since the La Honda retreat eight weeks earlier.

The first day, with the strong meditation energy in the hall, I sank deeply into inner silence. During the public sharing periods, many people spoke about their experiences with the awakened spiritual energy. People would raise their hands, someone would hand them a mic, they'd stand and describe their experiences. Many volunteered to share, but I held back, still uncomfortable with exposing my innermost experiences. Hearing others' shared experiences of inner growth and insights encouraged me to stay on the path. Through sharing, we became guides for each other, pointing out the sights as we climbed toward still-distant peaks.

Baba's complete honesty and dynamic presence sold me on his yoga, along with his ability to present spiritual teachings with great humor. In him, I saw someone supremely energetic yet calm, reflecting an unshakeable inner stillness. Watching him and listening to him, I experienced a true Master, always in complete command.

We followed Baba from Aspen at the end of August to one more week of programs in Norman, Oklahoma. After a weekend retreat there, we drove back to California and went back to work. It would be nearly six months before we would see him again, but seeds of love were sown, ready to blossom into flowers of devotion. We worked, came home, and meditated before dinner. We read Baba's books, discussed his teachings, and met with other students for chanting and meditation sessions. My yearning for deeper experiences increased.

HOW WILL I KNOW FOR SURE?

By year-end 1974, Elle and I had followed Baba for nearly nine months. I had great love for him, and I could sense positive inner changes in my outlook on life, but I still was holding myself back, not yet sure he was the right master to follow.

Baba advised everyone: take your time, follow the practices, turn within, and see if YOU change (for the better). In other words, wait a while, make sure of him, and only then make a serious commitment to his spiritual path. Baba often told the story of a man who dug many 50-foot wells, quitting each time he didn't find water. The water source was only 100 feet below the surface, but he never found it. I understood the message; don't shop around forever. Decide where to look for water and dig deep enough in one place to find it.

Toward the end of January 1975, we drove to Los Angeles to attend a weekend retreat at Saddle Rock Ranch in the Santa Monica Mountains near Malibu. With only about sixty people there, we loved being with Baba in such an intimate setting. During one meditation, I prayed intently for a sign. I sat in the back row of chairs, directly in front of the aisle Baba used to enter and leave the hall. At one point during the hour-long meditation period, Baba left the hall. As he walked behind me, he gently put his hand on my shoulder, confirming he had heard my prayer. Baba's touch clinched it; I knew he was my teacher.

I made some significant changes in my lifestyle to help my meditation practice. After spending a year with Baba, I became a vegetarian, at first only because Baba recommended it for meditators, but later because I recognized eating a vegetarian diet fit with my environmental values: eating lower on the food chain was its own virtue.

I stopped drinking alcohol about a year after meeting Baba. One evening, I shared a glass of wine with my former brother-in-law Bill aboard a boat in Sausalito where he lived. I got so sick from the wine I swore off alcohol forever, convinced Baba's Shakti energy wanted me to quit.

BABA'S UNIQUENESS

In the spring of 1975, Baba opened his first American ashram in Oakland, California. For many months he held satsangs on weekday evenings, with immersive meditation retreats most weekends. The ashram soon became a gathering place for thousands of spiritual seekers, not only from California, but from all over the world.

After giving a talk, leading us in a chant, and meditating with us, Baba would give darshan, a time when you could come forward to greet him, ask for a spiritual name, request a meditation mantra, pose questions, lift your baby or young child for him to bless, sometimes give him a hug, hold his hand, or drop a piece of fruit, a box of chocolates, or *dakshina* (an offering of money) in baskets at the foot of his chair.

During darshan, he held a peacock feather wand, scented with *heena* and *khus* oils, gently tapping or stroking each person's head as they came before him and bowed. The line often lasted for an hour or more, as people moved slowly toward him, four abreast. Each time I came before him, even if for a moment, my heart expanded. His love and compassion flowed like a gentle cool breeze on a warm day.

Standing in a line as it inched toward Baba's chair became an exercise not only in patience but in examining my inner state. Did I have a burning question? Did I simply want him to notice or acknowledge me? Why? If Baba was omniscient, he must already know everything about me. I learned to be quick with my occasional questions. But most nights, I only wanted to bow before him and express my gratitude for the great gift he had given me, an awakening to the inner life.

Once I had a moment of darshan, I would return to my seat, contemplate what I had experienced and watch him as the great line of humanity flowed toward and away from this simple man, as waves flow onto the shore and recede. I marveled at his steadiness, his ability to receive this great onrush of people and their problems, without moving or tiring, as fully present with the last person as with the first. When darshan finished, Baba would hand his peacock wand to someone and lean back for a moment, offering a final blessing—his steady, loving gaze—then leave the hall.

WHAT HAPPENED AFTER INITIATION

Before I met Baba, I had little connection with my own innermost feelings. I lived much of my life in surface thoughts and emotions, reacting habitually to words and situations, without real empathy for others. After I received his touch, I experienced my own awareness in numerous ways, in unusual places and at various times. I might be walking along a street, I'd sense my awareness subtly shift, and I'd be watching myself with detachment, from some higher place, as a witness.

Occasionally experiences would come in meditation. My mind would become still as a lake without ripples, or I would have an unexpected insight into an issue at home or a problem at work, often with only a single word or hint. Sometimes I would be at work and shift subtly into a witness state, observing a situation without habitually reacting to it, or shift into simply feeling love for the people around me. I could be talking with someone, my awareness would shift, and I'd sense a deeper connection.

In meditation or in programs with Baba, sometimes I would slip into a deep yogic sleep-state, wholly indrawn yet still aware of the world around me. At other times, I would have a sudden opening of the heart and experience love for God, something entirely new.

I kept journals during my early days as Baba's student. In them, I took many notes on scriptural teachings I heard during workshops, like being back in a classroom, but didn't note many inner experiences. I still believed in an old model of studentship, one I had practiced all my life: if I could only *comprehend* everything Baba taught, using my mind and intellect, I would make progress in spiritual life. Playing it safe with my ego, I still engaged with Baba on my terms instead of plunging into his radically distinct way of seeing and being.

I knew there was more to this practice, but I held back a part of myself. During the first retreat with Baba in July of 1974, I wrote in my journal: *Meditation is an inner pilgrimage and your outer research, study, and pursuits cannot help you in the realm of inner consciousness.* Though I knew I had to go beyond the mind, I was unwilling to let go of my reliance on the intellect, on my limited sense of "I-consciousness." I wasn't ready to enter the universal heart.

At the retreat in Aspen, during one deep meditation, I saw myself walking along a beach, looking at waves rolling in, one after another, experiencing great peace. Baba's face clearly emerged from the sea for a few seconds, then slowly faded back into the water. While Baba represented the ocean of supreme consciousness, I was only one small wave in the vastness. If I truly wanted to enjoy Baba's experience of life, I would have to leave the safe shore behind and become one with the ocean.

Finally, I figured out I had to *change myself* to gain what Baba offered: the continuous experience of my own innermost nature and the ongoing, ecstatic upsurge of love from the heart. I didn't stop taking notes in courses, but I searched deeper to extract meaning and guidance from my experiences.

I intuited I had to drop my ingrained sense of self-importance, my desire for name and fame, and live more honestly. Among other things, this meant offering my environmental work with a sincere spirit of service to others.

Some people are ripe for spiritual life and merely need to meet a Master to relinquish their old ways. Others, like me, require an extended period of daily practice, attenuating old habits and tendencies and adopting new behaviors before they can experience more subtle worlds. This process might continue for decades. It's like igniting a wet log in a fireplace: first you must dry it out by placing it close to the fire before it can burn cleanly.

After a while, Elle and I wanted to integrate Baba's teachings and practices more wholly into our lives. In August 1975, a year after initiation, we decided to take a monthlong retreat with Baba. This became the next inflection point in my relationship with Baba. I dove deeper into his ocean, harvesting pearls of wisdom from the depths of experience, unconcerned when or whether I might surface again.

TREE HUGGER

I N AUGUST 1975 ELLE AND I WERE IN ARCATA, California, at Humboldt State University for the year's highlight: a month-long retreat, spending quality time with Baba and fewer than a hundred other devotees.

Most of us at the retreat were from California, and a genteel hippie element still characterized Northern California's spiritual culture. People wandered around the retreat with nametags reading, for example, *Groovy* and *Dancing Bear*. Others wore tags with spiritual names Baba gave them, names that always seemed to fit. My friend Norman had retired as the CFO of a large hotel chain a few years before driving to Aspen to meet Baba. After a few months, he offered Baba his service full-time. From Baba, he received a name meaning Lord of Wealth.

We'd quit our jobs with ESA to attend. This year the boss wouldn't agree to give us a month off, even without pay. We decided we could always find other jobs, but we might never again have this much time to be with Baba and imbibe what he had to offer.

Baba fell seriously ill right before the retreat and didn't come until the end of the second week. At first, he gave darshan while sitting on his second-floor apartment balcony. It's hard to describe the experience of seeing a great soul. While watching him, his elevated and one-pointed awareness became my state. I felt uplifted, cleansed, and renewed by gazing at Baba even from a distance.

One morning, I had a strong experience of Baba's power. After he gave a short talk, we chanted. I experienced an ecstatic, drunken state throughout the chant. After chanting, we meditated, and I fell into this experience again. Baba's energy kept drawing me back into a deep state.

I vibrated with strong surges of inner bliss, love arising from deep within. After the meditation ended, I came out of this state with enormous mental clarity and an overflowing love. As I walked outdoors, the sweet inner sensation remained. With a tender touch, I caressed the forest plants around the meditation hall, marveling at their texture and structure. I put my arms around a redwood tree, hugged it, and experienced oneness with its strength and resolute nature. In that moment, I became—for real—a tree-hugging environmentalist.

Intuitively I understood the forest: with clear vision and clear hearing, I "got" it: the earth's clean smell, the bark's rough touch, the forest's quiet hum, birds singing to each other or singing for no reason at all except sheer bliss, joy outside and joy inside: a complete sensory experience. I experienced nature's power to evoke awe and reverence.

GETTING MARRIED

Several months later, not long before Baba left Oakland for New York, one day the ashram announced there would be a group wedding in February 1976 and Baba would conduct the ceremony.

Shortly before he died three years earlier, my father offered this advice about Elle: "If you love the girl, marry her."

Even though I wasn't sure I was ready for that commitment, I suggested to Elle that Baba should marry us. We'd been together almost five years. After meeting Baba, we had grown even closer through our shared spiritual explorations. Though we hadn't yet discussed our future in any depth, she agreed. We decided to take part in the wedding, joining eighteen other couples, hopeful that Baba's blessings would get us past her lingering uncertainty.

Because of her enchantment with New Mexico, especially Native American jewelry we had seen in Santa Fe, for a wedding ring she chose a large turquoise stone in a lovely silver setting. Each couple had their moment of *darshan* with Baba. He placed a chocolate truffle in our mouths. Quickly chewing the chocolate, we turned around and had our picture taken, smiling with delight, sitting at Baba's feet.

I assumed getting married would strengthen our bond and that our shared spiritual practices would magically make everything OK, but reality was more complicated. Outwardly a committed and socially engaged couple, we still had a fragile emotional relationship. Elle wanted to develop an independent career path, but at twenty-six she had yet to find her way.

We had spent enough time with Baba to yearn for deeper experiences. A month after getting married, we moved into the ashram in Oakland. As part of a spiritual community, we offered *seva*, or selfless service, each day doing practical things like cleaning and cooking.

For the next six months, I cooked breakfast, which meant rising before 4:00 daily to get the morning meal ready by 6:00, right after people finished their meditation session. For breakfast we served chai tea—sweet, spicy, caffeinated—fruit and a tasty whole-grain hot cereal. Baba had many unique recipes; the morning hot cereal was one. Everyone loved it. Using millet as a base, we cooked a combination of Indian spices and shredded coconut, blended in a mixture of tomatoes, dates, chilies, and ginger: sweet, spicy, and savory. People added nutritional yeast and crumbled croutons for a delicious vegetarian breakfast.

Between offering seva, attending the morning chant, sharing a spartan room with two twin beds and a small dresser, and working outside the ashram, we didn't have much time alone, time to talk about what we both wanted out of life. We still hadn't addressed one fundamental issue: what did it mean to be a couple? Instead of spending time simply *being* together, we were always *doing* something.

During our trips to New Mexico and Arizona, Elle had gotten interested in adobe building and in solar homes designed to work harmoniously with the sun's energy. She got a small assignment to write a chapter for an early solar design book. Her research for the book led to us talking about designing and building our own home using a passive solar design approach. As she developed a strong interest in solar home design, Elle came into her own as someone with a mission and well-defined purpose in life.

We shared our great love for Baba. Our spiritual explorations continued with courses and workshops, plus our daily meditation practice. We had worked hard for four years and had saved some money. We decided to use it for a trip to India, living with Baba in his ashram in the countryside of western India. It seemed idyllic, magical, mysterious, and adventurous. After Baba's second world tour ended, leaving behind its vibrant events, weekly meditation Intensives and colorful pageantry, the real inner work commenced.

PASSAGE TO INDIA

BABA'S SECOND WORLD TOUR MAY HAVE STARTED SMALL IN A LIVING ROOM in Piedmont, but by its third year, crowds were huge. During the summer of 1976, Baba held satsangs at the iconic DeVille Hotel in New York's Catskill mountains, a two-hour drive from New York City. That summer, seemingly *everyone* had to meet Baba, receive his grace, imbibe his wisdom. On weekends, the darshan lines were enormous as thousands drove from New York, Boston, Philadelphia, everywhere along the East Coast, even from the Midwest. Baba delighted in meeting people, whether rich and famous, poor and ordinary; it didn't matter. His mission was to awaken souls from the slumber of ages, and he embraced it with infectious enthusiasm, perpetual joy, overflowing love.

At the end of the summer, Baba planned to return to his ashram in India; he invited everyone to come live with him. By mid-summer, the number of residency applications from seekers grew so large that Baba's staff decided to charter an Air India 747 to take people from San Francisco to India. Elle and I eagerly paid the deposit, got visas and shots, and once more threw caution to the winds, leaving our new jobs to be with Baba.

In October 1976, with great anticipation, accompanied by a few hundred of Baba's American students, Elle and I boarded the plane in San Francisco, bound for India. Stopping briefly in London to gather Baba and his traveling party, we flew onward to Bombay (Mumbai). During the flight, Baba would occasionally walk around greeting us; his attendant would follow, offering us each a teaspoonful of Baba's *prasad*, blessed food.

THE ASHRAM

As our shuttle bus came around the last bend in the country road, forty bumpy miles outside Bombay, my heart leapt with joy and anticipation. In the distance I saw Baba's ashram, a gleaming presence set amid rice patties, sugar-cane fields and mango groves, an orange flag flying from the temple dome signifying Baba's presence. After two days of travel from the Bay Area, we were finally in Ganeshpuri, the fabled home not only for Baba but also for his Master, Bhagawan Nityananda. The air was warm and sticky in early October, with the summer monsoon weather lingering.

The ashram was large, with buildings constructed in a classical Indian temple format: arches, swirls and domes. The ashram's exquisite gardens had statues of Indian spiritual masters and images from Baba's teaching stories. Peacocks wandered noisily around the gardens. Spotted deer lived in a large fenced enclosure; in the distance I heard an elephant trumpeting. Baba had planted many varieties of mangoes and other trees to shade pathways and provide fruit for meals. The coolness of the beautiful marble courtyards and marble benches set around trunks of various trees tempered the heat.

The beauty of the ashram seemed otherworldly. During my graduate studies ten years earlier, I'd visited many leading museums of Europe and seen a thousand years of treasures, architecture, and great art. Elle and I had visited many beautiful natural areas in the West: Grand Canyon, Yosemite, Muir Woods. But Baba's ashram had a special beauty. In each museum or natural area, I'd see beauty with the eyes of a tourist or hiker, and I'd marvel at the skill of the artist or at a vast panorama of landscapes carved by millions of years of intense wind, heaving ice, and flowing water. In places of great beauty, I'd have a few thought-free minutes, but inevitably "worldly" thoughts would intrude on my inner peace.

In Baba's ashram, I experienced beauty in a new way. I could sense a vibrant spiritual energy pervading the ashram: palpable, calming, insightful, uplifting. As my heart opened, I stayed in the thought-free state for longer periods of time, and my aesthetic sense became more refined. I could perceive exquisite beauty in simpler things: peacock feathers, trailing vines, and deep green mango trees; rice paddies on the walk leading to the upper garden; curlicues along the roof lines; variegated patterns in the courtyard's marble patio; and the gold-leaf statue of his Guru sitting on a marble pedestal in the temple. I saw beauty in simple things in the ashram because I had learned to see with new eyes and a new sensibility.

THE SCHEDULE

To house Baba's Western students, the ashram had built a three-story dormitory with large open rooms and, as at a summer camp, spartan iron-frame beds with thin, striped cotton mattresses, one wing for men and the other for women. The ashram had no accommodations for couples, so Elle and I bunked apart. For all my stuff, I had a small gym locker: what didn't fit went into a suitcase shoved under the bed. Morning meditation began at 3:00 a.m. and finished at 5:00. After drinking a cup of *chai*, sweetened with sugar and buffalo milk, we gathered in the temple at 5:30 for a ninety-minute recitation of spiritual texts in Sanskrit. Afterward, we had time for breakfast (often a pastry or hot cereal and more chai tea in the Amrit, the ashram café), followed by a two-hour work period. At noontime, we chanted for another half-hour, then took our main meal at 12:30.

The Amrit was one of Baba's special creations. I'm sure he'd observed during his second world tour how the café kept people close to the ashram and encouraged them to share their spiritual experiences with each other. It functioned also as a safety valve for Westerners who wanted more variety than simple meals eaten at a set time. In Oakland, after Baba's spoke during the evening programs, since we weren't allowed to take notes, we'd often gather in the Amrit to share recollections and create a collective account of what he'd taught. Here, the ashram food was nutritious and plentiful, but Westerners often wanted something familiar, a taste of home, to break the routine. In India, the Amrit served salads, grilled cheese sandwiches, various Indian dishes such as *dosas*, and baked goodies like croissants (to die for!) and bear claws.

Baba designed the ashram schedule to keep us focused on inner work, leaving little time for gossip or idleness, his *bête noirs*. Offering a few hours of selfless service each morning and afternoon to maintain the ashram became integral to my experience, providing an avenue for experiencing bliss through work and overcoming my residual tendencies toward laziness and inattention.

After lunch we rested or studied for two hours until the afternoon work period began at 3:00. At 6:00, the ashram paused for the traditional evening *arati* (waving of lights and chanting), followed by a light supper at 6:30. A deeply moving event, prior to the arati a *pujari* (priest) walked around the ashram, stopping at each picture of Baba or his Master and waving before it a beautiful silver oil lamp lit with handmade cotton wicks soaked in ghee, containing a smoking clump of sweet-smelling *dhoop* (incense), which filled the air as he passed by. To begin the arati, a few minutes of loud musical sounds (people beating drums, blowing conch shells, ringing bells, banging tambourines, and clashing cymbals) stilled the mind, affected various inner spiritual centers, and focused our attention on the chant.

After supper, sometimes Baba would sit outside on a bench under a tree in the main courtyard and listen to the day's final chant in the temple, a melodious hymn composed (it is said) by celestial musicians. After the chant, I went to bed for six or seven hours before rising again for early morning meditation. I quickly fell into step with this daily rhythm. It became as natural as breathing.

I shared a large dorm room with a few dozen men. I usually rose at 3:00 or 3:30 for morning meditation, showered, and walked a few dozen yards to the meditation hall. Beyond experiencing the benefit of regular daily meditation, some mornings Baba would be there, giving the touch. One day flowed seamlessly into another, punctuated by occasional celebrations such as *Diwali*, the Indian New Year, held around the time of Halloween. The ashram routine maintained inner peace, fostered deep meditation and contemplation, accelerated changes in my outlook.

In the dorm, we took Navy showers with a small bucket (wet quickly, lather, rinse) and used an old-style squat toilet (a ceramic basin with a hole and steps on which to put your feet) with a bucket of water for wiping (always with the left hand.) But the drinking water was pure, and the food tasty even when eaten by hand (the right one) from banana-leaf plates, sitting on a thin fiber mat that barely cushioned the dining hall's stone floor.

For a month, I offered *seva* during meals, filling tall stainless-steel water cups during lunch and dinner. I would eat lunch and dinner early with other servers, Western and Indian, get a water pitcher and pour water. Drinking cups sat on the floor mat next to the food plate. If you wanted less water, you had to indicate it by putting your thumb and forefinger close or learn to say "chhota" (short or small in Hindi). As water pourers, we moved quickly along the rows, walking right behind food servers as they ladled out portions of rice, dal, vegetables, and puris or chapattis. The only way to avoid spilling water was to stay one-pointed on the task, moving easefully, thought-free. I was extraordinarily joyful during this walking and bowing meditation.

Joel, a Bay Area student whom I knew, saw me doing this seva. After several weeks, he pulled me aside one day. "Can I do what you're doing? You look so blissful." With only a moment's reluctance, I happily gave this seva to him.

DARSHAN

Baba could appear anywhere in the ashram at any time. I never knew when I'd see him, so I learned to stay conscious of my surroundings all the time. I wasn't ready for the strong, moment-by-moment commitment to inner work that Baba expected, but Baba's love and blissful presence kept me going. Most days, he would sit on a marble ledge along one side of the quiet, shaded courtyard during the late morning or early afternoon, offering darshan. When we heard Baba was there, we'd all quickly finish our seva, drop whatever else we were doing, and sit silently in the courtyard, watching him while he chatted with people, answered questions, took care of ashram business, or fed thick handfuls of chapattis to a young elephant someone had given him.

Many days, a *mahout* would lead the elephant into the courtyard, where it ceremoniously bowed to Baba. Baba would feed it and anoint its forehead with fragrant oils. For the grand finale, with its trunk it would gently place a flower garland around Baba's neck and once more bow to him, then follow the mahout back to the barn.

Baba's ashram was a living laboratory for yoga and meditation. As effortlessly as I could go into a meditative state pouring water in the dining hall, I could get into meditation anywhere on the grounds. Baba's state of divine intoxication permeated each plant, every statue, the stone benches and walls.

A large room below Baba's bedroom, called "the cave," where he had meditated for many years, was always open. When I descended into its cool darkness, lit only by a single candle, I paused a few seconds for my eyes to adjust, then moved slowly and carefully to avoid disturbing anyone. I silently slid into a sitting posture on a comfortable cushion and fell instantly into a quiet, thought-free, deeply indrawn meditation.

Entering the cave was like returning to the womb, each meditation a rebirth into the life of the spirit. In the cave, silence was deep, all-pervasive, primordial. At the heart of the ashram experience, inner silence resonated. Yogic scriptures describe ten classical divine sounds called *nada* arising from OM that become subtly audible in deep meditation. While meditating in the cave one day, from deep within I heard one of these sounds: a thunderclap. The loudest sound I'd ever experienced, it moved me to tears and opened yet another door into a deeper faith in Baba's grace and teachings.

Another day, in deep meditation in the cave, I saw an image of myself flying, as if on a magic carpet, to be with Baba. When I arrived where he was sitting, Baba held out a silver tray with a lid on it, like a platter on which my mother might serve the roast at a Christmas dinner. He lifted the lid and revealed a heart lying on the tray. I disappeared into ecstasy the rest of meditation. I understood Baba had given me back my heart, which I had lost touch with before meeting him, opening me to a fuller experience of love, love without object or desire, love as my innermost nature.

I had such revelations often enough that I began to shed the idea, ingrained by my entire education and upbringing, that the rational worldview was all there is, that it provided a complete description of this mysterious world we inhabit and the hidden inner life we all live. There was so much more. Baba's world richly embraced personal revelation, ancient experiences of intense longing for grace, transcendent moments of oneness with all creation, a belief in God's immanent presence in our lives, a view of the equality of all people in the Self, past lives that became living memories during times of intense meditation, immersion in an ancient time before history, before literature, before philosophers, almost before language itself.

In Baba's world, I understood that life could be simple: the student and the master; the natural world, the community, and the people around us; and my own sincere effort to make sense of life from its most basic element, the breath. Once I had this revelation, a sense of an unbroken succession of students and masters extending far back in time arose in me, and I began to settle into my spiritual journey. I regarded it as the essential work of this lifetime, a fountain of inexhaustible plenitude, and the most challenging personal mountain to summit. Unlike much in life I'd forgotten by chance or choice, through inattention or carelessness, I could not forget these insights; I kept them as cherished talismans.

INNER WORK

During work breaks, Elle and I would meet each day at the ashram café and share experiences. With friends, we'd discuss our meditations and changes in our inner state. We'd share stories of what Baba had said or done. For days at a time, I could stabilize my meditation and watch the subtler workings of the awakened energy as it purified my inner being. At other times, the mind would be doing its own thing: thinking nonstop during the entire meditation period.

My description for this process: "Watching and waiting."

I resolved to sit for meditation, repeatedly *watching* the play of the mind and the inner conscious awareness, and I committed myself to *waiting* for grace to reveal what I had to learn. Instead of *achieving* instant enlightenment, the real work became *letting go* of things like attitudes, assumptions, memories, desires, fears, and attachments to melodramas, all holding me back from knowing my true Self.

I would ask myself: What would I have to do, or *not do*, to get to a place of contentment on a permanent basis, to make it my continuing inner experience? In learning to swim at ten at the Rita Curtis Swim School in Van Nuys, I had to let go of my tight grip on the wall of the pool and trust the process I'd been taught, follow the instructor's guidance, and swim out into deeper water without fear. I knew I still clung tightly to my self-conception as a limited person, but what would it mean to let go of this small self, trust Baba's process and live freely in the great Self?

At the Ashram, the main meals were lunch and dinner. For a simple breakfast, you could buy a couple of bananas from street vendors outside the ashram entrance. You could also get a full breakfast at the Amrit, or more cheaply at an open-air restaurant with a dirt floor across the road from the ashram. There I would order a *masala dosa* (large rice or lentil crepes with a potato filling) or *idli sambar*, a south Indian dish of steamed rice-and-lentil cakes dipped in a spicy soup, tasty and delicious. There was only one slight problem.

You might guess the cleanliness there didn't meet Western standards. After eating an occasional breakfast across the road, a month later I developed amoebic dysentery and lost forty pounds over several weeks. Most of the day, I lay in bed. To control the diarrhea, I ate plain boiled basmati rice mixed with buffalo milk yogurt, which Elle brought from the Amrit. The prescribed drug, Flagyl, had side effects almost worse than the disease. I was miserable. The purge was both inner and outer. After the worst part of the illness passed and I could again walk around normally, I was relieved to be free of many mental and emotional burdens.

Elle and I lived eleven weeks at the ashram that fall. One morning we approached Baba in darshan to say good-bye and express our gratitude. As a parting gift he gave us each a knit cap and a yellow silk shawl to wear for meditation. We flew home in December, arriving a few days before Christmas. I didn't mind going home. Much had happened, far more than I could articulate or fully comprehend. I knew I'd need time, lots of it, to appreciate and assimilate what I had learned, what had changed in my approach to life.

Once back, to readjust to "civilian life" we returned to living at the ashram in Oakland. In India, Elle decided her personal and professional priority was building her own solar home. After returning, we used most of our remaining savings to buy a parcel of land for the home site. To replenish the bank account and get back into the flow of working for a living, for six months I commuted forty miles each way to San Jose to work as an environmental consultant on waste management projects. Elle networked with friends to find solar energy work that could pay her something.

After returning from India, Elle continued suffering back pain from falling off the horse and from the auto accident. She hoped that spending time with Baba in India would magically heal her; she invested a lot emotionally in that hope. Baba never posed as a healer—if healing happened around him, fine—but that wasn't the purpose of a Master.

In India, Elle got to know several American women who qualified as "old timers" around Baba because they had lived in the ashram before Baba's second world tour began in 1974. That gave them a certain credibility with "new timers" like Elle and me who had met Baba more recently. When you're new on the spiritual path and you don't yet have a firm grasp on your own experience, you tend to believe people who appear to have been at it longer, people with insider knowledge.

In India, she was particularly susceptible to their influence. One woman convinced Elle the reason her back hadn't healed was that she wasn't ready for a truly spiritual life, that she didn't "get it"; in other words, the problem was not that her back was injured, but that her faulty attitude kept her from healing. The woman might have meant her advice to be "helpful," but these cruel words entered Elle's awareness like a dagger.

She didn't understand how it could be *her* fault she hadn't healed. Not knowing whom to believe, at this point in her life Elle decided to focus more on her career, less on spiritual practices. This small seed of doubt planted by someone's insensitive remark sprouted and, within a few years, she moved away from regular engagement with the Oakland ashram community.

LAST YEARS WITH BABA

WHEN WE RETURNED FROM INDIA, we stayed in the ashram in Oakland for nine months. I thought I'd "achieved" something in India, as if there was ever anything to achieve in spiritual life. I soon found out how wrong I was. As I was already a three-year veteran of Baba's Oakland community, the ashram invited me to take part in an interview segment with the local public television station. Six of us shared our experiences. Afterward, another student, a well-known activist in the black community, someone about my age, pulled me aside. "You're very dry," she said with love but characteristic directness, "you have to learn how to open your heart when you talk about Baba."

Her assessment forced me to reflect on my real purpose. Was it still only to become a better version of "Jerry," to become a smooth talker about yet another "subject," or was it to transform myself into a beacon of love, as Baba clearly showed in his own person? The goal of Baba's yoga was experiencing the Master's state *as my own Self*. Better yet, experiencing myself naturally, moment to moment, living free of any attempt to *become* somebody. I still had much to learn.

BABA'S THIRD WORLD TOUR

For his third world tour, Baba returned to Oakland two years later, in October 1978. He gave regular evening programs for three months and most weekends held two-day meditation retreats called Shaktipat Intensives. I went to see him as often as I could, Elle less often. While she still loved Baba and meditated regularly, she wasn't as keen on actively participating in the Oakland spiritual community. I found it difficult to balance wanting to be with Baba those evenings, Elle's expressed desire for quality time as a couple, the work of preparing to build our solar adobe dream home, and my new day job in Sacramento, eighty miles away.

Baba was seventy when he returned to America. I'm sure he knew it would be his last tour, and he poured out his love in a flood. Night after night, he lectured to and met with more than a thousand people. Before evening satsangs in Oakland, the line outside the ashram would be several blocks long, people waiting patiently for a chance to be in his presence, if only for a fleeting moment, to sip wisdom from his bottomless cup. Often the darshan line lasted more than two hours.

I relished approaching Baba during darshan, often simply to offer my gratitude. Many times, when I looked carefully and deeply into his eyes, I saw only that familiar, but ever new, ecstatic presence, lost in divine bliss, yet paradoxically intimately present for each person. Each night, waiting in line to approach Baba's chair, I contemplated: What's my inner state right now? What do I want to say or to offer? What's on my mind? How's my heart?

I found Baba's teachings liberating on their face and motivating in practice. I could still work hard to create a better world through offering my work in renewable energy and environmental protection as service, while maintaining a meditation and devotional practice. This way, I could be *in* the world but not *of* it. So I thought; but life isn't always that simple.

I grappled with many habitual tendencies, especially anger when things didn't go my way. For a while, I could stay focused on Baba's elevated teachings and on the experience of peace and love I had around him. Invariably something would happen, a negative thought, something someone had said, a difficulty I faced, an old resentment, and I would get angry. Someone might praise me and I'd puff up, pulled back into my older (and still familiar) mindset of competing for attention with my siblings, classmates, or people at work. Thanks to Baba's teachings, I now had tools, especially daily meditation and mantra repetition, to get back to the state of peace, love, and steadiness, but I struggled even as I understood that I had to welcome this back-and-forth process as an essential element of the spiritual journey.

BLISS IS OUR VERY NATURE

Being around Baba became a daily feast for all senses, but it was also a celebration, like a wedding dinner where champagne flowed all night, everyone high on love and drunk on wisdom. In Baba's presence, the champagne gushed without ceasing, tiny bubbles of bliss tickling the mind and heart, erasing any concerns I might have brought with me to an evening satsang. Bottled under pressure, ordinary champagne releases its fizziness when you pop the cork, eventually going flat. Night after night, Baba's vintage bubbly sparkled with charisma, flowed out into the hall, and intoxicated us.

Baba insisted on the primacy of bliss, but when someone came to him experiencing suffering, perhaps grieving over the death of a loved one or lamenting an unexpected divorce, he would offer compassionate, visible, loving comfort. But while suffering pertains to the body, mind, and emotions, Baba maintained that bliss was the supreme principle—the very nature of the divine—an experience of the pulsating inner Self, which we could experience and on which we should focus.

Most of us love to talk about our suffering, our victimhood, our troubles and grievances; but we fail to seek out, experience, and live in our innermost nature, which is nothing but a body of bliss. I've had back pain most of my life from a pronounced scoliosis that developed during a growth spurt at about twelve, but I've never let it affect my inner life. In my experience, episodes of physical suffering vanish as quickly as the morning mist when I remember my own inner bliss. Being around Baba, I found bliss especially accessible through chanting, a practice well known in India as *namasankirtana*, chanting the divine name.

Before meeting Baba, I had never chanted, but I took to it easily, experiencing that it quieted the mind and opened the heart and then—surprise!—I would sense an upwelling bliss. It didn't matter what divine name we chanted; the syllables vibrated with

Shakti. Chanting had its own meaning, purpose, and reward. Unlike a champagne hangover with its attendant headache, after the chant ended, I found it easy to sink into a deep joyful meditation and then to take that state out into my life.

MAHASAMADHI

In the fall of 1981, after three years in America, Baba returned to India. A year later, in the early afternoon of October 2, 1982, I drove to the ashram in Oakland for a weekly one-on-one basketball game with one of the residents.

When I arrived to pick him up, he walked over to my car, looking very sad. As I leaned out the window, he told me quietly, "Baba has taken *mahasamadhi*; he's left his body, he's gone."

Mahasamadhi is the conscious merging of a great being into the Absolute. Baba had left his body. I would never see his beloved form again. A great light was gone, a light that had uplifted thousands, including myself, with its purity, depth, strength, and brilliance.

Shocked, surprised, and deeply saddened, I felt that my dearest one, my guide, my spiritual teacher, my great Friend, had left me. Only seventy-four, Baba had worn out his body by offering his great heart not only to multitudes in India, but to hundreds of thousands of ordinary people like me all over the world. Immediately I drove home and told Elle what had happened. When she heard the news, Elle burst into tears. I went back to the ashram that evening to mourn with the community.

We might have lost Baba, but people responded in an uplifting way. For seventeen days and nights, hundreds of Baba's students chanted, beginning with a slow mournful dirge, each person taking multiple shifts daily, so the chant never ceased. What could have been a funereal event soon evolved into a fast version of the chant, a joyful expression of Baba's continuing presence, an experience of love for God, and a harbinger of inner peace. By the chant's end, honoring Baba in this way had inspired and uplifted the entire community.

Still, I felt that the experienced engineer guiding my train toward the distant goal of liberation now had left it to run on its own. What now? What should I do? Where should I turn for inner inspiration, for the Master's love, for devotion? I felt I'd lost an essential connection to my spiritual master, to his living, loving presence. I experienced a void inside. Even though I practiced meditation as Baba taught and continued to attend satsangs at the Siddha Yoga ashram in Oakland, at times I felt distracted, adrift, floating alone in a vast sea of worldly concerns. For consolation, I threw myself into my work promoting solar power, which I'd begun five years earlier.

IV
SUN DAY

ELLE AND I SAT ON A LAWN AT UCLA IN AUGUST 1975, during a break in the biennial Solar World Congress of the International Solar Energy Society, engaged in a spirited discussion of English versus metric systems with scientists who favored metric. Joining us was Steve Baer, a solar energy inventor we'd met the year before in Albuquerque, who decided I was OK because I agreed with him that, for practical and historical reasons, we should still use the English system.

Beyond this banter we all shared a deeper agreement: if we wanted to cut dependence on foreign oil and reduce our exposure to future oil embargoes, we had to turn to the sun. As a society, we had to become as heliotropic as sunflowers.

But how? Solar technology was still primitive, good only for heating water and powering small spacecraft and ocean buoys. We all agreed it would take a massive national program, a Manhattan Project, to commercialize solar power. After the Apollo moon missions ended in 1973, the country wasn't ready for further mobilizations. But solar enthusiasts were passionate and persistent. We pushed ahead, developing innovative technologies, using government resources where we could.

The next year, as a solar expert, I joined Governor Jerry Brown's new administration, hoping to craft a uniquely California approach to implementing solar technology. Two years later, Elle and I decided to do what we could as individuals: build a passive solar home to demonstrate solar's feasibility. We bought some land and became solar pioneers, figuratively heading west again.

OAT FLAKES

THE BRITISH ECONOMIST E.F. SCHUMACHER'S 1973 COUNTERCULTURAL manifesto, *Small is Beautiful: Economics as if People Mattered*, a book about development economics in the Third World, galvanized many in the environmental movement to consider applying the message to our own country. Schumacher argued for a smaller-scale, more *appropriate technology*, one that included installing millions of rooftop solar electric panels to power our towns and cities instead of relying on a few large power plants. He urged us not to rely on big government and big corporations, a feeling shared by many in the Bay Area counterculture.

Sim van der Ryn became the California state architect after Jerry Brown took over as governor in 1975. Part of the countercul-ture himself, Sim brought Schumacher's ideas with him, and the iconoclastic Brown made *Small is Beautiful* required reading for his staff. Sim urged Brown to implement an appropriate technology program in state government. After we got acquainted at the In-tegral Urban House, Sim saw me as a kindred spirit and wanted me to help him implement this project. I got excited at the possi-bilities for translating Schumacher's ideas about urban ecology and appropriate energy technology into a state government ini-tiative. Perhaps we didn't have to view government as "the enemy" after all.

Beyond his interest in appropriate technology, Sim was a pio-neer in green building, a strong advocate for ecological design, a mentor to many, and a memorable character. He always wore a silk foulard, never a tie, more like a college professor than a typical architect. He often spoke haltingly, pausing while talking, as if he expected you'd be listening carefully and could fill in the blanks. Short, energetic, intuitive, wise like a shaman, Sim radiated charisma.

He committed the state architect's office to energy-efficient commercial building design at a time when most architects wouldn't consider it. He designed a new state office building in downtown Sacramento using passive solar and ecological design principles, naming it the Bateson Building after renowned social scientist and systems thinker Gregory Bateson, a professor at Santa Cruz. It was the most ecologically advanced government office in the country, remarkable for its low energy use, abundant daylighting, and natural ventilation scheme.

After considering Sim's proposal for an office devoted to appropriate technology, Brown agreed to let him try it out. In January 1976 Sim brought me in as a consultant to develop the idea into a workable government program. After a few months of discussions, I drafted an executive order for the governor to establish this new office. The order spelled out an exciting mandate:

"Promote less complex, less capital-intensive, more labor-intensive, frequently smaller, more decentralized and environmentally benign technologies, more appropriate to the needs of communities."

In early May 1976, Governor Brown created the Office of Appropriate Technology (OAT), and I became its first director. He placed OAT in the Governor's Office of Planning and Research, giving us direct access to the governor's top people.

OAT fit in nicely with my liberal politics at the time. The Vietnam War and Watergate scandal made many young people distrust large corporations, including oil companies and electric utilities. We yearned for more control over our lives. After living in the Bay Area for five years, I'd imbibed the prevailing political thesis: offering *radical* solutions meant getting to the *root* of problems and addressing them by creating institutions and supporting technologies better fitted for new economic, energy, and political realities.

I loved doing what I considered important environmental work, in a setting I thought would make a real difference in how we treated the planet and each other. Elle also wanted to be part of it. I pitched Sim on bringing her in as my assistant, but he wouldn't hear of it.

"Too much like nepotism—wouldn't look good, can't do it," he responded.

Sorely disappointed, Elle now had to find her own work in the solar energy field, an effort that took her a full year.

I wanted OAT to push state government into a stronger environmental commitment and to influence trends in the larger society. Initiating OAT as a pilot project reflected Jerry Brown's approach to changing state government. If people proposed innovative ideas, he'd nod favorably, tell them to go ahead, and his team would scramble to find resources to develop the idea. If it went well, Brown would take the credit. If it didn't work out, well, it was only some staffer's dumb idea, not something he endorsed or knew much about.

I was still naïve to a fault at this time, but I soon learned two basic rules of the political game. First rule: make the boss look good. Second rule: above all do no harm to the boss's image, a form of the Hippocratic oath taken by all political appointees. If you hurt his image or reputation, you're soon out. I didn't know it, but almost every neophyte political appointee gets thrown under the bus at least once early in their career. That's how they learn the game; there's no instruction manual.

With Sim leading the way and providing access to the governor, we launched OAT. We began with a staff of five and a small budget, producing publications that encouraged Californians to adopt small-scale renewable energy and natural living solutions.

The real estate team found office space for OAT in the choir loft of a former mortuary. This setup hinted at the relative importance state bureaucrats placed on this initiative; from the outset, we had only secondhand furniture and improvised space. Was OAT's fate to be determined by this inauspicious beginning?

I wanted the chance to make something good happen for solar energy and alternatives to the prevailing vision, a future powered by fossil fuels and nuclear power. I wanted to craft a new message of decentralized, lower-impact energy and environmental technologies. With only a small staff, we had to be selective about what we chose to do, careful in defining our mission. At the beginning, even though we had an executive order from the governor with ambitious language and high-level goals, we still had to work out every detail. Once launched, we spent a few months developing a more specific plan for OAT.

With me working in Sacramento, for the first time in years Elle and I weren't spending much time together. To avoid driving 150 miles per day round-trip from Oakland, I rented a room in a friend's house along tree-shaded 28th Street in Sacramento, a mile from the Capitol. At the outset, Elle and I could cope with being apart a few days a week, but after a few months of my week-long absences our once-strong relationship started unraveling at the edges.

OAT exemplified Brown's plan for changing society, using state government in a positive way to showcase new ideas and behaviors, making it a laboratory for encouraging changes in the larger economy.

Beyond little money, OAT had a more significant institutional problem: in 1975, the California Energy Commission began operations with a large staff and a mandate to address the state's energy supply problems. OAT got leftovers, essentially a mishmash of small-scale solar and wind technologies, suitable mostly for rural areas, appealing primarily to social change agents, hippies, and young people in places like Santa Cruz, Berkeley, and the northern California countryside.

Because many people called those on the ultra-liberal and hippie fringe "flakes," with our initials we quickly became known as the OAT Flakes. Despite the negative connotation, we adopted it as our proud identity. After nine months of working with Sim to get OAT off the ground, I left government work behind to go to India with Elle, to deepen my connection with Baba and meditation practice.

In one of life's odd coincidences, even though I left it behind, my work at OAT connected me with the governor and other top people in state government. A year after I returned from India, Sim and Governor Brown invited me back, this time to create a new program focused on developing a vibrant solar industry in California.

There I got my first exposure to insider political maneuvering and learned valuable lessons about how hard it is for government agencies to midwife new industries.

SOLAR HEGEMONISTS

SACRAMENTO IN JANUARY CAN BE DREARY. One afternoon, the Tule fog descended at about four o'clock, as it did almost every day, and before dinnertime it was chilly, dark, and damp. At six, as I walked over from my apartment to join Wilson Clark for dinner, I could taste the damp air; I couldn't see more than a block in any direction. We ate dinner at a small vegetarian restaurant near the Capitol and finalized our presentation for Governor Jerry Brown later that evening. Wilson served as the governor's energy advisor and, as a consultant, I'd recently come on board to help him create a solar industry commercialization program.

Wilson found out earlier that day from friends in the governor's office that Brown would eat dinner later at Frank Fat's Chinese restaurant, a hangout for lobbyists and politicians on L Street, a block from the Capitol. Fat liked having the governor there—it was good for business—and reserved a booth for him at the back of the restaurant. The semi-circular booths with their 1950s-style padded, burgundy leather kept conversations private, a necessity with politicians and lobbyists wheeling and dealing (and eavesdropping) most evenings. Wilson and I planned to get the governor good press as a leading supporter of solar energy. We needed his OK to move ahead. After we finished our dinner, we walked over to Fat's.

"Here come the solar hegemonists," announced the governor loudly, with characteristic irony, as we entered the restaurant.

Wilson and I made our way to his booth at the back. At several tables, I could see people eating the house specialty, sweet and sour spareribs. Fat's served good food; the setting projected intimacy, power, and privacy. The bachelor governor liked to hang out there whenever he spent time in Sacramento. To capture his attention and get his buy-in, Wilson and I wanted to meet him in a more relaxed setting rather than making a formal presentation in his office.

President Jimmy Carter had already agreed to sponsor a national "Sun Day" to promote solar energy, on May 3, 1978. We saw this as a terrific opportunity, perhaps as significant as the first Earth Day in 1970, to move Jerry Brown and California's approach to promoting solar energy to the forefront of national awareness. Brown and Carter both had campaigned for the 1976 Democratic presidential nomination, eventually won by Carter. After that, Brown welcomed any chance to steal the national spotlight from the president.

I was nervous. I'd had several meetings and a couple of dinners with the governor at Sim's apartment two years before when I ran the OAT program, but I had left after only nine months on the job. I hadn't talked to him in over a year. I knew if we got his OK, I'd have a steady and highly visible job running the program.

Brown and two of his sidekicks occupied the booth. We pulled two chairs over from a neighboring table and sat opposite him. The waiters brought menus, but we waved them off; we didn't plan to stay long.

As a key advisor to the governor, Wilson did most of the talking. Sitting across from us, the trio looked like judges at a tribunal who would render a verdict on my ideas, with Wilson serving as my lawyer. He quickly laid out the approach:

"We'll create a small new office for commercializing solar energy, we'll have a solar advisory commission, and we'll develop a state plan for all this within a year."

Brown asked, "What do you want to call it?"

"We'll call it Solar California, or SolarCal for short," I said.

"It sounds OK," he responded. "Can you get it organized by May?"

Wilson: "Yes, Sim and I will make sure it gets done; Yudelson here will do the day-to-day work."

"Don't forget to get input from the union guys, homebuilders, manufacturers, local government—get everyone involved," Brown said.

He signed off on the concept, asked a few more questions, offered advice about where in state government to place the office, and signaled the end of the conversation by turning to talk to one of his associates. With nothing more to discuss, we stood and quickly left.

Once outside, Wilson looked at me coolly: "It's yours now, buddy. Don't fuck it up. Come by my office in the morning. We'll call Sim and flesh out the details."

I walked back to my apartment, elated, breathing the cool night air. I mentally thanked Baba for getting me back into the middle of the action, this time around my passion for solar energy.

As a young journalist from North Carolina, Wilson's claim to fame came from a 1974 book, *Energy for Survival: The Alternative to Extinction*, researched and written quickly after the first Arab oil embargo in 1973. The book made a compelling case for including domestic and renewable energy resources in a new and expanded definition of national security. We shared a strong mutual interest in advancing solar energy, seeing it as an alternative energy source with an unlimited future. We had spent a lot of time developing an approach for putting California in the vanguard of the anticipated solar revolution. Now I'd get a chance to put this approach into practice.

Jerry Brown attracted many intellectuals like Clark during his first term. Brown appeared to be a breath of fresh air in the stilted, post-Watergate national political landscape. Media-savvy, Brown used the press adroitly; it loved to report on his unusual ways. His inaugural address as governor in 1975 ran for only seven minutes, brevity noteworthy enough to be a story on national TV during the evening news. As a speech, it ended almost before the audience settled in. As for impact, it never intended to have any; the main goal was getting press attention.

Like many younger people, after a decade of war and the Watergate scandal, I appreciated fresh faces in politics. Almost 40,

Brown fulfilled our psychic need for a new beginning. People fancifully saw him as a philosopher-king, both intellectually astute and politically effective. Political reality was more prosaic. Brown won the 1974 election largely on his father's name—Pat Brown had been an effective governor whose two terms had ended only eight years earlier—and the elder Brown's influence with powerful campaign supporters—California's unions—coupled with a Democratic Party newly energized by the Watergate scandal.

On various occasions when I spent time alone with the governor or met with him and Sim to discuss appropriate technology or solar energy, I'd face a barrage of questions. Brown was usually well informed, probing for details about what we proposed, reflecting in his questioning his upbringing in politics and time in a Jesuit seminary. I didn't have many one-on-one meetings with the governor, so when they occurred, I had to be prepared or he'd dismiss me quickly as a lightweight.

An acknowledged energy expert, Wilson liked Brown's intellect, his willingness to try new things, and to take reasoned but unconventional positions: for example, to come out against nuclear energy and for solar power. Still under 30, Wilson looked older: he wore glasses, sported a moustache, and always had a serious expression around Brown. For someone that young, he was remarkably crusty and wouldn't tolerate lazy thinking, reflecting his journalistic training: no BS.

He memorably introduced me to the ethics of Brown's team. First, he instructed, don't confuse your personal life with working for the state government, especially at a prominent level. He looked at me squarely one day and delivered specific advice about dealing with women in the Brown administration: "Don't shit where you eat." I got the message. Newly married to Elle and actively practicing meditation, that was one temptation I could surely resist.

Brown's use of the phrase "solar hegemonists" when he saw Wilson and me that night did not strike me as a term of endearment, especially since it used outdated Chinese Communist rhetoric. In principle, Brown strongly supported the search for alternative energy sources after the 1973 oil crisis, but he wanted us to make a rational case for a major reliance on renewable energy.

For decades, few companies had tried to improve solar heating technology. As a result, in 1978, solar technology was mostly good for providing hot water for households and swimming pools. Brown opposed nuclear power, but solar would have to survive serious economic and technical scrutiny before he'd advocate too strenuously for it as THE solution to the oil crisis. Still, he had an open mind on the issue and thought we should at least give solar a chance.

Beyond solar enthusiasts—mostly architects, engineers, and activists—serious political players saw how solar power could combat our growing reliance on nuclear energy. Many activists regarded nuclear power as inherently dangerous because of potential accidents; it could also open the door to further spreading of nuclear weapons. After the Vietnam War ended in 1975, the 1960s anti-war crowd morphed into an anti-nuclear-power force in California, led by Tom Hayden.

A dedicated socialist and antiwar activist then married to the actress Jane Fonda, Hayden forced Brown's hand on solar power. Hayden promoted progressive politics through his 5,000-member Campaign for Economic Democracy (CED), an anti-corporatist group. CED released a report in 1977 claiming solar power could create hundreds of thousands of new jobs in manufacturing and installation, something sorely needed during that time of economic hardship.

As a centrist and pragmatist, Brown thought Hayden might run against him from the left in the Democratic primary for Governor in 1978, potentially spoiling his reelection prospects. If Hayden wanted only a leadership role and some credit for making solar energy a reality in California, Brown would happily give it to him.

Brown's drive to make California a leader in renewable energy received a boost from a 55% tax credit for solar and wind energy installations created by the state legislature in the fall of 1977. For the first time, instead of putting a red light in front of polluters to stop bad things from happening, the state put a green light in the form of tax incentives to accelerate development of renewable energy as a positive alternative to over-reliance on fossil fuels.

The largest tax credit ever, the state incentive far surpassed the 25% federal solar tax credit, also passed in 1977. We had the incentive, but we had no industry in place to implement it. Finding ways to support growth of the solar industry and removing the barriers to consumer solar adoption became SolarCal's primary tasks.

After Sim and Wilson persuaded Governor Brown to create SolarCal, they hired me to run it, naming me as the Director of what we called the SolarCal Office.

SUN DAY ARRIVES

On May 3, 1978, Sun Day celebrations took place around the country. Sun Day's chief organizer, Denis Hayes, had persuaded President Jimmy Carter to endorse this event, modeled after 1970's successful Earth Day efforts that Hayes also organized. But Earth Day had entirely different origins; strong grassroots support from millions of participants resulted in a permanent national environmental movement. By contrast, local, state, and federal governments provided the big push behind Sun Day, not the public, the grassroots backbone of Earth Day.

Sun Day came and went without much fanfare or follow through. Crowds were light, only hundreds of people, compared with thousands we'd seen everywhere on Earth Day. Why? People relate to Gaia, the earth goddess, far more emotionally than to Apollo, the sun god. Environment is visceral, solar cerebral.

The national Sun Day celebration began inauspiciously. To emphasize solar energy's importance to our future, the president visited the Solar Energy Research Institute's new campus in Golden, Colorado. In his speech, Carter proclaimed a new day in America for solar power. It rained throughout the day. Undeterred, Carter later showed his commitment to solar power by directing the White House staff to install 32 solar panels for water heating.

Wilson and I had worked hard for the past three months putting SolarCal together. I did most of the day-to-day work, but

Wilson regularly reported to the governor on our progress, which made him the key liaison for moving forward. I drafted the executive order creating the office. To keep the Energy Commission from messing with it, we put SolarCal in the office of the cabinet secretary for business. We networked throughout state government and among Brown's leading political and business supporters to get names of prominent people to serve on the Council.

We wanted a broad-based group that would meet a few times over the next nine months, providing input for developing a state solar program. After we had most people on board, we showed the list to the governor and got a few more suggestions for people to add. We needed to get all the pieces in place before May, launching SolarCal for maximum PR exposure during the national event.

On Sun Day in California, Governor Brown signed and promoted the executive order establishing a *SolarCal Office and Council*. Brown charged the 26-member council with developing state policy for "maximum feasible solar commercialization." Sim became chair of the council; Wilson was executive secretary. Governor Brown appointed me as director of the office. Brown gave Tom Hayden a prominent role as vice-chair of the Council. The governor set a goal of 50,000 solar installations in California in 1978 and 1.5 million by 1985. These numbers would create 60,000 new jobs in the solar industry.

In serving the governor's agenda, I traded my idealism about renewable energy and solar power for realism. I had to produce specific results, working with leaders from labor, business, government, and environmental groups. I had to be accountable for what we could accomplish over the next few years, unlike at OAT where I'd bailed out after nine months to go to India. The first deliverable: an ambitious but realistic state plan for solar energy development. Spending time promoting the governor's agenda taught me to be practical with my recommendations, and I learned how to get buy-in from diverse stakeholders.

On Sun Day, Governor Brown and I traveled to three separate solar-related events in the state, flying in a state plane from a morning event in Sacramento to two more events, first at noon to visit a solar installation at Corcoran in the Central Valley, and onward to a rally later in the afternoon in Los Angeles. The morning was overcast, but by the time we arrived in southern California in the early afternoon, the sun shone brightly. During the flights, I briefed the governor about each upcoming event and gave him a few talking points. We found modest crowds of a few hundred at each rally. Sun Day didn't have Earth Day's infectious enthusiasm, teach-in focus, and outpouring of public support.

SOLARCAL

As the head of the SolarCal Office, I sometimes worked with state legislators to develop bills facilitating the growth of solar power. One day, I learned a lesson in practical politics. Many legislators, both Democrats and Republicans, wanted a piece of the action, introducing numerous bills to help create a vibrant solar industry. A young Republican Assemblyman from southern California submitted a draft solar bill that we at SolarCal didn't like, mostly for technical reasons. When an Assembly committee scheduled the bill for a hearing, I got the (not so) bright idea to testify against it.

After the hearing, this Assemblyman rushed up to me outside the committee room, red-faced, mustache bristling like an angry boar, eyes bulging behind his thick glasses. He shouted angrily, "Don't ever do that again. If you have a problem with my bills, come talk to me first!"

Ouch! As with most of life, politics is primarily a conversation. If you have an issue with someone's proposal, talk to them and try to appreciate what they want to accomplish. If you later must oppose it, at least they had a chance to argue for their viewpoint. I learned the hard way: saving face plays a leading role in politics. (Yes, even at thrity-four I was still that naïve.)

The solar energy spotlight clearly shone on Hayden, but I had a tough time getting along with him. He led a statewide political movement and, in his eyes, I was merely another technical flunky he expected to support him, no matter what I thought about his ideas. Through his wife he had acquired money, celebrity, and an imperious manner in dealing with Sacramento staffers. This was another way life served my meditation practice, challenging me to give up my still-inflated ego and offer my help wherever I could.

Wayne Parker, a young Georgia Tech grad, served as my Deputy Director. He could easily have had a cushy job in the Jimmy Carter administration since his former boss in Georgia was now an Assistant Secretary of Energy. Instead, he came west, drawn by Brown's image as a fresh voice. One day, Hayden came by my office looking for me, but I was away. He made himself at home, barely acknowledging Wayne.

"He strutted around like he owned the place while waiting for you," Wayne later told me.

Hayden quickly looked at things, picking up objects and putting them down, restless in the way of politicians and celebrities when there's no one around either important to talk with or to fawn over them.

He saw the back of a picture frame on my desk, grabbed it and turned it around. Instead of seeing my parents, children, or wife in the photo, he looked straight into Baba's face.

He replaced the picture, saying, "Well, I guess that's not his father."

It goes to show: spirituality and politics don't often mix.

During the SolarCal plan's development, I wanted to run the whole show, but Hayden persuaded Wilson and Sim to split the SolarCal job into two positions: one to serve as secretary of the SolarCal Council and one to run the SolarCal Office. For the Council secretary's role, Hayden chose Ron Lipton, effectively to serve as his personal assistant. Ron was a balding, soft-spoken, but savvy man in his early 30s who had recently and (to my mind) mysteriously arrived in Sacramento, managed to get introduced into Brown's inner circle, and befriended Hayden's key people.

When people wanted to know about his background, he claimed to have worked for the CIA, an assertion with two significant virtues: it impressed people in a government town like Sacramento and there was no way to verify it. I mean, who would you call to find out if Ron was once a secret CIA agent? He could have been—at times he looked and acted shell-shocked, sometimes speaking only in a barely audible whisper, sometimes moving his lips without any sound coming out, perhaps displaying a residual trauma from things he'd witnessed. Who knew? I still had doubts he was legit, but in the interests of team harmony, I let them go. If he was a phony, Hayden could figure it out and deal with it.

After working out our separate roles in promoting state support for solar energy and leaving Ron to deal with Hayden, I moved the SolarCal Office team under the auspices of the head of the Business and Transportation Agency. For nearly three years I directed the renamed *Solar Business Office*, responsible for doing everything we could to foster a vibrant solar industry in California.

Even with these intense political goings-on, I still meditated regularly and went to see Baba at the ashram in Oakland during the fall of 1978. I found it hard at times to reconcile these two vastly different worlds, even though I rationalized that my intention at work was to help create a better world. In Sacramento, I again found myself competing, sometimes subtly, sometimes overtly, with others for recognition and advancement: this time with Ron, to see who the top dog in our small solar energy world would be.

I read once a quote from Baba: *To compete with anyone shows your unworthiness.* After contemplating this situation, I figured out a better approach. I decided to do my job the best I could and let results manifest however they would. In this way, I could practice the yogic virtues of detachment and non-action. I understood Baba's simple message: don't try to become more important by diminishing anyone else's importance. The corollary: by promoting others' good work that supports causes you believe in, you create "win/win" situations for everyone.

What good came out of this conflict over the top role in the fledgling state solar bureaucracy? Although I lost some clout from Ron's political maneuvering, I gained a solid portfolio with staying power (and one that didn't challenge the Energy Commission's technical mandate in solar.) I learned about solar as a business, not only as a technological solution. I met solar industry people from around California and beyond, and I acquired a reputation as a practical guy and solar business expert.

After we launched SolarCal, I thought we could speed up the solar revolution by getting homebuilders to put solar water heaters on all new homes. I shared this idea with Dale Stuard, a SolarCal Council member and the president of a large homebuilding company in Orange County.

He listened politely and responded, "Jerry, let me tell you how our business works. If the first ten homebuyers who come into one of my model homes this weekend ask for solar, I'll call you on Monday to learn how to get started. Otherwise, I'm telling you there's no market for it and, as a company, we're can't afford to be out in front of consumer demand on this."

Bottom line: homebuyers weren't demanding solar water heating in new homes. To advance the solar agenda, we'd have to focus on existing homes.

After eight months of intense work, we released *Toward a Solar California: The SolarCal Council Action Program* in January 1979, the first state-level plan in the U.S. The plan offered a detailed program for developing California's solar energy industry. My small team wrote and produced it, got it approved by the SolarCal Council, and published it to serve as a model for other states' efforts.

Beyond continuing the state's generous tax credits, the SolarCal Plan recommended forty-six action steps, including removing impediments to solar use, training a workforce, using government projects as demonstrations, etc. But we all knew state government alone couldn't usher in a solar revolution. At best, it could be a facilitator, a remover of obstacles, and a strong voice to encourage property owners, government agencies, and businesses to use solar technology. The private sector responded and by 1980 California's solar industry was booming.

While developing the SolarCal plan, I met dozens of business leaders from California's solar industry. At one point, I had an epiphany: these folks were the true solar revolutionaries, not the Jerry Browns, Wilson Clarks, Tom Haydens (and Jerry Yudelsons) of the world. As doers, not talkers, they put their money, time, energy, and talent on the line to create a better world. Once I understood this, I developed enormous regard for their contributions.

I knew I would also be a more effective solar advocate if I stopped talking and started selling. To do this, I'd have to leave government and enter the private sector.

If I had read everything Baba wrote about the benefits of meditation, but never meditated, what would I have gained? I could talk about solar's benefits all day, but shouldn't I also "walk the talk"? As a first step, Elle and I began building our long-delayed passive solar house, wanting to walk the talk in our private lives.

A PASSIVE SOLAR HOME

ELLE PASSIONATELY WANTED TO DESIGN AND BUILD A HOME DISPLAYING our environmental values. When she was young, she wanted to learn how to build things, but her traditional father believed girls shouldn't learn practical things like hammering and sawing. He refused to teach her what he knew, something she deeply resented. Once our home construction began, Elle gradually picked up practical skills from the guys we hired. She managed to look simultaneously sexy and capable in a T-shirt, cut-off jeans, a baseball cap, and work boots, holding a hammer and wearing a leather tool belt.

I couldn't offer much help, though I had learned rudiments of carpentry helping Stewart renovate his house in Felton. My father was a lawyer with few household-level practical skills, except he'd learned to replace windowpanes in the French doors facing our backyard, glass which my brothers and I regularly broke with errant throws while playing catch with a baseball or football.

But could Elle and I afford to build a house? Most people wait until they're rich or well settled in life, usually in their 40s or 50s, before building their own home. When we began planning the home, Elle was 26, I was 32. We didn't have much money, hardly the best time to plan a home. We'd spent most of our savings buying the property when we returned from India. But we wanted to be authentic, showing that our passion for solar homes wasn't only hot air: something we talked about only to impress friends in the environmental movement.

To deepen our comprehension of solar home technology, in the spring of 1976, we flew to Albuquerque to attend the first Passive

Solar Conference, sponsored by Los Alamos National Laboratory. There we met researchers and practitioners, passionate advocates for low-energy homes.

Early work by scientists at Los Alamos showed that passive solar homes used less energy than conventional homes and typically didn't cost more to build, which encouraged us to move ahead with what we had planned. During our trips to New Mexico, we studied traditional methods of building. We visited passive solar adobe homes that were quiet and comfortable, like living in a light-filled cave.

After we returned from the conference, Elle insisted on building something ourselves as an example of what people could do about addressing energy problems. We learned it was far cheaper to make bricks using onsite clay (aka "mud"), the way people typically built adobe homes in New Mexico. From our earlier environmental consulting work, we knew Bay Area hills consisted mostly of clay soil, so we decided to build in the foothills.

We found the site, but without regular income, we couldn't qualify for a construction loan. Elle hadn't yet produced design and construction drawings; without those, there would be no building permit and no loan. After I landed the full-time position with SolarCal, we had enough steady income to get the loan and Elle began designing the home in detail.

BUILDING THE SOLAR HOME

Elle had studied the home site. The property had a regional-water supply canal on the north side, so site geometry dictated we place the rear of the home facing the canal for privacy and move it far away from trees on the west side that could block the afternoon sun. For optimum solar gain we wanted our living room windows facing south.

Elle's design featured a post-and-beam structure, with wooden beams supporting the roof's weight. As a result, we had non-load-bearing walls, especially important for withstanding an earthquake. Not wanting to stack adobe bricks in the traditional style, Elle developed an innovative approach to making adobe, creating a slurry mixture with clay, sand, straw, and water, which she poured between expanded-metal-lath forms to make the walls. This represented a marked departure from the conventional method. Because it rains more in northern California than in New Mexico, she added a waterproofing asphalt binder to the slurry.

After two years of planning, we got a building permit in October 1979. We bought a new ¾-ton Chevy pickup to haul building materials and moved to the building site with our cat Kokopelli, where we lived in a 10-foot-wide, 70-foot-long old mobile home. Every day, I commuted sixty-one miles each way to Sacramento. When commuting got too tiring, I stayed in Sacramento, living for a year in the basement of a friend's house. I traveled frequently for my work at SolarCal. We had no mobile phones, internet or PCs, and no one worked from home then, so I was gone (and out of touch) a lot.

This 700-square foot, poorly insulated trailer served as both our home and the construction office, muddy during winter rains and dusty most of the time, with our two-man crew, Ed and Jamie, coming in and out of the kitchen and bathroom each weekday. Kokopelli spent most of her time outside the trailer, hunting mice in the tall grass on the hillside. One day, she didn't return for dinner. We searched the neighborhood for a week, posted flyers on telephone poles, and asked neighbors for help, but we never found her. I felt sad for days; losing an animal is hard, especially when you don't know her fate. For weeks, Elle and I sensed something missing each night when we went to sleep without a small furry creature curled between us on top of the blanket.

Elle worked on the construction site either all day, or late afternoons after working at her design studio. I helped on weekends and summer evenings whenever I could. Because we used the innovative technology of poured adobe, things didn't always go as planned, and we ran out of money before we finished construction. We went back to the bank for an additional construction loan that added twenty-five percent to the mortgage. In 1980, interest rates were above 10.5 percent. With my steady job with the state, we qualified for the add-on loan, but it added to our financial burden.

LIVING IN A SOLAR HOME

Living in an earth-sheltered home is a unique experience, whether it's made from adobe, rammed earth, or similar materials. It's like living in a cave. Inside temperatures change slowly. The heavy mass absorbs much of the heat gain or heat loss during the day and radiates heat or coolness back into the space during the evening. Sometime, during the late afternoon, stand near a concrete or brick wall that's had sun on it all day and you'll feel the radiant heat. The major drawback? This slow-to-heat, slow-to-cool characteristic requires more patience than most people have.

Because Elle had chosen post-and-beam construction and designed an exposed vaulted ceiling, we had natural wood everywhere: window frames, doors, posts, cabinets, the roof deck, and exposed ceiling beams. If you wanted to design a home for optimum physical and psychological well-being, you'd build it mainly from earth and wood, with lots of daylighting and only a few manufactured products like faucets, toilets, sinks, and brass hardware.

After two years' living in a small, singlewide trailer during construction, we relished once again having normal living space. We made our offices in two smaller bedrooms on the east side, with good morning sun, working again side by side, though our differences remained. Once settled, we held a party and celebrated achieving Elle's dream of building and living in her own passive solar home.

To cool the home and keep it ventilated at night, we left open two windows in the living room on the north side facing the canal. A public walkway ran alongside the canal, separated from our site only by a five-foot-tall chain-link fence. At night, anyone walking alongside the canal could see if windows were open.

One morning I woke slowly with a headache, feeling groggy. Sometime during the night, burglars had cut the screen and got in through the open window. Someone had clubbed me, knocking me unconscious, opening a cut on my left ear. In the morning, after I got out of bed and went into the living room, I saw right away that Elle's purse was gone from its usual spot on the dining table.

I shouted, "We've been robbed!"

Still sleepy, she sat up in bed. "What did they take?"

I looked around the living room and went into the two offices. "Looks like all they took was your purse. They cut the screen. I guess we left the window open."

We called the sheriff 's office and filed a crime report. I went to an outpatient clinic to get the cut stitched. My meditation practice came to the rescue. I remained calm, unconcerned about what could have happened to Elle or me had we woken up and confronted the robbers. Throughout the day I kept repeating the mantra I'd received from Baba, staying centered. We both credited Baba's grace for saving us from far worse consequences than replacing credit cards.

TROUBLE IN OUR RELATIONSHIP

Building a new home didn't bring us closer, as we had hoped. We continued drifting apart. The adobe house functioned not only as our home but to help build Elle's career as a passive solar home designer. Gradually we stopped spending quality time together. I stayed more often in Sacramento to avoid the hassle of a daily two-hour commute. Our originally close relationship deteriorated. Even after eight years as a couple we hadn't committed to a life together. I began to question what I wanted from the relationship, and Elle wanted to get on with her career without having to deal with our occasional emotional melodramas.

Even though I considered myself Baba's student, I hadn't yet assimilated or implemented certain core teachings very well into my life. I experienced too many conflicts such as I had with Ron in organizing SolarCal or in arguments with Elle over personal priorities, such as where to go on vacation.

One of Baba's core teachings is *See God in each other*. Sounds easy enough, but I had difficulty practicing it consistently, especially with people who (I thought) didn't have advanced spiritual knowledge. I found it hard to admit that maybe I was the one who wasn't advanced, or whether I could determine who was a spiritual adept.

For months at a time, Elle's design studio and workshop business didn't make enough money to cover expenses. Without telling me, she withdrew a little money regularly from our checking account to cover her office payroll. Eventually the hidden losses exceeded $10,000, more than three months' salary. When I figured it out and confronted her, we had a nasty fight. She felt I was suppressing her career aspirations, but I thought if she wanted to have her own business it should be self-supporting. This incident showed me we already led separate lives and had lost the implicit trust we once shared.

Because of money stresses from going way over budget during construction, plus the time we had spent apart during those three years, we couldn't (or didn't try to) reconstruct our once-close relationship and, through inaction, decided not to try to refresh or redefine it. The bloom was off the rose, but it was still stuck in the vase. Over time, we gradually withdrew from each other, pursuing our separate interests.

By the time we moved into the new home, in the summer of 1981, even after ten years together, we hadn't decided what we wanted from our marriage. Though we still liked and respected each other, at times our connection seemed more like a truce between warring factions than a committed, long-term loving relationship.

I was determined to get on with my career in the solar industry. I knew I couldn't learn how to get the public to buy solar while I held onto a cushy job in state government, but I needed a vehicle to ride into the private sector.

THE ENERGY CLINIC

O N ONE OF MY TRIPS TO WASHINGTON, DC, in the run-up to Sun Day, I met Jackson Gouraud, the Deputy Undersecretary of Energy. A pioneering ad man, in the early sixties Gouraud was one of the first corporate marketing consultants in the United States, helping companies sell L&M cigarettes, Valium, and Smirnoff vodka. A vigorous man in his late 50s, he could easily have had a role in *Mad Men*. An influential senator convinced President Carter to appoint Gouraud to bring his advertising smarts to the job of selling energy conservation to the public.

After two years in government, Gouraud was itching to get back to the private sector. He conceived of a new company called The Energy Clinic to sell solar and conservation via a network of retail stores. He set about organizing the company, planning an Initial Public Offering (IPO) to raise $4 million in late 1980 from the stock market. Because California had the largest solar market in the country, he wanted me involved and called me in the spring.

"You really should join me if you want to get this solar thing going. I'll show you how it's done in business."

My initial response was noncommittal. "I've still got things I want to do with Jerry Brown. Let's talk again in a month or two."

He kept calling. By late summer, I'd given the idea more thought, convincing myself now was the time to leave state government and learn about business.

Jackson's final pitch sold me: "We'll match your state salary and benefits and give you some stock options." I thought maybe I could get something beyond a salary, some valuable stock, if the company succeeded.

When I agreed to leave the state government to take the Energy Clinic position, I left an easy job I could have held for two more years until the governor's term expired at the end of 1982. I had become well established in the solar industry. But I wanted a change. I have a lot of Mercury in my chart (perhaps from that long prenatal journey), which subtly pushed me to keep moving, restlessly looking for the next important thing.

I have always made key decisions with my gut, not fearing consequences, assuming if I followed my passion of the moment, things would turn out all right in the end. When I decided to leave graduate school after Earth Day, I didn't know where I would land, only that it was time to move on and take a more active role in the environmental movement; it was a decision that led me to Elle and eventually to Baba. Now I was ready for a new phase, trusting once again my heart's direction.

Leaving state government meant, in less than five years, quitting a second position to which the governor had appointed me. I knew there would be no going back, and I knew any new company posed a risk. Would it be competitive with existing solar companies, many of which had a three-year lead in serving the market? Was I cut out for the rough-and-tumble world of running a small business, especially a startup, instead of the high-level, slow-moving, policy and political environment of state government?

For many reasons, The Energy Clinic concept flopped. The meager profits from selling a few solar systems a week couldn't pay for a manager and staff, salaried salespeople, and the overhead of a retail store. Despite his experience, Gouraud apparently hadn't done much market research. We launched the business in a tough economy. Retail sales experienced an economic recession that began in the second quarter of 1980 and continued mostly throughout 1981. We never found a way to overcome the skill and experience of the established competition.

I had failed in my first private sector venture after leaving government, but I decided to treat it as a "learning experience," a popular term for "turning lemons into lemonade."

Gifted with new-found street smarts about the solar business,

I sold my expertise as a consultant to companies planning to enter the California solar industry. Over the next two years, I became known as an industry guru, my reputation spreading even to foreign companies. One day I got a large check in the mail, unsolicited, from an Australian company wanting a California market study for their solar water heaters. Gradually, I developed expertise as a market analyst and marketing consultant for selling new renewable energy technologies. Within a year, I was able to turn the Energy Clinic failure into a stroke of good fortune.

BECOMING AN EFFECTIVE SOLAR ADVOCATE

From 1982 to 1985, as part of my consulting business, I worked part time as a solar industry lobbyist in Sacramento, promoting (and protecting) the nascent California solar energy industry.

After Jerry Brown left office at the end of 1982, George Deukmejian, the new Republican governor, and Willie Brown, the state assembly leader (a liberal Democrat) tried each year to kill the 55% state solar tax credit. The new governor thought it was a waste of public money and Brown objected, in principle, to giving state incentives to wealthy homeowners when there were more pressing social needs.

Fortunately, we had enough bipartisan legislative support from our SolarCal efforts to keep the credits in force until the originally scheduled sunset date at the end of 1985.

I found getting a reputation as an expert, a thought leader, or an important person (and working to maintain it) represented a challenge for the ego. For someone pursuing spiritual practices, as I got stroked with praise, I found it difficult to maintain detachment from results, positive or negative, the ups and downs endemic to political and business life.

I had learned from Baba that a main goal of meditation is to retain a steady focus while enduring the pairs of opposites: praise and blame, success and failure. The side benefit of having a good reputation, hard to overlook for a committed solar advocate: I could get good things done for a cause I believed in. The trick was not to get too high with praise and too upset with blame.

Baba's advice was crystal clear: if I put my small ego aside—my often understated but insistent need for recognition and appreciation—the work would become great, it would serve many people, and in time I would gain recognition.

Even as the solar industry grew as planned, because the state and federal "solar" tax credits also applied to all forms of renewable energy, another new industry emerged in an unanticipated way from something blowing in the wind: free, renewable energy captured by wind turbines and fed into the electricity grid. With a little luck and a few connections from the Brown Administration, I found I could extend my solar consulting work to include wind power.

But first I had to take care of the situation with Elle, something I'd been putting off for a year-and-a-half after moving into our new adobe home.

BLOWING IN THE WIND

IN THE SPRING OF 1983, after twelve years together, I told Elle I wanted a divorce. She was angry but also relieved to put an end to our strained relationship and get more control over her life. In our separation agreement, she got the house and I moved out. I agreed to pay half the mortgage for three years, to keep the peace and not leave her stranded financially. I found an apartment on the ground floor of an older house in Oakland's Rockridge neighborhood, ten minutes' drive from the ashram.

I felt the loss keenly, mourning the end of a twelve-year relationship into which we each had poured our hearts and souls, an ending resembling more a balloon slowly deflating than some dramatic rupture. Less than two years after the failure of The Energy Clinic, I faced another disappointment, this time more personal. I became depressed for a month, losing touch with my once upbeat and confident self. I didn't want to leave my apartment except on weekends to go to the ashram to chant and meditate. I couldn't work. I moped around. During this time, I failed to complete a large consulting assignment, the only time in my life that had ever happened: a sure sign of my sorrowful state. With apologies, I returned the client's fee.

Still I continued my spiritual practices; gradually they lifted me out of this sadness. By meditating, participating in satsangs, chanting *namasankirtana,* hanging around people at the ashram who practiced living with boundless joy and great enthusiasm, gradually my spirits brightened. I resumed working with new energy and creative delight.

AN UPTICK IN MY FORTUNES

In 1980, I'd met Tom Flynn soon after he'd landed an appointment in Jerry Brown's administration following his work in Brown's abortive 1980 presidential primary campaign. After working two years for Brown, Tom moved back to New York to join a small investment firm. One day in October 1982, he called from New York, wanting me to be a consultant to investigate the wind energy industry. He and his new business partners wanted to syndicate an investment partnership to deploy wind turbines in California, in Palm Springs and Tehachapi, two of the largest wind resource areas in the country.

Sophisticated investors had figured out that combining state and federal tax credits with accelerated deprecation amounted to a "half-off sale," immediately reducing more than 50 cents in tax liability for each dollar invested in a wind farm. To qualify for tax write-offs, developers had to install and operate them each year by December 31st; there wasn't much time left in 1982 to get in on the action.

One Bay Area Congressman, Fortney (Pete) Stark, claimed at the time, "These aren't wind farms, they're tax farms." It was a quip that later became a telling blow. He was right, at least for some projects. As I learned with solar energy, using tax credits to spur industry growth often draws in quick-buck operators and leaves behind a mess for others to clean up. Someone had sold my investor clients on a wind technology with only one working prototype installed in Palm Springs. They sent me there to investigate whether to invest in it.

Palm Springs is a perfect wind resource area. If you drive east from the Los Angeles basin on a summer afternoon you will experience how fiercely wind blows through the San Gorgonio Pass, framed by two 10,000-foot mountain peaks, San Jacinto and San Gorgonio. As the desert warms during the morning, the heated air rises, replaced by cooler air drawn inland from the Pacific Ocean, about a hundred miles away. Flowing into the desert between the mountains, the cooler air accelerates to about 30 miles per hour. It usually takes three to four hours for ocean breezes to get to the pass, but by early afternoon, the wind is howling. Find a good place to install wind turbines and, if they work, you're guaranteed to make electricity.

At the time, many wind machines didn't work; experimentation ruled. Developers installed wind farms quickly, as the tax credits would expire at year-end 1985; it was as chaotic as any gold rush. At one point in the mid-1980s, as Palm Springs sported dozens of varieties of wind power technology, it looked analogous to historic villages you see all over Europe, with housing types from various centuries, along with a blacksmith, wool spinner, and glass blower.

After some searching, I found a few people knowledgeable about wind technology. Based on these conversations, my consulting report recommended against backing the specific device Tom's team wanted to invest in, but as there wasn't anything else available at that late date, they went ahead.

The next year, I continued my wind power investigations for Tom and his investors. This assignment had three benefits: I got paid, I got to visit New York often (always fun, especially when someone else foots the bill) to brief the investment group, and eventually I landed a consulting assignment with a new wind power manufacturer that Tom's partners took public in a 1984 IPO. Behind this turn of events I saw the grace of my meditation practice. I had acquired mental and emotional flexibility, allowing me easily to make changes in business direction.

By investigating wind power, I got acquainted with Zond Systems, which in 1980 pioneered wind power development in Tehachapi. With its early entry into the business, Zond secured a steady supply of sturdy Danish *Vestas* wind turbines. For decades, Danes had generated electricity from wind power. They made wind turbines like farm machinery, with heavy metal construction and rugged electronics able to function in wind, rain, and cold for many years. Contrasting with smaller but more rugged Danish turbines, American-made machines were often ten times larger, made with high-tech composite materials, and developed primarily for government demonstration projects. In daily use, they broke down repeatedly.

Later in 1984, I began working with Zond as a consultant in government relations. After a year, Jim Dehlsen, Zond's CEO and founder, called me. "We like working with you, but we can't keep paying you as a consultant; you're too expensive. Why don't you come here and work for us? You can use your lobbying experience to work on getting the federal tax credit extended."

I considered his offer for a few weeks. Leaving the Bay Area would mean leaving the Oakland ashram community. But I was ready to move on and leave behind the uncertain life of a lone consultant, never sure when or where I'd find the next client. In the summer of 1985, I signed a year's contract as Zond's marketing and lobbying director. With a few regrets, I left northern California, where I had lived fifteen years, and moved to Tehachapi, 100 miles north of Los Angeles: a dusty rural town I'd never visited, located at 4,000 feet elevation in the southern Sierra.

After I arrived, Dehlsen took me for an updated wind-farm tour in his blue Chevy Suburban. For moving crews out to the turbines and back, Zond owned a half-dozen Suburbans, all of them perpetually dusty and needing new shocks because of the rough terrain.

Tall, lanky, and handsome, with looks reflecting his Danish heritage, Dehlsen was a no-nonsense business owner who could turn on the charm when he had something to sell, reflecting his earlier career as a stockbroker.

Zond was racing to complete two wind farm installations to beat the December 1985 deadline, when the state and federal tax credits would expire. If the credits expired, Zond would have to switch from sales into a maintenance mode.

Jim wanted me to lead a lobbying effort to extend federal tax credits beyond the end of 1985. We knew we couldn't extend the state's 55 percent tax credit. After three years battling California's new governor to keep them in force, that wasn't going to happen. We hired a lobbying firm in Washington DC, headed by Jim Corman, my father's old friend and my former hometown

congressman. I went to DC several times to lobby key Congress-
men, even met with senior officials at the West Wing, working to
convince the Reagan Administration to help our new industry.

I tried getting Congressional leaders to listen to our story,
stressing the importance of renewable electricity to our nation's
energy supply. Pete Stark's old comment characterizing our projects as "tax farms" created a high hurdle. We failed to change the
law; federal tax credits for wind expired at year-end.

Beyond a steady paycheck, Zond offered me an unexpected
opportunity for spiritual growth, not only because I lived alone in
a small apartment. In moving to Tehachapi, I expected to be working directly with Dehlsen, the CEO, but instead I had to work under
Ken, the number two executive. Ten years younger than I was,
Ken was an aggressive guy with an MBA, a former banker who
surrounded himself with similar high-testosterone types. Our
styles clashed immediately, but I couldn't do much about it; he
was my direct boss.

In Carlos Castaneda's books about his apprenticeship with a
Yaqui Indian shaman, Don Juan forces Carlos on several occasions
to confront his nemesis, an adversary who would push him beyond
his narrow sense of himself. As an academic, Carlos always expected to receive rational treatment from others. Instead, Don
Juan warned him the nemesis might choose to kill him, maybe for
no reason. He warned Carlos to stay alert. Initially this revelation
upset Carlos. *It wasn't fair!*

Don Juan taught Carlos he should *welcome* the nemesis, because
he could play a positive role in Carlos's spiritual evolution, forcing
him out of his mental rigidity and into moving with the flow of
life in each moment.

I'd often heard from people around Baba that the essence of
spiritual attainment was to have no preconceived opinions or preferences, to be willing to accept and live in harmony with whatever
life presented in each moment. In this sense, my younger boss
was a perfect nemesis.

After a while, because this had happened several times before
in my life, I had to take stock of my role in creating this situation

and make peace with it, at least for the moment. If I considered Ken to be a jerk (the exact opposite of Baba's teaching to see everyone as God), I reasoned, I only had to deal with him 40 hours a week, but he had to deal with himself all the time. In this way, I worked to smooth out our relationship from one of conflict (in my view) to one more businesslike.

After further reflection, I came to see HE was perfectly normal; my outlook was flawed. I knew I could change how I saw him if I wanted to, so gradually I did. We finished the year on respectful terms after I stopped resenting his oversight and accepted the situation as an important learning experience.

One defining characteristic of the spiritual path I'd chosen is how often I found opportunities to make sweet lemonade from life's bitter lemons. Once I saw what was happening, I welcomed this situation as essential to my spiritual growth. But I had more important work ahead than nourishing an inner conflict in a remote corner of California. I had to get back to my spiritual practices.

V
A NEW LIFE

DIVORCE IS A CLOSE COUSIN TO DEATH. The relationship dies; the grieving begins. After I left Elle, I wallowed in this process, becoming unsteady, like a top losing momentum and wobbling after spinning fast. With new relationships, I reverted to old habits, starting them as casually as I would buy a T-shirt, wearing them a few times, discarding them as readily as I had done before meeting Elle. After eight months living this way, an inner voice prompted me to stop and assess how I was living.

I recalled an analogy I'd heard Baba use a few times. It went like this: If you have a dog with a curly tail (he'd draw a few circles in the air with his index finger to illustrate how curly) and you want to straighten it, you could put the tail in a pipe. That would work for a while, but as soon as you removed the pipe, the tail would curl again. I understood the analogy: the pipe represented the discipline of yoga and the curly tail my wayward tendencies. I knew I had to get control over the grieving.

In the same way as coaches, when they see their team getting tired, flustered, or out of sync, call a time-out to regroup, my inner coach called "time." I grasped I had to create space for myself to heal, to let go of twelve years spent with Elle. Pursuing new relationships wasn't the right way to go about it. Realizing it's always darkest right before dawn, my intuition told me I needed time to myself. I needed to wait for the dawn, for the darkness to disappear naturally in brilliant sunlight. I rededicated myself to spiritual practices, to purifying myself on a deeper level. After a few months, I felt refreshed, ready to take the next step on the path.

GURUMAYI

I MOVED TOWARD GURUMAYI CHIDVILASANANDA, Baba's leading disciple and his designated spiritual heir, in the darshan line at the Siddha Yoga Ashram in Oakland. Gurumayi offered darshan the same way Baba did, blessing people with a peacock-feather wand, listening to their concerns, accepting their gifts, putting shawls around people's shoulders on special occasions. During these satsangs, she lectured on spiritual topics and each night led us in chanting and meditation sessions. She was young—not yet thirty—exquisitely beautiful and clearly in command. There was one big change: I could talk to her. As Baba's main translator during his third world tour, Gurumayi spoke excellent English.

During meditation with her the day before, I had seen Baba's form vividly, exactly as when he was alive. As I watched, Baba's image faded, slowly changing into Gurumayi's form. In the same way Baba gave me a sign during the retreat in Malibu a decade earlier, I felt he has given me explicit direction to take Gurumayi as my spiritual guide.

I was nervous as I moved slowly toward her seat. From my experience with Baba, I knew this was a momentous decision, something each seeker had to face, outwardly and inwardly. It contained my deep personal commitment and my reverence for the role of the spiritual Master, the guide, the teacher, the source of wisdom, the ultimate refuge.

Now I was directly in front of her, kneeling at her feet.

After bowing low, I said, "Gurumayi, I want you to be my Guru."

She responded immediately: "Did Baba come in your dream?"

"Yes." In response, she nodded. That was it; I walked back to my seat, relieved and elated. She knew what I had experienced. We had already connected in the heart. We didn't have to say anything more.

Gurumayi had attracted many of Baba's students right after his passing eighteen months earlier, but I hadn't connected with her until then. Baba had initiated me, and I regarded him as my spiritual Master even after he took mahasamadhi. Now he'd clearly handed me over to Gurumayi, whom he had chosen to continue his mission. If I had faith in this path and conviction in my commitment, I felt I had to embrace this instruction as Baba's parting gift, pointing me in the right direction.

In Gurumayi's presence I experienced her as ancient, wise, all-knowing. She lacked nothing; through her years of dedicated service to Baba, Gurumayi had become a perfect spiritual Master: compassionate, freely joyful, insightful, able to give spiritual initiation with a look, a thought, a word, or a touch of the peacock feathers. I could see she was deeply committed to her students.

Around Gurumayi, I understood ineffable truths. When I was with her, joy arose spontaneously, and I experienced subtle knowledge bubbling from within. After I had this meditation experience, I knew she and Baba were essentially identical as Masters. I experienced great love for her. Even away from her physical presence, I had similar elevated experiences whenever I took time to remember her or to recall a resonant teaching I'd heard or read.

By spending time with Gurumayi, my meditations deepened, and my spiritual understanding grew. While I practiced daily meditation, I still had my consulting work for solar and wind power companies, which required a lot of travel. There wasn't much time for relationships.

After I left Elle and before I connected with Gurumayi, for six months I'd dated and slept with several women, whenever I could fit them into my schedule. But something changed within; I decided one day I had to remake myself, both within and outside. To honor this insight, during the next six months, I made a conscious choice to remain single and unattached.

For the first time in my adult life, I went cold-turkey celibate, acting like a "real yogi," and didn't date anyone. I decided to look for satisfaction not in the arms of a lover, but in a gentler embrace of my spiritual practices. If I found a woman attractive, I would view it dispassionately as only a karmic impulse, a worldly samskara, and let the impulse subside without acting on it. Confusion I'd had about relationships vanished as I connected with my inner joy and with the subtle energy of meditation. I trusted that if I allowed grace to dictate my course, I'd eventually find a beneficial relationship.

I still lived in the rented house in Oakland. A woman in her late thirties lived in a small apartment behind and adjoining mine. At some point, the owner had added this apartment to the house, without spending much to soundproof the walls between these two units. How did I know? She had a regular boyfriend; I'd see them going out most weekend evenings. My bathroom wall adjoined her bedroom wall. Anytime I used the bathroom on Saturday night (often after returning from chanting at the ashram), I heard through the wall the familiar loud sounds of a couple fucking with great abandon. I'd laugh, smiling, relieved for the first time to feel no attraction for bedroom passions. My attitude toward sex had changed. I'd let go of feelings of lust that had gripped me for the past twenty years, had pushed me into poor relationship choices. Better to be slow to change than never!

During this time, I would drive away from the city to visit beautiful and inspiring natural areas in northern California. I found writing poems about these places encouraged me to go deeper into my inner experience, connecting their physical beauty with the longings of my heart. Here are two poems inspired by those visits.

Carmel Postcard

Wind in my face, hungry gulls circling.
Rocky outcrop—poet's chair.
Treasure hunters roam—shells and coins.

Steep path down to the beach.
Facing into strong North Pacific winds.
Smell of sushi drifting over
ten thousand miles of open ocean.
I see a sign—*Danger—Intermittent waves*
Of unusual size and force.
We need a sign like that in the meditation hall:
Danger—Large waves of joy
May overcome you at any time.
It's a steep path down to that essential shore.

Thought pebbles
smoothed by wind and surf, polished
into tokens of pure love.
You always find them on this beach.
If you take a walk along the coast,
"Go as far as you can without getting killed,
then come back."
And send this postcard to your heart!

Point Lobos

Granite outcrops
mix in with surf.
Shades of blue and green.
Millions of years,
hard stone, ground and
caressed by the sea.

Our hearts are like that:
All around us
the sea of love,
yet we stay cold,
only softening a little now and then.

Baba's path was total openness.
Embracing rock and water,
he was salt spray,
the sound of breakers.

We all remember
these elemental sounds,
remember ourselves as ocean waves,
breaking eternally on the soft sands of existence.

Once in meditation, I heard deep within
a thunderclap so loud
I began to cry—
The immensity of my own Self.

JESSICA

EACH FRIDAY NIGHT, I'd leave Zond at five and head out of town going south on Willow Springs Road on my way to Los Angeles. It was exactly 100 miles to the Siddha Yoga ashram in Santa Monica, barely a two-hour drive (against the traffic) even on Fridays. In the desert, I usually drove well over the speed limit to make the trip in two hours. One Friday in September, I turned left onto Highway 138 toward Palmdale and put the pedal to the metal, accelerating above 75 on my way to the Antelope Valley Freeway leading into L.A. One car headed toward me from the opposite direction. As it passed, I saw it was a black and white: Highway Patrol. I slowed the car immediately but watched in my rearview mirror as the patrol car did a magnificent U-turn, raising a cloud of dust, and came rapidly toward me, red lights flashing. I pulled over and took my medicine like a man. The officer and I had a brief, polite, but ultimately expensive conversation. After that encounter, I tried harder to adhere to the speed limit. Hadn't Baba always taught us to obey the law?

Going to the ashram to attend satsang and spend time with Gurumayi's students became a weekend ritual. Afterward, I'd stay at the ashram or go to my mother's house in Van Nuys twenty miles away, killing two birds with one stone: visiting Mom, then in her seventies, and going to the ashram.

A few months after I began this routine, in October 1985, the ashram celebrated the third anniversary of Baba's mahasamadhi, the date of his passing. I went there for an evening of my favorite activity, chanting. For a great saint like Baba, each year devotees celebrate the anniversary of his death, using the occasion to remember him with love and to renew their focus on his life and teachings.

Before the program, I went to the Amrit café for dinner. The café had been the breakfast room of the hotel located there before it became an ashram. I stood in the serving line for dinner, drinking in the calm but energizing atmosphere. I loved ashram food: vegetarian, delicious, cooked with love. I filled my tray, paid for the food, and walked into the main dining area. In the crowded dining hall, I saw only one open seat. Fortune smiled.

At a table near the window, I spotted an attractive woman sitting with someone I knew from Oakland. As it turned out, there was an open seat directly across from her. I hurried over, careful not to spill my soup while I swerved through the crowd. As I got closer, I could see her more clearly: a beautiful redhead.

I approached the table hesitantly. "Is this seat taken?"

In the ashram, it was OK to sit with people you didn't know, but I thought maybe they'd reserved the seat for someone getting dinner. I raised an eyebrow, asking; my friend motioned me to sit with her and Jessica.

We introduced ourselves and started talking. She captivated me right away. After a half-hour of light conversation, dinnertime ended and we both went into the program. During the next few hours, whenever I took a break from chanting to have tea in the café, she'd also be taking a break. Synchronicity? My good karma? Who knew? We talked some more and exchanged phone numbers.

As I drove back to Tehachapi, I was intrigued, excited, filled with anticipation, certain I had met someone special. I got even more interested when I inquired the next week among mutual friends at the ashram and found out Jessica was single and (as far as anyone knew) not in a relationship. I could see only one drawback: at the time, she was temporarily sharing an apartment in West Hollywood with her mother, after moving out of her beachfront cottage in Venice. But nature and fate provided a perfectly adequate work-around: that month, she was housesitting nearby.

I went to see her the next weekend, this time for lunch. She was taking care of a friend's house in Palms near the Santa Monica airport. I soon learned she was serious about food. Jessica looked ten years younger than her age, owing to her disciplined approach to eating; maybe it was also good genes. She studied with a nutritionist, Cristopher Gian-Cursio, a New York-based doctor from Italy who crafted a mostly plant-based diet for each patient, a form of Natural Hygiene popular in the 1980s.

When I arrived for lunch, she wanted to know, "Do you like blended salads?"

"Of course, sounds great," I said, lying through my smile; I'd never had one.

I wanted to please her and would eat whatever she served. I thought, "It's only lunch; how bad can it be?"

She acted delighted to hear this, and we ate the way she liked: first, a glass of fresh carrot juice, followed by a blended salad (imagine a thick cold green porridge, like gazpacho), followed by dessert: a blended orange mashed into raw cashew butter, all organic. For sure I liked cashew butter and oranges. In this diet, for dinner you could add a tossed salad to the carrot juice and blended salad, then have two steamed vegetables, with a grain or lentils. The diet allowed two seasonings, olive oil and lemon juice, no salt. You could eat cheese, but only an unsalted raw-milk cheddar or jack cheese mail-ordered from a specific dairy in upstate New York approved by the good doctor. Despite my initial skepticism, I found the food filling, nutritious, and tasty and, though I had more interest in the woman than the meal, I ate with my customary gusto.

This was all new. Growing up, I ate SAD: my mother's Standard American Diet of meat and potatoes with boiled frozen vegetables, mostly peas, corn, and green beans. I'd become a vegetarian twelve years earlier. While I ate properly when I was in the ashram, I still had a fondness for the four major food groups: coffee and doughnuts, diet Coke and nachos, grilled cheese sandwiches, and Yoplait fruit yogurt eaten straight from the cup; not much had changed since my college days.

As we got better acquainted the next few weeks, I fell in love with Jessica. I looked forward to eating her food. On her diet, for the last course on certain days after a salad-only meal, she could choose to eat three bananas, a whole avocado, or twelve dates. As I learned more about it, I decided it was strict but sensible.

Jessica later admitted she knew right away we were meant for each other. We shared similar views on many levels: intellectually, spiritually, sexually, and politically. We even shared a similar sense of humor. But more than two years after leaving Elle, my divorce still hadn't become final, and I hesitated to leap into another relationship.

After our first date, we talked daily by phone. I went to L.A. every weekend to see her. Because she was house-sitting, we could be alone. Our first kiss happened on a sofa Baba had sat on in 1980. (The woman who owned this house had loaned it to his tour for Baba to use, getting it back after his Bay Area visit ended.) We became lovers that night—there seemed little point in waiting. Via that couch, we fancied that Baba had blessed our relationship. Things between us flowed naturally, but there was one big issue holding us back: legally I was still married.

A SPEED BUMP

After our first weekend together, we decided to go away the next weekend to Santa Barbara. We both wanted the relationship to blossom and began disclosing more about our life situations. After leaving her cottage near the beach in Venice because of increasing crime, Jessica moved into her mother's two-bedroom apartment in West Hollywood. I was committed to living in Tehachapi until my contract with Zond finished in nine months. Living together was not going to happen, not for a while, perhaps not for a long while. But two intuitive friends had recently predicted that she'd soon meet her husband, who would be a businessman (like me), not the types she had been dating: actors and others in her field. As a result, she was open to the possibility something might develop.

We walked along the beachfront holding hands. She looked at me, and asked,

"Are you really single?"

"Sort of; I'm getting divorced."

I was uncomfortable; I could see I'd have to tell her the whole story, even though it might not put me in the best light.

"What happened?"

"We had good times and not-so-good times. We stayed together a long time, built a house, and had a lot of common intellectual interests. But after we finished the house, the relationship soured; we'd been together since she was very young. Gradually we grew apart. Toward the end, I could see that neither of us was happy. We had nothing to keep us together—no kids, no business, few common friends, so I took the initiative to end it."

She persisted, "But what does it mean, 'sort of' getting divorced?' How long has this been going on?"

I took a deep breath before telling her, "It's been a while. it's complicated because there's this house we both own, and she wasn't making a lot of money at the time I left. We're separated, and I filed for divorce two years ago. I don't know when it will be final."

As much as I wanted to be with Jessica, right now I was stuck in this uncomfortable middle ground.

She asked, "Can you guess?"

I fidgeted. "I don't know. I've done everything I can to move things along. I gave her the house, but I've been paying half the mortgage since I moved out."

Jessica pressed the point: "So, you're single, but you're still married, and you have to send her money every month?"

"Yes, no, and yes. Under the divorce arrangement, I can stop sending her the mortgage money next summer. Our deal was for three years, so she'd have time to start making enough money to support the mortgage by herself."

Expectantly, with what I hoped had the right mix of reality and intention, I offered, "We can still be together until the divorce is final."

We kept walking. She was quiet for a while. I could tell she wasn't pleased. She had to decide if she should get more involved with what might become a sticky relationship. She had never been married, hadn't lived with anyone more than a year. I could sense my current situation was a big issue. I didn't blame her for being cautious, but I couldn't do anything about it at the moment.

I felt stuck, as did she, each in our own way. Even though the situation was muddy, we wanted to be together, to move toward a committed relationship.

I needed a miracle, and I got it. Barely two weeks after we met, the divorce decree arrived by mail from the Contra Costa County clerk's office: I was a free man! After work, I phoned and told Jessica. I could tell she was relieved and happy. Week by week, we grew steadily closer, but it would still require a nudge from a higher power to get us to take next step.

GETTING BETTER ACQUAINTED

Around Thanksgiving, barely a month after we'd met, I took Jessica to meet my mother, my younger brother and older sister who, after thirty-five years, still lived at the family home in Van Nuys. My sister later told me that she knew immediately this was a serious relationship. I hadn't brought anyone home to meet Mom besides my college girlfriend and Elle. But they were both very young at the time. In Jessica, they saw a beautiful, accomplished, mature woman; my sister and Jessica liked each other immediately. Later she told me that seeing the loving relationship I had with my family put her mind at ease.

Now that the divorce was final, we were ready to put the show on the road: the actors had finished rehearsals, the play was ready to open, but the script still needed work.

After she stopped house-sitting, Jessica went back to living with her mother again, and I got to know her mom better. Jessica and Bea were close. Jessica's parents had separated when she was an infant; Bea mostly raised her as a single mom. When Jessica was nine, Bea remarried and had another child, Jessica's half-brother Danny.

As a child, Jessica saw her father only on Saturdays. He paid for her to attend summer camps, to attend Bard College, and to rent an apartment in New York City. Because of a bitter custody battle that cast her father as the villain, Jessica long harbored resentment toward him. The relationship improved after Jessica met Baba. From being around him, she gradually understood she had to fix her relationship with her father to make progress in the spiritual life.

Bea Marcus was a stereotypical Jewish mother: outspoken, fixated on her daughter's welfare, and, as I quickly learned (and came to appreciate), an excellent cook and baker. After her second husband died, she moved to L.A. to be close to Jessica. To get her out of the house (and out of her hair), Jessica pushed a producer friend to give Bea a small role in one of his movies. In her mid-sixties, Bea took to acting and became a "type," someone seen in commercials that needed an older woman, as an extra in sitcoms like *Golden Girls* (she often stood behind the stars in group scenes), and in a movie where she played the lead, a grandmotherly killer.

On one of her visits to L.A., Bea saw that Jessica was involved in a "yoga thing," with Baba's pictures all over her apartment. Bea decided right away she'd better go with Jessica to Oakland to see this Baba, vowing, "I'm going to give him a piece of my mind."

They went to Oakland, stood in the darshan line, and Jessica nervously introduced her mother to Baba, concerned with what Bea might say. Momentarily stunned by Baba's radiance and warmth, Bea broke out in tears and fell at his feet, sobbing, overcome by the love she experienced in Baba's presence. After that, she meditated and accompanied Jessica on summer retreats, first with Baba and later with Gurumayi. For her Ashram service, she would bake signature pastries such as rugelach and hamantashen for sale in the Amrit café.

In some ways, Jessica and I shared similar backgrounds, both attending small elite colleges. She was intelligent, charismatic, full of love for people and animals, had many friends, and was deeply committed to the same spiritual path. She was also a talented actress. She had studied in New York with several renowned teachers including Lee Strasberg, founder of the Actor's Studio. Her early work as a theater actress led her into jobs teaching acting, coaching speakers, screenwriting, and a few minor film roles.

Over the Christmas and New Year's holidays in 1985 and into 1986, Gurumayi held satsangs in Hawaii. In those days, to get cheap tickets you had to buy them months in advance and couldn't make any changes without losing the ticket. Before we met, Jessica and Bea had already planned to fly there in mid-December for two weeks. In one of those uncanny coincidences that highlighted the early days of our relationship, the month before I met Jessica, I also had bought a ticket to visit Gurumayi, arriving the same day that Bea left. With the divorce issue now happily in the past, I flew to Hawaii, planning to spend a week with both Jessica and Gurumayi. That next week became a turning point in our relationship.

GETTING MARRIED

I HADN'T SEEN GURUMAYI SINCE BEFORE I MET JESSICA. I arrived in Honolulu in the afternoon, took a cab to the hotel, washed, and changed clothes before we headed to the evening satsang. After meditation, we joined the darshan line and approached Gurumayi. I was excited to see Gurumayi again but concerned with how we would explain our relationship: knowing each other only a few months, we still hadn't decided where it was heading. Now we went forward together to greet our teacher.

We didn't hold hands as we approached her chair, but Gurumayi didn't wait around for us to tell her. She asked, "Are you two together?" I guess it was obvious.

"Yes," we replied as one.

"When did this happen?"

Jessica responded, "During the mahasamadhi chant at the ashram in LA."

Gurumayi turned to several people sitting close to her, people who knew both of us.

She acted surprised: "Can you believe it?"

Then she threw up her arms, saying "They're together! They're together!"

For the moment that was it. We went back to our seats, not sure what had happened.

There was a backstory. Jessica had written a letter to Baba three years earlier, a month before his passing, asking him for a husband. She wanted a man who was strong and could help with her service as a traveling meditation teacher. Later, she learned that Baba had taken mahasamadhi before seeing the letter. In his place, Gurumayi

THE GODFATHER OF GREEN

responded indirectly to her secret wish. One day, in all innocence, like a good mother, Bea asked Gurumayi, "When is Jessica going to get married?"

Gurumayi turned to Jessica: "Why *haven't* you gotten married yet?"

"I haven't found the right man."

Gurumayi responded it was less about finding the right man and more about her intention: "You haven't made up your mind. Jessica, you have to make up your mind."

Surprisingly, Jessica and I hadn't met before. In 1974, we were both at the La Honda retreat with Baba, and we both received initiation the same day. We attended the small retreat at Saddle Rock Ranch in Malibu in 1975. For twelve years, as students of Baba and Gurumayi, we attended dozens of the same events and unknowingly shared mutual friends. We must have noticed each other at these programs, but we never met until that night in the Amrit café. The likely reason was that I was with Elle and living in the Bay Area. Like a fine wine, our relationship apparently required proper aging.

Now, barely two months after our first date, we stood in front of our teacher as a couple. The next evening, we went forward to greet Gurumayi again.

We bowed. In a soft voice, Gurumayi asked, "When's the wedding?"

I heard the question but didn't answer. With a pronounced and longstanding hearing loss, Jessica hadn't heard Gurumayi. I thought that sometimes it's best to keep silent when the Master asks you an important question, that you should take time to reflect before responding.

The next morning, we left the hotel after breakfast and drove along the North Shore of Oahu. Near the Polynesian Cultural Center, I pulled over and stopped the car so we could look at the ocean. The waves sparkled, the sun shone, the air was balmy for January: an idyllic Hawaiian day. During the drive out from the hotel, I thought about how I would respond to Gurumayi's question, how I should ask Jessica to marry me. I couldn't figure out a better approach, so I casually asked Jessica if she had any response to Gurumayi's question last night.

"No, I didn't hear what she said; there was too much background music."

Sheepishly, I told her, "Well, what she said was, 'When's the wedding?' "

For a moment Jessica looked shocked, then quickly regained her composure.

"Why didn't you tell me right away?"

I didn't have a good response, but right there, inside a rental car parked alongside a busy highway, looking into her beautiful eyes, I popped the question,

"Would you like to get married?"

She laughed. "Yes, of course, but why didn't you tell me last night?"

"Well, I wasn't sure if this is the right time to get married again, so soon after my divorce."

"That's only an excuse. It's your secretive Pisces nature, wanting to keep some things to yourself rather than sharing them right away."

I had to admit she was right. This had been a life-long tendency, an old *samskara* arising from who knew where. I was always cautious, non-committal, wanting to keep my options open, maybe afraid of having my ego bruised if things didn't turn out the way I expected.

We held hands and went out to the beach, looking out at the infinite expanse of sea and sky, a symbol of a world about to unfold, a world impatiently awaiting us.

The next night, when we approached Gurumayi in darshan, she didn't ask about the wedding.

She knew intuitively what we had decided and said, quietly but directly, "Go see the astrologer and get your time."

Conveniently, an astrologer named Neelima was visiting from Texas, so we met her in the lobby after the program. She told us about a spiritual bookstore in town that prepared charts using a computer, so we went there the next morning. A few hours later, full of anticipation, we got the charts, gave them to Neelima to review, and arranged to return later for the reading.

I had been to an astrologer only once, ten years ago, when Elle persuaded me to have a reading from one of Baba's longtime devotees, an Indian astrologer. My chart showed I'd live a long life, into my eighties—that sounded good—but I was a rational guy and didn't put much trust in astrologers. Jessica was more open to intuitive guidance when she felt a strong connection with the person offering it.

Because we had given our birth dates for our charts, to my surprise I found out Jessica was nearly five years older than me. She jokingly tried to hide it by holding her thumb over the birthdate when she showed me the astrologer's chart, but I peeked. She looked so beautiful, so young, so fresh, I had assumed she was several years younger than I was. It didn't matter. I found her incredibly attractive not only for her looks, but for her inner beauty, the product of twelve years of meditation and loving service she had offered to Baba and Gurumayi.

When Neelima interpreted our charts, she was incredulous.

"I have never seen two people this perfectly matched. You two were meant for each other; you complement each other perfectly."

But the chart showed something else, a strong warning.

"You must avoid conflict if you want to be happy and stay together."

No problem, we thought; even though two strong-willed people in their forties who barely knew each other might reasonably expect to have a little conflict after they got married. But we ignored the warning, already reveling in a gauzy, dreamlike honeymoon phase.

For the wedding, the astrologer gave us four auspicious dates that we took to Gurumayi that evening.

Her first question was, "What's best for the family?"

She chose two dates, one in mid-February, five weeks away, for a family wedding in Los Angeles, the other in July for a spiritual wedding at the ashram in South Fallsburg, in upstate New York.

My brief and happy bachelorhood vanished like early morning

mist on a warm sunny day. Over the space of four days, I had agreed to marry a woman I'd known barely two months: a big risk, a decision I couldn't easily walk away from. Marrying Jessica so soon after meeting her was another leap into the unknown, another huge life choice based on limited information. As with the love I felt upon first meeting Baba, my strong love for Jessica encouraged me to take this gamble.

I wasn't alone with my concerns this mid-life marriage might be chancy. Jessica was taking the bigger risk. She was getting married for the first time to a man she barely knew, someone she now talked to each evening, but whom she saw only on weekends. She might have had second thoughts whether the marriage would work out so easily. For my part, though I had concerns, I was confident this was the right relationship at the right time in my life, and I knew Jessica was the perfect mate. Strong coincidences had joined us together. I was sure things would work out.

Jessica had barely five weeks to arrange the big wedding she'd always wanted. Busy with planning, she held any concerns at arm's length. Away working in Tehachapi and in town only on weekends, I couldn't offer much assistance. Her girlfriends and her mother helped with preparations: finding a florist, buying a beautiful dress, arranging a band, securing a ballroom for the reception and dinner, and myriad other details. Jessica managed to accommodate dozens of East Coast relatives and most of our L.A. friends. With plenty of grace, everything came together on time.

When she first met him, Jessica asked Baba for a spiritual name, something people often did to symbolize their commitment to change themselves. Baba gave her the name Maitreyi, a great seeker in ancient India. In the *Brihadaranyaka Upanishad*, a three-thousand-year-old scripture, the sage Yajnavalkya prepared to finish his life's journey by retiring to the forest to meditate. He planned to divide his considerable property between two wives, Katyayani and Maitreyi, so they could live comfortably the rest of their lives.

Katyayani eagerly accepted his gift, but Maitreyi immediately asked, "Will your wealth make me happy?"

Yajnavalkya didn't expect this question but was pleased. In response, he explained that the source of true happiness was Self-knowledge, not wealth.

"All things are dear, not for their own sake, but for the sake of the Self."

And this Self was the inner divine principle that exists everywhere, in all beings, eternally. After hearing this teaching, Maitreyi told him firmly she didn't want his wealth.

"Take me to the forest with you. I want your knowledge."

Gurumayi told this story during one of her evening satsangs shortly after we'd decided to get married.

At the end of the story, looking directly at me, in an audience of hundreds of people, she remarked, "Ah, there are not many wives like Maitreyi."

I have thought about this remark often (and Jessica reminds me about it periodically), but I recognized right away I had received, in one beautiful package, all bundled together, a great gift, a significant challenge, and a divine blessing.

Returning home, I had no misgivings about the upcoming wedding. It had my teacher's blessings, we loved each other deeply, and, besides, Jessica was the most beautiful woman I had ever known. Still, much like my parents, brought together by the exigencies of wartime, in our case we had led different lives, in my case more technical and rational, in hers more artistic and emotional. Our different experiences and approaches offered a built-in recipe for conflict, even for two people committed to spiritual practices.

During our reading, the astrologer insisted we had to be married on February 16th at the most auspicious time: 4:30 in the afternoon. We found out there wasn't any venue that would accommodate this time, as it fell between a hotel's lunch and dinner shifts. Instead, we held the ceremony at the auspicious hour at my aunt and uncle's house in Brentwood with forty guests seated in the living room. At 80 years old, Jessica's father finally got to walk her down the aisle, after a fashion, holding her elbow to steady himself as they descended slowly from upstairs into the living room.

My uncle recruited a retired judge, his friend and neighbor, to perform the ceremony. Then well into his 70s, the judge hadn't done a wedding for years, if ever.

At the end of his textbook script, he forgot to utter the words, "I now pronounce you husband and wife." Instead he closed his notebook and turned to me, one eyebrow raised, saying, "That's it. It's done. You can now kiss the bride," which I did.

None of this seemed kosher to Jessica's conservative father. He wasn't convinced the wedding was official without the traditional pronouncement, so we had to show him the marriage license from L.A. County, signed by the judge.

Right after the ceremony, we had a reception and dinner for more than a hundred people at the Beverly Hills Hotel (paid for by Jessica's father, to my relief.) Jessica's friends and relatives dominated the guest list. She had a knack for friendships and for staying in touch with people, a practice I had never mastered. Moreover, her friends loved and supported her. Like most weddings, it was the bride's day and the husband only present as an afterthought; a necessary element, like the formally dressed groom perched on top of the wedding cake.

The next day we departed for our honeymoon at the *Las Hadas* resort in Manzanillo, Mexico, famous as the setting for a scene in the 1979 movie *10*, starring Bo Derek in various states of duress and undress. I had only a week's vacation, so we had barely six days in Mexico before I returned to work in Tehachapi. As easeful as the wedding and reception were, the honeymoon was the opposite.

My friend William offered to let us stay on his 40-foot boat moored at the Las Hadas marina. With this gift, we wouldn't have to pay exorbitant room rates at the upscale resort. I had sailed before with William in San Francisco Bay and knew this boat, and I jumped at the opportunity. After spending our wedding night in bliss at the Beverly Hills Hotel, the next day we flew from Los Angeles, got a taxi at the airport, and arrived late in Manzanillo.

The first night, we slept at a rented villa so we could board the boat in daylight. With February's cool nights, Jessica turned on the heater. In the middle of the night we smelled a gas leak. That kept us awake until we got the staff to turn off the gas. Moreover, the room had only two immovable single beds. Miraculously, we survived the honeymoon's second night. In the morning, we took a taxi to the boat, with our suitcases, swimsuits, sunscreen, and high expectations.

When we got to the boat, we found out the first mate had departed for Tahiti a few days earlier (which was fine) but had taken the mosquito netting and insect repellent (which was not); we had not thought to bring either. Beyond the inconvenience, we learned that the cook lived on board, was perpetually stoned, and didn't want to move out to accommodate us, a small glitch William perhaps didn't know about or had avoided telling us. To have the boat to ourselves, we gave the cook a hundred dollars as a bribe to stay in a hotel room in town for the week.

The next day, right after breakfast on board, I decided to show off my athletic skill to my new bride by jumping off the stern of the boat onto the metal dock. Instead of a graceful leap, I caught my foot on a rope and stumbled, landing awkwardly on the metal dock, in the process badly cutting my knee. The cut stung whenever I went into the ocean, so I stayed out of the water and sunbathed on the beach the rest of the trip.

After two nights of swatting at mosquitoes and sleeping in a narrow double bed in the boat, we gave up and took a room at Las Hadas, which we should have done all along. We enjoyed the last three days of our honeymoon at the resort. Despite all the mishaps, we loved being with each other; we found we could both laugh at our troubles, even as they happened. Twelve years of meditation practice had given us the gift of more easily stepping back and seeing things in perspective.

On our last day in Las Hadas, Jessica pronounced, "If we can survive this disaster of a honeymoon and still laugh, the marriage will surely last." After breezing through a string of near disasters, I agreed with her. But bigger challenges lay ahead.

OUR SPIRITUAL WEDDING

SET IN THE CATSKILLS OF NEW YORK, the ashram was beautifully decorated for the upcoming *Guru Purnima* celebration, the one day each year when devotees specifically honor the Guru. Six months earlier, Gurumayi had invited us to take our vows a second time in a traditional Brahmin wedding. July 8th was the auspicious day, approved by both Western and Indian astrologers after an extended negotiation. Although we married in February in Los Angeles, this day felt like an initiation into an altogether different relationship.

At mid-morning. Jessica and I walked slowly downhill from the main building toward the Shakti Mandap, an open-air pavilion where Gurumayi held satsangs each evening during the summer months. The Mandap was large, easily accommodating more than a thousand people for evening satsangs with Gurumayi. That morning it was almost empty, except for our wedding guests and twelve Brahmin priests from India who had traveled here to participate in Guru Purnima. A small stream ran behind the Mandap; tall fir trees flanked the stream, all visible through tall glass walls. The weather was warm and not too humid. A few white clouds scudded across the sky dome. The setting was idyllic, a picture-book summer wedding day.

I wore a light beige wedding suit, recycled from the February wedding, and Jessica wore a traditional and exquisitely beautiful red silk sari. We each held decorated coconuts to offer during the ceremony.

Jessica had a garland of gardenias in her hair, with curlicues of red and white decorations painted on her forehead. On my head, I had a borrowed (and stiff) golden turban, one size too small. A small garland of red and white carnations hung from each side, swaying side to side as we descended the hill toward the Mandap.

We entered a beautifully decorated area in the center of the pavilion. The Brahmin priests and our translator sat around the fire, already burning in a large metal pan. We sat cross-legged on cushions close to the fire, so we could make offerings when it was time. Our wedding guests and some ashram friends sat on folding chairs facing the fire. The setting was intimate and ancient.

During the ceremony, a chorus of eleven Brahmins chanted Vedic mantras. One old and revered Brahmin priest, a long-time devotee of Baba's, officiated and conducted a traditional fire ceremony with the small fire at the center of the ceremony. Divorced forty years earlier, Jessica's mother and father looked happy to see each other. Weddings are sacred occasions; those with the Master's blessings offer immense joy to everyone.

Because the head Brahmin priest spoke Hindi, one swami had to translate every instruction for the fire ceremony (throw the rice into the fire, throw in the turmeric, feed coconut sweets to each other, etc.) into English, which we then quickly implemented. I focused intently, my awareness indrawn from the ecstasy of powerful Vedic chanting, yet outwardly present each moment throughout the ceremony.

The ceremony ended on a blissful note. With a traditional Indian wedding flourish, we stood facing one another. Two priests held a shawl between us, obscuring our view. The priests chanted powerful mantras. When the chant reached a crescendo, they lifted the shawl. We saw each other, as if for the first time, united forever in the eyes of God. As they lifted the shawl and we looked into the other's eyes, now as husband and wife, I felt we had become one in spirit, experiencing incredible bliss as I gazed at Jessica. We exchanged rings again, garlanded each other and stood for a moment facing our guests while they gleefully threw rice at us. We left the pavilion in an ecstatic state.

SACRED MARRIAGE VOWS

After the fire ceremony we walked uphill to the ashram temple to have our rings blessed. I could sense the temple's spiritual power: an electric and vibrant energy filled the entire space. Through the interpreter, the head Brahmin priest asked us to accept four vows representing a householder couple's *dharma*, their duties to one another and to the community. The vows were simple, practical, and powerful. They came in rapid fire, one after the other.

After each vow, he asked: "Do you accept this vow?"

In unison: "Yes."

We had now taken a sacred oath to observe the dharma of marriage. In our hearts we meant it. Only in the following months, after we began our married life, did we experience how challenging it could be to practice one specific vow in our daily life. Can you guess which one it was? Here they are:

Always speaks the truth.

Never fight; never have strife between each other. Never find fault with each other.

Always welcome other people into your home with love and respect; always offer what you have to others.

Be good to people; never hurt anyone.

At the end of the blessing ceremony, the priest offered his blessing. "If you follow this dharma and observe these vows, you'll become liberated." We agreed, with great intention.

Following our visit to the temple, we returned to our guests to eat a catered lunch under an outdoor tent, along with Jessica's mother, father, stepmother, and our friends. We were still swimming in the ecstatic sea generated by the ceremony. At the end of the lunch someone came and invited us to visit privately with Gurumayi. As we knelt in front of her, she wrapped beautiful woolen meditation shawls around our shoulders and carefully examined Jessica's jewelry, mostly family heirlooms from her mother and grandmother. She commented on how beautiful the old jewelry was, saying, "Everything old is good."

To make the point clearer, she asked me, "Who is older?"

I gestured toward Jessica. "She is."

With a beautiful smile, Gurumayi said, "Older is better."

Following that blessing, Gurumayi gave us a box of chocolate truffles to share with our wedding guests and sent us out to join them for dessert.

MARRIED, NO CHILDREN

THE FOLLOWING MONTH, I left my job at Zond. Eight months earlier, the phase-out of solar and wind tax credits had decimated the renewable energy industry. Since Zond couldn't sell new turbines to investors without tax credits, the wind industry went into several years of maintenance mode, and the company didn't need my marketing or government-relations skills. I had to find a new job, so shortly after the New York wedding, I began looking for work in Southern California.

I still wanted to stay involved with the alternative energy business, but I couldn't find many openings. The best business opportunities focused on industrial cogeneration, using natural gas to provide electricity and hot water for manufacturers. After searching for a while, I found a marketing VP position with Micro Cogen Systems, a company in Irvine manufacturing energy-efficient small cogeneration systems. There I could use my business skills and technical knowledge to sell an environmentally beneficial product that used eighty percent of the energy in the input fuel, clean-burning natural gas.

With a decent job in hand, Jessica and I moved into a home in Costa Mesa, forty miles south of Los Angeles near Newport Beach. We no longer regularly saw close friends from L.A., but there was an upside: clean air, the ocean close by, and a vibrant spiritual community. First, we had to get to know each other better; after our spiritual wedding we were living together daily for the first time.

MARRIED LIFE BEGINS

Once I read that a TV news reporter interviewed Baba, asking him, "You have thousands of followers. How do you work on all of them?"

Baba purportedly responded, "I don't have to. I just put them together and they work on each other."

It's the same way river rocks get smooth by rubbing against each other until the sharp edges disappear. As serious students of yoga and meditation, Jessica and I supported each other and tried to be aware of when we might be falling short of our ideals. One of them: Take life seriously but deal with each other lightly, realizing we're in this for the long haul. This commitment meant to be honest and direct about our feelings, which I found challenging, preferring to keep mine to myself. The other part was to be kind and gentle in expressing them.

I quickly found out we had a lot to learn to have a long-lasting and happy marriage. We found this testing clearly profiled by two white, formally attired small teddy bears Gurumayi gave to us at the wedding, one dressed as a bride and the other as a groom. We put them on the top of our bedroom dresser facing Gurumayi's framed photo; we knew devotees (and their bears) should always face the Master.

Several times when we had disagreements, we'd notice the bears facing each other, as if they too were arguing. We carefully repositioned them to face toward Gurumayi's photo, and there would be a period of peace. A few weeks later, we'd be bickering again. When we looked at the dresser, we'd notice the bears again facing each other; we turned them around once more to face the picture.

We felt the Shakti, the spiritual power of the teacher, was working on us through those two cute little white bears, pushing us continually to remember our wedding vows. We got an unmistakable message from an unlikely source: harmony had to be the primary goal in our marriage, exactly as the astrologer in Hawaii said.

The novelist Javier Marías wrote, "We always arrive late in people's lives." They have a personal history before we meet, largely unknown to us, sometimes obscured by misunderstandings or hidden by the pale, poorly visible light of the past, often deliberately misrepresented, as if to tell the truth would inevitably discredit them in our eyes and cast doubt on the present relationship. Jessica and I met in our forties, so we knew nothing of each other's personal history before our shared history began only a few months before the wedding. We were ignorant of each other's first twenty years of adulthood, except what the other had freely shared or (in my case) that Jessica heard about from my sister.

Perhaps it was her nature, or she felt more at ease with her own past, but she was more open than I was about sharing details. One thing especially surprised me, endeared her to me even more. I'd had the habit of burning my bridges in personal relationships—it was all or nothing; once it was over, it was over forever—but Jessica was on speaking terms, friendly with several former boyfriends, people who had been, perhaps still were important in her life. I found out more about her history than she did about mine, because she freely offered the complete (well, almost complete) "backstory" before I met any of them. Her openness prompted me to be more forthcoming about my own past relationships, although I still found it difficult to talk about how my first marriage had hit the rocks.

Our shared history of engagement with the Siddha Yoga community meant we were not strangers to each other's spiritual practices, and we'd had many similar experiences with Baba and Gurumayi. We knew what it meant to be a serious student of yoga and meditation, something difficult to communicate to someone who hadn't had those experiences. Her involvement with the spiritual community was more extensive, because she'd offered her loving service for a longer period. She especially had shared her love for Baba and Gurumayi with friends in the film and theater world and had organized several events in L.A., introducing people in the arts to Siddha Yoga meditation.

In many respects our "courtship" began after the wedding, because we'd spent little time together beforehand. Her openness about her feelings, along with our mutually shared yogic understandings, helped smooth the way forward for what could have been a much rockier beginning for a marriage between virtual strangers.

WHAT ARE YOU HIDING?

THE NEXT YEAR, we took a teachers' training course at Gurumayi's ashram in New York along with a few dozen other meditation teachers. For the concluding ceremony, the group wanted to give her a small gift of appreciation; they asked me to present it. I sat cross-legged on the carpet near the front of the room to make it easier to give the gift when the opportunity arose. Being a clever student, I stuck the small gift-wrapped box under one leg so Gurumayi wouldn't see it until the time came to give it to her.

Masters are far cleverer than students, however, even if the students have advanced degrees. When Gurumayi walked in, what did she notice right away? The gift I was awkwardly concealing.

She asked, "What are you hiding?"

"That's something for later."

At the appropriate time I presented the gift to her and the course concluded.

For acquiring self-knowledge, I'd heard that even the master's casual remarks have great power and can give important guidance if contemplated and put into practice. I thought about her remark, "What are you hiding?" and my response, "That's something for later." I recognized I had hidden my true feelings for a long time behind a false façade of cleverness, humor or other means of dodging them, always intending *later* to tell someone how much I loved or appreciated them. I feared expressing the *feeling* of love, fearing being open would require me to let go of my strong masculine personality: cool, rational, detached, invulnerable. Intuitively I knew it was only the ego wanting to stay in charge, but I often reverted to this older and more comfortable behavior.

A few years later, Gurumayi offered a resolution for her students to contemplate and put into practice: *I will not hide my perfect love from the world*. This instruction resonated. I decided to take it seriously and open my heart to other people, to genuinely love them, not always by expressing it (which might be unwelcome or misinterpreted), but simply by valuing them for their unique qualities. We all know the experience of receiving genuine love from others; words are mostly unnecessary.

This period marked the time Jessica and I coalesced. We could openly express our love and deeper feelings, but still deal with practical situations without emotional struggles, which had in the past often led to egotistical melodramas.

I understood a further teaching; it's one I have had to relearn many times in practicing yoga and meditation. I couldn't save anything for later; I had to deal with everything in the present moment. That didn't mean troublesome situations would automatically resolve themselves, but it did mean I shouldn't avoid dealing with them in the moment, no matter how inconvenient. On a karmic level, it meant these situations would keep recurring in different guises until I dealt with them.

I knew I had to examine each aspect of my life, especially things I was avoiding. I saw how a careful observation of my mental and emotional tendencies represented true self-inquiry, a practice I could and should do all the time. I heard that Gurumayi once said that you should carefully watch each gesture you make, even if it's merely moving your finger to turn off a light switch. In other words, stay in the present moment, stay in touch with the inner awareness, connect with the energy of the situation, and respond from a place of inner stillness, no matter what else you're doing or what is happening around you. This inner awareness became my key to conscious living.

I had received a great lesson in staying in touch with this awareness a few years earlier. In 1984 I visited the ashram in India for a few weeks. During my previous stay eight years before, I experienced that the spiritual energy in the ashram quickly found submerged issues and brought them to the surface. This meant I could see them, face them, and figure out how to deal with them on the spot. That year, during the full moon in October, we celebrated the second anniversary of Baba's mahasamadhi, the day he left his body, said to be the most auspicious one.

After having accepted Gurumayi as my spiritual guide a few months earlier, I decided to go to India for this celebration and to express my gratitude to Baba by visiting his *samadhi shrine*, his burial place. For my service during the celebration satsang, I became a welcome host. Visitors came into a large central courtyard to have darshan with Gurumayi. I had little to do but stand there and, if needed, help people get seated comfortably. Most Indian devotees had visited the ashram frequently. They didn't need any instruction about where to sit. As a host, I had only to provide oversight, stand off to the side, offer a gentle presence, and keep an eye on things.

As the courtyard became more crowded and things got busier, I got a little too involved in directing people where to sit, perhaps making too many sweeping arm gestures. At one point, my supervisor, Matt, another American, came over.

He asked, "Do you like coffee?"

I didn't respond; I wasn't sure what he meant.

He repeated, "Do you like coffee?"

I hedged, still unsure where he was going, "It's OK, I guess."

Since I still wasn't getting it, he became more direct.

"Why don't you take a break now and get a coffee in the Amrit?"

I finally got the message: Step back, take a deep breath, go for a break, and reconnect with the inner energy. Don't get attached to your role as a host: it's not who you are. Try not to stand out; people aren't here to see you. Stay focused within, move about quietly and humbly as you offer your service.

I often took multiple lessons from things occurring in the ashram. Reflecting later, I understood I had always tried to be in charge, to make things happen, instead of flowing with what was going on in each situation. I knew I needed to move away from my habitual reliance on my ego-mind and assertive personality, focusing instead on remaining anchored in the heart and acting in alignment with the energy present in each situation. After ten years of meditation practice, I had to ask myself again: did I fundamentally want to change? As I contemplated my spiritual practices, this question stood at the forefront of my awareness.

Through my commitment to Gurumayi as my teacher, I had already agreed (with myself) to make this change. I recall her saying something like, *A devotee can do whatever he wants, but a disciple (student) must follow the rules, inside and out.*

I contemplated the situation. Did I want to remain a devotee, standing on the sidelines, as I had done mentally and emotionally for the past ten years? Or did I instead want to take what she offered and enter the game, take her way of being as my own and accept the *inner discipline,* the essential meaning of *disciple*? With Baba, although I deeply loved him and practiced meditation regularly, I kept a lot of my habitual tendencies; but with Gurumayi I knew I had to make stronger efforts to get rid of them right now.

Resolving to get rid of my old patterns didn't make them disappear overnight, but it did accelerate the process of attenuating them. I became more conscious when an old tendency would assert itself, such as becoming impatient with others or indulging my sense of self-importance. With this awareness, I could decide *in the moment* to act on it or not, to silently witness it and let it go away. Each time I chose to witness old tendencies and not to act on their impulses, I could sense myself becoming clearer, purer, and more anchored in my practice.

BALANCE

DURING THE LATE 1990s, Gurumayi toured California several times. For each tour, I offered service as a welcome host, usually standing outside the hall, greeting people who came to be with her in satsang, staying there until the very last person had arrived. I'd adopted this service over several years and delighted in practicing Baba's teaching *See God in each other* as I welcomed each person with love. This simple practice opened my heart. Everyone and anyone could come to see Gurumayi, and I was often the first person they encountered. I learned not to form judgments about how people looked or acted. I reminded myself that these people were all coming to a "universal costume party," dressed and acting exactly as themselves; what could possibly be wrong with that?

One evening I stood outside the large hall of the Santa Clara, California, convention center. Gurumayi was on a teaching visit, holding several evening satsangs at this place. Inside the hall, several hundred people chanted joyfully, awaiting her appearance. As usual, I welcomed people. I was the last person still standing outside the hall, waiting for her to arrive.

One-on-one encounters with Gurumayi were delicious and rewarding. There she was, walking toward me, two assistants trailing a few steps behind. As I watched her coming, her orange robes rippling with the slight movement of her walk, I felt incredible love arising and pulsating within. I stood there calmly, smiling, focused on her. She was holding a rock in each hand, caressing it, rolling it around with her fingers, imparting her Shakti energy to the stone.

As she approached me, she asked, "Would you like a rock?"

"Yes." I cupped my hands, right over left, in the traditional way of receiving her *prasad*, this unexpected gift.

She softly placed a palm-sized stone in my upturned hand: a purple amethyst, oval-shaped, polished smooth, engraved on one flat side with the word *Balance* in gold letters. Then she turned and went into the hall. Receiving something directly from the master's hand is always special, and I was grateful. At the same time, what I was I supposed to learn from this succinct message: *Balance*?

As much as I might try to remain balanced, I often found myself chasing after things I should leave alone or conversely holding back from opportunities I should pursue. Naturally enthusiastic, many times I'd found myself carried away by the excitement of a new venture without seriously contemplating in the moment if it's something I *should* be doing.

Balance is a life art. It's a spiritual practice all its own and, I've discovered, an essential quality for success in life. The *Balance* rock became a meter to measure my inner state. Is my mind balanced right now? Am I maintaining my commitment to treating everyone and everything that happens with respect? Am I offering my service with humility, seeing whatever is happening in the world as imbued with God's grace? Life's a roller coaster, with ups and downs, exaltations and disappointments, inner and outer dramas. I know it's important to have a balanced perspective, not to get too high on the highs or too low on the lows, but I've also found it's hard to practice this simple art, moment by moment.

Gurumayi and Baba also taught how to use balance to enter a state of deep meditation, using the metronome of the breath, an instrument we carry with us all the time. I learned how to let myself glide into the pauses between the breaths, entering an altered state of awareness, slipping behind the busyness of the mind like a cat burglar intent on entering a house without awakening the occupants. Like a Surrealist painting in which opening a closet door leads into a vast expanse of blue sky, simply balancing on the knife edge of the breath, as it turns from outbreath to inbreath, inbreath to outbreath, I could enjoy absolute stillness, harvesting in season a bounty of insights about my life. Often after such med-itations I'd recall one word or a subtle hint that would give me guidance about what to do next.

With a balanced mind, natural joy suffuses life's every aspect and provides radiant happiness, no matter what outer circum-stances arise. I've understood that a balanced mind and optimistic outlook are keys to keeping a storehouse of joy full all the time. Clearly, balance was a habit I needed to cultivate as I would a gar-den, giving careful attention to providing water and nourishment at the right time and continually searching for weeds to remove. One of the weeds that kept sprouting, my competitive nature, still pushed me to want to come out on top in whatever I did.

BALL DON'T LIE

I HAD LONG BOUGHT INTO THE IDEA I HAD TO COMPETE WITH OTHERS TO accomplish anything worthwhile, to win at life's game. Hidden within this feeling was a worldview depicting life as a Darwinian struggle: he wins who competes best.

I loved especially basketball for its competitive nature and team approach. I started playing in the seventh grade. To help me develop my skills, my father nailed a 4' x 4' plywood board with an orange metal rim to the wall of the garage behind the boys' bedroom. I spent hours outside shooting buckets through that rim, whether it had a net or not, in all kinds of weather. With less than twenty feet of space between the house and the garage, it was a small court, but I could still practice free throws and jump shots. A tall white wooden fence stood between the house and the garage, hemming in the court on the left, which meant most of my shots had to come from the right side. It didn't matter. I got hooked. You can play basketball by yourself: only you, the ball and the basket. Either it goes in or it doesn't—ball don't lie. Immediate feedback adds to the joy.

At my tallest I was 6'3" and weighed only 185 pounds as a college athlete. I played organized basketball from the age of 14, first in a local YMCA league, then in high school, college, and even a year in graduate school in West Germany. Overall, I played competitively—with referees, whistles, and uniforms—for ten years.

My best friend Stewart and I were co-captains of the Van Nuys High School varsity team. In our senior year, we had a new coach, Recently arrived from Missouri, the coach was a stocky 5'8" transplant in his 50s with a gray crewcut, an old-school approach, and some barnyard phrases that suburban kids in L.A. had never heard. My favorite was, "That pass was as worthless as tits on a boar hog." I had to ask a teammate to interpret, because I had no clue what a "boar hog" was or why it would have (or not have) tits. With no star player to help the rest of the team (like me) get better, we finished with six wins and eight losses in the highly competitive Los Angeles city leagues.

The best part of playing on the high school varsity was that I convinced Mom that the coach wanted us to eat meat the morning of each game, so we'd be stronger for the afternoon contest. (This was long before anyone knew carbohydrate loading was far better preparation.) She was happy to cook me a T-bone or rib-eye steak those fourteen game mornings, which I ate with relish, the meat even more delicious as I watched my siblings eat cold cereal for breakfast.

To build my shooting and dribbling skills and to develop court sense, I played nearly every day, often at the high school during the summers as a "gym rat," sweating heavily in a stuffy gym at least forty years old and smelling like a hundred, without air-conditioning or even decent ventilation. I shot 100 free throws a day in practice for years and became proficient at that art. Once in college, I hit eleven in a row during a game. I got good at rebounding, but sometimes didn't score much.

Before our senior year, the high-school varsity squad decided to play in a summer league in Compton to get in shape for the fall season. The previous year, as a junior varsity team, we'd been undefeated and thought we were pretty good. *We were in for a big surprise.* The movie *Straight Outta Compton* gives a general idea of the environment we encountered. Here we were, a half-dozen white guys from the suburbs thirty miles away, playing all-black teams on their home turf.

We were maybe a little crazy, naïve for sure, going so far from home to play ball, but it was 1961, several years before the Watts riots. Race relations were not yet combustible, and we wanted to play against good competition before the season began.

We played a deliberate, structured game, with lots of passing, pick-and-rolls, backdoor cuts to the basket, that kind of thing. They played freelance, loose, and much faster. We lost every game. The black teams were better, but I also felt an uncomfortable undercurrent. Before the game, the other team clearly hinted with body language and a little trash talk: *if you win, we'll see you in the parking lot after the game and it won't be to talk basketball.*

I loved competition in all forms, especially academic. My father made it clear he expected all five children to get good grades. For his oldest son, Dad set the highest expectations. All through school, I was the top student and graduated high school as class valedictorian. I thought *learning* meant scoring high on tests and meeting teachers' expectations.

Only after I met Baba did I grasp that learning about life meant real *studentship*, a commitment to studying my own inner nature. I finally understood that passing classroom tests didn't guarantee success in life.

I went to the most demanding college I could find, Caltech, which for decades had the country's highest SAT (test) scores for incoming freshmen. Caltech teams played basketball in a lower-tier college division against other small schools. For four years, I toiled for Caltech teams that won 13 games and lost 69, each Fall a twice-weekly exercise in character building.

Showing up for a game I knew we'd likely lose, but still playing hard, I learned perseverance in the face of adversity. As a discipline, practicing for two hours every afternoon during the season, and many hours a week the other months, helped me to stay healthy and build a strong body. In my senior year at Caltech, I averaged 11 points and 8 rebounds: not too shabby. I had a 22-point game and a 22-rebound game. When we won those 13 games, it was usually through defeating local Bible colleges with stronger faith but even fewer decent players.

Ball don't lie. Either the ball goes into the basket or it doesn't. Either the rebound lands in my hands or it doesn't. Either it's a foul or it's not. Either you win or you lose; no ties allowed. Basketball delivered everything I wanted in a team sport. After college, during my fellowship year, I was on the university team in Aachen, playing a dozen games in Luxembourg, Holland, and nearby German cities.

After ten years, I left organized team sports behind. For the next 15 years, I played occasional pick-up basketball. Though I retreated from basketball, I found my competitive spirit useful in business and politics, both organized team sports.

After practicing Siddha Yoga Meditation for many years, I reconsidered the notion of competition. I had learned that the best way to compete was to become better, stronger, more astute, etc., and not to spend time overly concerned with what anyone else was doing. After all, if there is only one supreme Consciousness ever-present in ALL of creation, who is the *other* I'm competing against?

I gradually understood the notion of competing against anyone (as opposed to doing your best) was antithetical to a genuinely spiritual life. In my own life, competition was an old *samskara* (deeply embedded tendency) coming not only from my father, but from the entire society, from school, from work, from politics, from business. In this worldview, I could win life's game by accumulating lots of money, a beautiful wife, smart and successful children, and a higher social status. But these things would only serve to bind me more tightly to a limited experience of life because I'd have to take my eyes off the real prize, the goal pointed to by saints and sages in every tradition: Self-knowledge.

In this regard, the Master is like a basketball coach, but with an essential difference: unlike a coach, she is a complete master of the game, teaching by example and advising from the highest perspective. The Master invites us to share her view of life, her constant and unlimited experience of inner Awareness, her joy, her bliss in the moment-by-moment recognition of the supreme reality behind all outward experiences. As I entered her world of conscious awareness, gradually I came to see the world differently.

I learned, as William Blake wrote, "To see a World in a Grain of Sand and a Heaven in a Wild Flower, hold Infinity in the palm of your hand and Eternity in an hour."

Over time, as my awareness shifted this way, I became more loving to others and intimately aware of the beauty of each moment.

In this sense, the ball DID lie. In life, there is no basket, no goal, no one keeping score, no visiting team, only the dance of universal energy we are all invited to join, a dance that is all there ever is. In this game, you win only by participating fully in the dance. *Love* is the name for merging with the dancing energy of life. At the end of each season, at the end of life, love alone remains undefeated.

VI
POLITICS

POLITICS IS A CONVEX LENS, a reality coherence system like economics or philosophy, a filter that focuses and helps make sense of the world's incessant and noisy signals. Since my late teens, politics had engaged, entranced, and frequently disappointed me. I thought I'd put politics and government behind me in 1980 when I left the Brown Administration for The Energy Clinic, but my karma pursued me like a hungry ghost.

During the next five years, as a consultant I lobbied state and federal governments on behalf of continuing solar and wind tax credits. By 1985, we'd run into a buzz saw of opposition to supporting the solar industry, my bread and butter. The tax credits disappeared, consulting income vanished, and I searched for other work.

But politics still had a hold on me, an itch that demanded scratching. After we moved to Costa Mesa in Orange County, I explored the local political scene. In 1988, the 40th Congressional District seat opened when the long-time Republican incumbent retired. An open congressional seat is a rarity. I lived there and immediately thought of running, of taking my environmentalist bent into politics. I went to see the local Democratic Party's leader. He discouraged me. "We already have a good candidate."

He suggested instead, "Why don't you move to Santa Ana and run against Bob Dornan? He hasn't done a thing for the past four years. If you decide to do it, we'll support you." I said I'd consider it. At forty-four, time for beginning a political career was running out. Jessica and I discussed it; we'd have to move to Santa Ana and campaign while I kept my job. If ever any life decision called for practical thinking and spiritual contemplation, this was it.

THE FIRST (AND LAST) HURRAH

WHEN WE MOVED TO ORANGE COUNTY, MY FRIEND TOM FLYNN SUGGESTED I attend monthly luncheons in Irvine with a club of local Democratic Party donors, if I wanted to get familiar with the political scene. It cost $1,000, but I decided to join. At our lunch meetings in 1987, we discussed the upcoming 1988 elections. I learned more about local issues and politicians, and I met people who shared my passion for politics and progressive change. I got interested in running myself. I thought I could do a better job for the environment if I held an office. I soon got the opportunity.

Robert Dornan was the Congressman representing central Orange County, the archetypal outspoken archconservative Republican any good liberal loves to hate. Nicknamed "B-1 Bob" after his vocal support for an expensive new Air Force weapons system, the B-1 bomber, Dornan had been a provocative L.A. radio talk show host before becoming a three-term Congressman in Los Angeles County. After the 1980 Census, the Democratic leadership in Sacramento took revenge on him by redrawing his district's boundaries to give it a strong Democratic majority, effectively forcing him out of office in 1982.

After scouting several possible new electoral districts, Dornan moved to central Orange County in 1984 and defeated the five-term Democratic incumbent to win his way back to Congress. In 1986, the long-serving Democratic state Assemblyman challenged Dornan but also lost. In 1988, the 38th Congressional District still had a nominal Democratic voter registration advantage (49% to 41%). Such a slender advantage usually wasn't enough. Democrats usually need to have 55% to 60% of total registration in a district to win, as many registered Democrats don't vote.

Early in 1988, after local Democratic Party officials convinced me to enter the race against Dornan, I began to understand their reasons. At every level, politics is a team sport. Party operatives love it when they find candidates who have or can raise their own money. An active, well-funded challenger forces the other side to spend money defending the seat, which means there's less money to spend on other races. Reading Chris Matthews' book, *Hardball*, chronicling his years as an assistant to U.S. House Speaker Tip O'Neill, told me all I needed to know about the professional politician's mindset—the purpose of a political party is simple: win elections.

But why did *I* want to run for office? I wanted to show that a candidate with a strong environmental commitment could win elective office. After spending a decade working with politicians in Sacramento, I thought I could be more effective if I were "inside the club," casting votes to support environmental protection and renewable energy development. A few Caltech grads had become Republican politicians: Ed Reinecke, a Pasadena Congressman during my student days (and later California's Lieutenant Governor), and Harrison Schmitt, an Apollo 17 astronaut and one-term U.S. Senator from New Mexico. From their examples, I thought I could make a greater difference if I held elective office. This belief got me past many obstacles.

At the beginning of 1988, I still worked at Micro Cogen Systems, marketing our energy-efficient cogeneration technology to industry. I should have been content with what I had in my life. I was happily married and working in a field reflecting my passion for alternative energy. But an old bug in my ear, leftover from the Jerry Brown days and even from my time as an Earth Day activist, whispered (to me alone; no one else heard it) that I could make more of a difference in elective office than in business.

I saw two clear choices: I could either run a token effort or else run to win. As a token candidate, I'd get my name on the ballot, spend some evenings and weekends politicking, gain practical experience, and keep my job. Jessica had a job teaching acting at a local theater. She also worked for a Santa Ana nonprofit, leading drama therapy workshops for high-risk teens, terminally ill children, battered women, and similar disadvantaged groups. If I chose the token path, she could keep doing the work she loved and not spend time helping me with the campaign.

The second choice would be far more ego-gratifying: go all-in and try to pull off a stunning upset. The problem? B-1 Bob had twice defeated more experienced local politicians, people with money, contacts, name recognition, and far better knowledge of the district. Still, I could make a persuasive case to myself for "go-all-in." Because this was a presidential election year with no incumbent, we expected Democratic voters to turn out in far larger numbers than in the previous two elections, in which Dornan had won his seat. Since the district had a Democratic registration edge, we might have a chance.

Jessica had valuable contacts in the liberal Hollywood community, all of whom detested B-1 Bob. We thought we could raise enough for a credible campaign.

Faced with making such a critical decision, we went to visit Gurumayi to ask for her blessings for the effort. I asked if I should run for Congress.

She had a prescient, practical question: "Do you have the funds?"

I didn't answer, but over the next few days, I considered her question. We were working people. There was no family money. We had to fund a campaign from scratch and do it ourselves. If I had more deeply contemplated the situation, I might have chosen the token effort, had fun giving speeches and meeting people, built name recognition for future elections, and accepted a loss with equanimity.

There was one problem with this approach: choosing a token effort didn't fit with my energetic, optimistic outlook. If I was determined to advocate for a better world, I wanted to do it with all my strength. I wanted to learn how to blow the trumpet of my passionate environmental concerns in a public setting. This wasn't easy. I hadn't worked as a theater actor or carnival barker and, outside of solar power, had little experience speaking publicly with real conviction about my core beliefs.

After weighing these considerations for a few weeks, I decided to run a serious campaign. We hired a campaign consultant from San Diego with solid experience in local and state races, but none in a Congressional campaign. He had two overriding virtues: we could afford his fee and he detested Dornan. We set out to raise money and build a campaign organization, rented an office in downtown Santa Ana, and met with local elected Democratic officials throughout the district.

As energizing as it could be at times, I found campaigning mostly hard work. It put a lot of stress on our marriage, then only two years old. What had we gotten ourselves into? It took a small dog to show us the right approach.

Before Jessica and I got married, she told me she'd had Scottish terriers since she was a child. Her last Scottie had passed several years before. Heartbroken, she wasn't ready for another, but soon after we got married, she announced she wanted one and hoped I would be OK with it. I'd never had a dog, but I wanted to please my new bride, so I agreed.

The next year, we got a female Scottie puppy from a local breeder. We named her Mukti, "the liberated one." I fell in love. Caring for her opened my heart in a new way. Over time, my love for Mukti made me a warmer person, more emotionally available to Jessica and others. Besides, Mukti and I had fun playing together!

During the initial stages of the campaign, when she was less than a year old, we took Mukti to meet Gurumayi during a teaching visit to Orange County. She stroked Mukti's head, petted her, and made a big fuss over her.

For the next few days, filled with Gurumayi's energy, Mukti ran around the house like a crazed person. Early in the Congressional campaign, Jessica resisted for a while doing all the work she had naïvely agreed to. She wanted to focus on what she cared most about, her work using drama therapy to help troubled teens gain more control over their lives. But I needed Jessica's participation to run a serious campaign. How could I convince her to help more?

The day after Mukti met Gurumayi, we were sitting in our bedroom discussing (arguing, really) Jessica's resistance to getting further involved. Suddenly, Mukti strutted in, holding a scrap of paper in her mouth. She had torn it from a notebook in which I had collected some quotes from the conversation between Lord Krishna and his disciple Arjuna from the *Bhagavad Gita*. (I'm not making this up—we were shocked.)

The scrap read, *You must have strong resolution; you must have firm conviction*, part of a section in which Lord Krishna tells Arjuna it is his righteous duty as a warrior, his *dharma*, to fight in the battle ahead.

We interpreted this message as coming directly from the Master: stay firm in what you have decided to do; be strong and resolved. Whether you win or lose, your actions will be righteous.

I went all in. I worked hard and ran as an energetic urban liberal; for credibility, I cited my background as a strong environmentalist and my service as a solar energy leader for Jerry Brown. Jessica used her contacts in show business to get people in Hollywood and the wealthier precincts of west Los Angeles interested enough in the race to contribute the legal maximum in the general election. Many people offered to hold fund-raising events for us. Slowly I got known in places outside the district, helped by Dornan's notoriety and because many people in the late 1980s knew we had fallen behind in environmental protection.

I had to learn new skills: fundraising, speaking as a candidate, and connecting with voters from every possible background. Being the candidate, "the man who is actually in the arena," represented a major departure from my previous work advancing public policy positions for the governor or the solar industry. There I could stay more in the background and let the governor or a state legislator advocate publicly for these positions.

This time, I had to put myself forward in a way I found initially uncomfortable, especially asking people for money or speaking in public. To get better, I hired Midge Costanza as a speech coach and set out to refine my "pitch."

A decade earlier, Midge served as a special assistant to President Jimmy Carter. A recognized leader in the 1970s women's movement, she was an effective public speaker. Midge and I began crafting a public and political persona we hoped would move people to support me. I had to get comfortable with speaking from the heart about issues I cared about. My meditation practice made it easier to do this, but I still found it difficult to harness the mind, the heart, and the voice into a convincing display of political rhetoric. The practical solution: speak often, to audiences large and small, and get better each time. After working with Midge and her partner for two months, I got much better, but we stopped these coaching sessions because our campaign budget was so limited.

Instead, my talented "running mate," coached me. Jessica had trained in New York as a theater actress and as a speaking voice coach. She could hear in my voice when I connected with my heart during a talk and provide immediate feedback. I quickly learned she had an intuitive approach to political speaking and decided to let her coach me for the rest of the campaign.

Using Jessica's contact network and my newly found strong voice as a candidate, we held successful campaign fund-raisers in New York City, in Orange County, and West Los Angeles, the liberal bastion of financial support for Democratic candidates. We had a good friend starring in a hit TV series who agreed to have a fundraiser at his home in Brentwood. As the guest of honor, we invited L.A. Mayor Tom Bradley, who came in part because he remembered that I had invited him to speak at Caltech twenty-five years earlier when he was a city councilman.

The actor Leonard Nimoy, *Star Trek's* beloved Spock and a committed environmentalist, held a fundraiser for the campaign at his home in Beverly Hills. The well-known actress, dancer, and singer Rita Moreno hosted an event at the Magic Castle in Hollywood, a hangout for professional magicians and showbiz types. People in L.A. wanted to support a committed environmentalist in Orange County, but they didn't live in the district and couldn't vote. I could only ask for their money.

We had another fund-raiser in Orange County at which former Governor Pat Brown, already in his early 80s, served as the featured attraction. He came because I had worked for his son Jerry. A frequent candidate once told me getting into politics is like joining the Mafia: once you're in, it's incredibly hard to leave. For successful politicians like Pat Brown, it's their life. They believe in the "cause" (or the party) and they like the action, the "high" they get from being around likeminded people and speaking to audiences about things they believe in strongly.

I made several trips to Washington to solicit contributions. One afternoon I went to see Congressman George Brown Jr., our Earth Day keynoter at Caltech, in his Capitol Hill office. Seated with his feet on his desk, leaning back, puffing on a cigar, the archetypal image of a long-time politician, he represented someone who got things done in the imperfect world of national politics. He remembered that I had invited him to keynote the Earth Day event at Caltech almost two decades earlier.

"I'm a man with firm principles," he intoned, pausing between puffs as he spoke, "and my first principle is flexibility."

I asked a favor: "Would you be the guest of honor at a fundraiser for my campaign?"

"I'll do it if we can agree on dates." And he did.

Favor given—favor repaid. The laws of reciprocity and abundance work the same way in politics as in life.

With these fundraisers, I cashed in all my political chips from nearly two decades of environmental and renewable energy work. We raised (and spent) $250,000 on the campaign, good for a beginner in a Congressional campaign, but we didn't know if it would be enough to overcome Dornan's name recognition, even with the higher turnout we expected for the presidential election.

Unfortunately, my boss at the cogeneration company didn't appreciate my political activity, as I occasionally took vacation time to attend a campaign-related event. In the end, I had to choose between running a serious race and keeping my job. I quit the job in May to allow me to campaign full-time until the November election.

After twelve years in national politics, Dornan undoubtedly saw me as an inexperienced newcomer. He must have found out I didn't have a personal fortune to commit, so he ignored me. A first-class demagogue who had built a national direct-mail fundraising base, Dornan used fiery speeches on the floor of the House of Representatives, broadcast on C-SPAN late at night, to excite right-wing contributors across the country. He had far better name recognition and a bigger war chest. Why should he even bother to campaign? He never accepted my debate challenge and only scheduled one local public appearance during the campaign.

Jessica believed this mostly working-class district didn't respond to an unusual name like mine, Yudelson, neither Hispanic nor WASP-y, the two largest voter groups in the district. Because I hadn't lived there long, I didn't have a significant local record or name recognition to rely upon. Where could I get standing quickly enough with voters to have a chance in the election?

My credibility with campaign supporters was based largely on my work in the Jerry Brown administration, already six years in the past, ancient history in most voters' memories. Most people vote their economic interests; environmental issues seldom change voting behavior. My background turned out to be useful in fundraising but not in gathering votes, absent any pressing local environmental issues.

It didn't matter; I plunged ahead and did the work of a politician seeking votes. It didn't seem like work—I loved every moment. Being around people energized me; I loved talking to the diverse types I encountered. I dove into it, meeting city officials, union leaders, teachers, trailer park residents, school cafeteria workers, animal rights activists, Democratic clubs, and myriad formal and informal groups.

I hung out at a barbershop in downtown Santa Ana with the owner Rueben Martinez, a Latino activist who knew every key political player in town. I learned some colloquial Spanish sitting in his barber chair, listening to him talk on the phone. Rueben introduced me to key players in the fast-growing Latino population in central Orange County. There's an underground force in ethnic politics everywhere, invisible to outsiders, well known to insiders. I spent enough time with these Latino leaders for them to accept me as a useful friend; sometimes they invited me to their private breakfast meetings, which I took as a sign of trust.

In the fall, I went to Washington to get endorsements from prominent Democratic politicians such as the former astronaut and Ohio Senator John Glenn and to raise money from national union political funds. One day I went to the Democratic Congressional Campaign Committee, looking for money. There I met with a young staffer, Rahm Emanuel, who told me outright I didn't have a chance and I wouldn't get any money from them, a cold turndown but a practical lesson. Politics is all about winning and, in this case, *ball don't lie.*

A seasoned operative will usually say, "Show me a poll (or two) that says you can win, and I may be able to help you. Otherwise, let's be friends, have a beer after work, and talk politics." Most union political funds were barely more generous; they'd give $500 to any Democrat congressional candidate who asked, on the off chance you might be someone who could help them in the future, perhaps as a presidential appointee. Unions play a long game; political parties' campaign committees focus by necessity only on the upcoming election.

While we lacked lots of money, we had enthusiastic volunteers. Jessica proved adept at finding and organizing them. In a low-budget campaign like ours, we welcomed anyone. In October, we organized volunteers to walk precincts on weekends and evenings, knock on doors, and hand out literature to voters. In the end, we only had enough money for two district-wide mailers. Instead, we tried to tell my story one-to-one, a longshot strategy for a district with 500,000 people.

Some volunteers didn't match up well with the district's demographics, but we used them anyway. A Beverly Hills matron, the widow of a famous actor, came one Saturday to walk precincts in Garden Grove decked out in high heels, wearing heavy makeup and carrying a large Prada bag with a small Yorkie's head sticking out. It wasn't exactly the image we wanted to present to our working-class voters—a pit bull (on a leash) might have looked better—but we were grateful for anyone who wanted to help. We gave her a voter list, stuffed some pamphlets in the Prada bag, and sent her out with the Yorkie to knock on doors.

The campaign's best outcome was unexpected. To get closer to people in the Congressional district, we moved from Costa Mesa into a rented home in a modest Santa Ana neighborhood near the Santa Ana River. A homeless pit-bull mix lived by the river, a place where people often dumped unwanted dogs. She began hanging out on our block and in our unfenced front yard. She had recently had pups and was still lactating. We searched the nearby riverbed, but never found them. Sadly, she was lame in one back leg, holding it up as she hopped on three legs.

When we found her on the street, she was starving. We left food out for her. Gradually, we won her trust and took her in, first into the rear yard, later into the house. She and Mukti became instant friends. Even our two cats accepted her. We named her Lady because she had an elegant look and a sweet disposition to match.

Lady spent most of her time standing on the living room couch looking out the front window, as if guarding us. If you looked in from the street, you saw a pit bull's face. We welcomed this image, because strange cars (we were sure they belonged to Dornan supporters) would cruise slowly by our house several times a week.

Our wariness was not paranoia. Jessica had loaned her new Honda to two young campaign workers distributing lawn signs at night. After they returned one evening, we noticed a dozen BB pellet marks on one side of the car. At the beginning of the campaign, experienced local political hands had cautioned us: there was a group of young Republican volunteers working for Dornan who harassed any opponent. This personal experience of "dirty tricks" put us on guard.

After Lady moved into our house, we took her to a vet who diagnosed a rare and painful hip disease. To overcome it, she needed a specialized operation, so we took her to the area's top local or-thopedic vet. When Jessica told the vet I was running against Dornan, he responded, "I'm a Republican but I hate that guy!" He performed the operation and when it came time to pay the bill, it was much less than we expected.

The operation was a success, but Lady needed months of phys-ical therapy to regain use of her leg and build muscle mass. We bonded during her rehabilitation. For therapy, I took her to walk on the beach early each day, forcing her to use her atrophied back leg by lifting her front legs, making her walk on two legs in soft sand. We became a team. The rehab was challenging; it was a 30-minute drive to the beach and dogs had to be off the beach before 9:00 am. In a few months, she recovered full use of her bum leg.

One morning at the beach, she slipped her collar and got away. I chased after her, running along the beach, but she ran faster, en-joying her newfound freedom and mobility. A lifeguard in a jeep saw us and joined the chase. He'd drive the jeep fast and get ahead of her; she'd turn around and run the other way, playing a "chase me" game with us. After five minutes of running back and forth, she got winded and slowed enough so I could catch her and put the collar back on. I got an expensive citation for having a dog off-leash on the beach, but it was worth it because Lady became an extraordinary companion.

Jessica and I worked hard to raise money and to campaign. For nine months, I spoke out forcefully for causes I believed in: environmental protection, women's rights, and animal welfare. A few weeks before the election, the *Los Angeles Times* endorsed me, which I thought might help with undecided voters. One ominous sign emerged during the last month of the campaign. In national polls, the Democratic candidate Michael Dukakis fell farther be-hind Vice President George Bush each week as Election Day neared. If he was sure to lose, the Democratic turnout would likely be lower than we needed to win, especially since the TV news would call the national election for Bush long before people in California finished voting. We could only guess where we stood because there wasn't any campaign money for polling.

On election night, Jessica and I had an early dinner with a reporter covering the campaign who wanted a human-interest angle. We went to the Democratic victory party (it's always called a "victory party" at the beginning of the evening) at a local hotel. In the ballroom, we thanked our supporters and enjoyed a few dances. Shortly after eight, the polls closed. On a large TV screen, the early results from absentee ballots came in. Dornan led with more than 60 percent of the early vote. Dukakis was getting shellacked by Bush in most of the U.S. About nine, I had seen enough; we went home.

I turned on the TV and the local results showed Dornan with a mounting lead. It became clear I wasn't going to win, Worse, I might lose by a sizable margin. I was momentarily shocked, stunned, saddened, speechless. For the first time, Jessica saw me visibly upset.

She responded from the heart: "Remember who you are. You're in this to help people; don't lose your center."

Her words sunk in, touched me to the core, took me away from my concern about the results, and steered me back to my broader goals. The gloomy mist quickly dissipated. For half the candidates in each election, life goes on after losing. I experienced this as letting go of both ambition and false hope. My meditation practice came to the fore; after all, meditation is a daily practice of letting go: of ego-attachments, dreams, and fantasies.

Dornan received 59% of votes cast to my 36%. After getting over the initial shock, I had to take stock: there was no way to sugarcoat such a decisive loss. The gauzy dream of a political career ended abruptly in the harsh morning light of vote-counting. I knew I had to get back to work. We had accumulated debt by taking time off from work to campaign, and we had to pay it off.

Gurumayi's prescient question lingered: *Do you have the funds?*

THE AFTERMATH

After losing an election, it's easy to take it hard, but I knew I didn't have to accept it as the only thing in my life. I recognized I could learn from it. The Dalai Lama once wrote: *When you lose, don't lose the lesson.* I knew I still had to discover the right *dharma*, or duty, the way in which I could best offer my service to environmental causes. After going through the process, seeing campaigning firsthand, giving it my all but getting a poor result, I wasn't sure I should continue in electoral politics.

During this time, Jessica and I became a team, a committed couple ready to take on any challenge. She became my ally for both spiritual and practical work. She had a keen mind for detail and was much better at reading people. And she remembered *everything.*

Jessica could see behind façades more easily than I could and was quick to discern people's real intentions, forcing me to become more realistic. It is a delicate balance: see God in everyone but be aware they might have their own agendas, their own karmas to work out, which might not be in your best interest. In the words of a World War II song, when you're in a fight, "Praise the Lord and pass the ammunition."

DIRTY JOBS: CLEANING UP
THE ENVIRONMENT

HOW COULD I TAKE MY STRONG INTEREST IN WORKING IN THE ENVIRON-
mental field in a positive direction? I took on short-term
management consulting assignments to pay the bills and waited
for a good opportunity. I joined the board of the Citizens for Clean
Air, the largest air-pollution lobbying group in California and
helped it develop the country's first system for selling emission
permits, a step toward more cost-effective air pollution control.
But I still needed a real job.

Before the Internet, *The Wall Street Journal* was the best place to
look for a marketing job. After the election, I scoured its help-
wanted ads daily for anything in renewable energy or
environmental work. I faxed resumes by the dozen, but nothing
materialized. If I heard back at all, it was that I was too old,
overqualified, didn't have enough relevant experience, etc.

Early one morning in March 1991, scanning the *Journal,* I saw
an ad for a marketing director position at an environmental remediation contractor, Pacific Coast Environmental (PCE), based
in Portland, Oregon. I thought I could get back to my environmental roots by working with companies cleaning up hazardous
wastes, a big opportunity after laws against toxic wastes passed in
the mid-eighties. I faxed my resume to the company. It arrived
first and went on top of the pile. They called back a few days later,
and we had a good phone interview. A week later I went there for
an in-person interview.

I flew into Portland and met the owners for lunch at a restaurant on Swan Island in the Willamette River industrial area. At 45

degrees, windy and raining heavily (a typical March day in Portland), the weather was bracing. Three of the four owners wore brown coveralls with a PCE logo over their white crew-neck T-shirts. The other guy, the accountant and CFO, wore a suit and tie. Wearing an overcoat, I must have looked like a real weather wimp and, with a suit and tie, sartorially out of place, but maybe that's what they wanted.

Relatively small, with 20 employees, PCE wanted to grow and needed a marketing expert. They worked mostly at the Port of Portland, remediating hazardous wastes from shipbuilding and ship repair but wanted someone to help the company expand into new markets. I was intrigued by the challenge of growing an environmental company and in working alongside practical people without intellectual pretentions. A week later they offered me the job.

Jessica and I discussed the opportunity. We didn't know a soul in Oregon, we'd be leaving behind our families and longtime friends, but we'd be moving to a place with clean air, little traffic, and lots of wide-open spaces offering a better lifestyle. There were many students of the Siddha Yoga path in Portland, which meant we could still be part of a spiritual community. We decided, let's try it. We can always come back.

The next month, Jessica and I left California and moved to Oregon. In beautiful spring weather, with two dogs in the back seat, we drove a thousand miles north to Portland. We rented a home in Beaverton, and I started at PCE.

I loved working alongside people doing the "dirty job" of remediating hazardous wastes. A month later, I landed a million-dollar-plus contract, PCE's largest ever, to clean up a contaminated site in Honolulu that had once been a motor pool owned by the Navy. Considered a mildly hazardous waste, most petroleum-contaminated soil usually went to landfills for disposal. However, local authorities in Hawaii banned disposal of such waste, fearing contamination of groundwater, Oahu's only water source. The state mandated that we had to send it to the mainland for burial. Ultimately, we barged 3,000 tons of contaminated soil from Hawaii for final disposal at a new, environmentally friendly landfill in southeast Washington state.

The Hawaii project became an environmental success story, at the time the largest remediation project in the state's history. In 2006, I went to Honolulu to give a talk at an architectural conference held in the new Hawaii Convention Center. I noticed something oddly familiar about its location along Ala Moana Boulevard. After checking a map, I soon recognized the convention center sat on the contaminated site I had cleaned up fifteen years earlier. Our remediation project restored it to an economically beneficial use: Brownfields had become Greenfields.

HITTING THE WALL AT 50

The next few years, I completed an MBA degree, left PCE for another environmental company, took on gigs as a management consultant, and started a small business to commercialize a new environmental biotechnology.

When I finished the Oregon Executive MBA program in 1993, I thought I could make more money as an entrepreneur. For three years, I tried hard, bringing to market an innovative technology called aerobic biofiltration, to help remediate gas stations with leaking underground storage tanks. We sold a few units, but not enough to stay in business. Sometimes, especially in middle age, the level of energy and commitment required to succeed as an entrepreneur puts everything else on hold, including married life.

By 1997, we'd been married for eleven years. We wanted it to continue; we deeply loved each other. But something had to give. I decided to surrender the fantasy of being a success in my own business. Putting aside Colonel Harlan Sanders (Kentucky Fried Chicken) and Ray Kroc (McDonalds), if success as an entrepreneur hasn't happened by age 50, it isn't likely to happen.

Eventually I admitted to myself that I was most productive as part of a team, not necessarily as the head person. After I got my MBA, my ego became entangled in being the leader, the head guy, and I'd buried this realization. I could see this entanglement happening, especially during meditation where I witnessed the mind and ego still lusting after outside approval. Stopping the fantasy was easier said than done, but eventually I got there. After closing the technology business, I had to find a real job. We loved living in Oregon and didn't want to move, so I kept looking. Soon we had to deal with a family matter requiring most of Jessica's time and energy.

Jessica's mother Bea was not doing well by herself in L.A. When Jessica visited her in the spring, she realized that Bea, then eighty-five, couldn't live alone any longer. From Bea's many friends who kept an eye on her, Jessica found out she was often making poor decisions and becoming confused, symptoms of a growing dementia. She had to assume Bea's care.

While this drama with Bea unfolded week by week in our personal life, one day I found my niche. Call it grace, the luck of the Irish (Mom's favorite phrase), talent, being in the right spot at the right time—it doesn't matter. One day, the marketing director at Glumac, a local consulting engineering firm, quit without giving notice.

They advertised for a replacement. I responded and got an interview right away. I put on a coat and tie, drove downtown, and met with one owner, James Thomas. I found out he was passionate about designing energy-efficient buildings.

Instead of a traditional interview, we talked shop about energy issues, one engineer to another. Even though I was mainly a marketing guy, he liked that I knew the technical side of the business. He introduced me to Steve Straus, the main decision-maker, who would be my direct boss. We clicked. I got the job. My environmentalist passion found a new outlet: promoting more energy-efficient buildings.

At Glumac, I soon got engaged with green building, which combined disparate pieces of my lifelong passion for environmental protection and renewable energy. In green building, I could again contribute to the environmental movement.

About the same time as I got the job, Jessica flew to L.A. to get Bea and bring her to Portland to live in an assisted-living apartment nearby. With our two-story house on a hillside lot and lots of stairs inside and outside, it wasn't practical to have Bea live with us. When relocating her mother, Jessica donated what she couldn't move and opened a new phase in her life: caregiver. She visited Bea almost daily; they bonded once again as mother and daughter, but in new, inverted roles. Bea lived three more years, eventually passing at eighty-eight in the summer of 2000.

On Bea's last night, Jessica lovingly rubbed an aromatherapy oil onto her feet and held her hand, sitting by her mom's bedside with her brother on the other side. They stayed with Bea until almost three in the morning, when she passed quietly, gently, and greatly loved into that good night.

VII
GREEN BUILDING

SOON AFTER TAKING OFFICE IN 1993, President Bill Clinton hired a team of architects and building experts to help "green" the White House. That simple gesture kick-started the U.S. green building movement, providing a cover of legitimacy for environmentalists, developers, and designers concerned with the environmental impact of buildings.

Not much had changed in the building industry since air-conditioning became standard practice in the 1950s. With A/C to cool them, concrete, steel, and glass skyscrapers rose everywhere. Architects, engineers, and contractors still used paper "blueprints" for design and construction. Designing with the environment in mind was not in anyone's playbook.

But times had changed. In the 1990s, sustainability became a buzzword as concern grew that humanity was heading into a box canyon, with population growth and economic development using far more resources than the earth could sustain. People began talking openly about global warming. One big question loomed: could we dramatically reduce human impact on the environment while still providing a high quality of life for everyone on Earth?

As the journey of a thousand miles begins with a single step, the journey toward sustainability began with a few adventurous leaders who responded by saying, "Why not?" They designed buildings, reoriented companies, developed new products, all with far fewer environmental impacts. A ray of hope glimmered; seeds of change sprouted and grew. I knew immediately that sustainability was the environmental mission for the times. Could I find a place in this movement? I decided to investigate.

THE GREEN BUILDING MOVEMENT BEGINS

AFTER I JOINED GLUMAC, Steve Straus was the first person I ever heard use the term, "green building." Steve saw it as a coming trend in the design and construction business. But what did it mean? In its simplest form, it meant designing commercial buildings to be much more energy-saving and resource-efficient than the norm. Steve wanted me to explore what Glumac could do in green building, so in the fall of 1997, I began attending sustainability meetings in Portland, meeting architects and engineers with equally strong beliefs about the importance of sustainable design.

The next year, interest in green building and sustainability grew stronger and I helped organize the U.S. Green Building Council's first chapter, *Cascadia*, based concurrently in Portland, Seattle, and Vancouver, BC. In a dynamic interplay between theory and practice, members included professors, universities, architects, engineers, contractors, government agencies, and others engaged with building design, construction, operations, and research.

After a year at Glumac, I had my first real introduction to green building during a Sustainable Building conference at the University of British Columbia (UBC) campus in Vancouver. I took a field trip with a few dozen attendees to see a new green building, the C.K. Choi building. UBC built this three-story research center on an existing parking lot without disturbing any large trees already there. The designers incorporated these trees into the design, using them to provide afternoon shade to reduce heat gain in summer. They recycled or salvaged fifty percent of the building materials. To save water, they used composting toilets and collected rainfall onsite for use in landscape watering during the dry summer months. The project cut total energy use by twenty percent compared with a standard building. During the next few years almost every measure in this project became part of the green building playbook in the Pacific Northwest.

Excited to encounter people who shared the same environmentalist mindset, I listened as they told how they approached ecological building design. As I listened, I thought, "This sounds exactly like what Sim van der Ryn talked about in the 1970s." What I had learned twenty years before was newly relevant—what a gift!

At Glumac, green building projects constituted only a small part of our business. With initial cost as the major issue, we mostly designed what we could call *brown* buildings, which met the local building code without any real effort to further reduce energy or water use. My job as Glumac's marketing director meant I had to serve the needs of the entire 40-person business. Beyond green building, I had to know about all kinds of projects and clients in a new industry, with its own structure, norms, language, experts, and client base.

I got first-hand marketing lessons from Steve, the firm's chief marketer. One sunny fall morning, as I arrived at work, Steve walked into my office.

"Let's go visit some architects."

"We don't have any appointments."

"It doesn't matter; we'll buy some lattes and show up. They'll talk to us."

We bought two lattes for them and two for us at a nearby Starbucks, and set out in his vintage yellow convertible, a 1961 Buick Invicta. With a full-sized set of Texas steer horns wired to the front bumper and its huge size, the 4,000-pound muscle car stood out as we drove off a few blocks into downtown, top down and radio blaring, looking and sounding like a giant musical banana in a parade float.

We dropped in on two architects, offered them each a latte, talked about their future projects, and suggested we should do the mechanical and electrical engineering for those projects. Steve was an incurable optimist, an essential trait for any marketer, which he demonstrated by owning a convertible in a city averaging 150 days a year of measurable rainfall.

Known for visiting architects' offices and wandering around looking at design drawings, Steve might stop a nearby architect and ask, "Why aren't we doing this project?" (he meant, of course, instead of our competitors.)

He was pushy, but knowledgeable enough about building design that architects recognized he knew his stuff and could show them some new tricks. With a staccato laugh and a bold manner, over the past twelve years in Portland he'd grown the business from a two-person office to more than forty professionals.

After Steve graduated from UC Berkeley in mechanical engineering, he worked for a few years in Glumac's San Francisco office. The firm's founder, Dick Glumac, then sent Steve to Portland to open an office, with the implication, "Make it work or don't come back." He'd make sales calls most of the day and work on engineering designs until late at night. After a few years, the office prospered. Steve had made it work.

I had worked at professional consulting firms before, but it had been twenty years earlier. It took me a while to get back into the daily rhythms of marketing meetings, sales calls, client relationships, proposals, and projects.

At Glumac, three partners ran the show. Even though I nominally reported to Steve, the other owners regularly demanded my attention. One day another partner hurried into my office and asked me to fax something to a client, saying he was late to a meeting, and abruptly left. My ego bristled and I tensed up.

I was going to reply, "I don't do secretarial work," when I recalled a core lesson from my meditation practice: be humble. I knew I was there to serve people. I figured a little humility would go a long way, and I faxed it without comment. Right then, I could almost hear an inner voice saying, "This was only a test of your state."

Engineers at the firm soon learned that I had two engineering degrees, but questioned why I wasn't a licensed Professional Engineer, a PE. That was the mark of distinction in the office, where there was a clear caste system. If you weren't licensed, by law you couldn't call yourself an "engineer;" in that case, you were a mere "designer." One engineer working downstairs loved to call me with some question and announce himself dryly as "Jess Williams, *PE*," to yank my chain.

He was right: I could talk like an engineer, but I wasn't one, in his eyes or anyone else's. I was only another marketing guy with engineering pretensions. His frequent reminder that I lacked a credential strengthened my resolve to get one. How? I had to pass Oregon's professional engineering exam. I found out that Oregon was one of only seventeen states licensing environmental engineers, lucky for me. I thought I could pass the exam if I worked at it. Fortunately, I had already taken the required preliminary engineering exam, the EIT, thirty years earlier as a graduate student, so I was eligible to sit for this test.

The exam was barely three months off. After studying intensively all summer, I took it, answering 80 questions, many with calculations, over eight hours, one question every six minutes. Through meditating and offering my service at the ashram and on Gurumayi's tours, I had learned to work calmly under pressure. At 53, twice as old as other test-takers, I hadn't done problem sets since college. I scored barely high enough to pass.

A few months later, I got the official "good news—you passed" letter from the State of Oregon. I waited for an opportune moment to show it to Steve.

One day after a large meeting, after most people had left, I approached him and casually asked, "Just out of curiosity, what happens when someone gets their PE license?"

"They get a two percent raise."

I pulled the letter from my jacket pocket and showed it to him. "You owe me."

He was delighted and told everyone about it. I was the only marketing director in Portland with an engineering license, and Steve made a big deal out of it. This changed how the firm's other engineers regarded me, now that I was also a PE. Jess Williams stopped saying "PE" when he called.

For three months' effort, I got an extra $100 a month take-home pay, enough to take Jessica out to dinner twice a month. More importantly, the "PE" after my name on a business card gave me credibility working with architects, contractors, and developers. With Glumac's growing green building business, I gained greater freedom to pursue my new passion.

THE GREEN BUILDING MOVEMENT
TAKES OFF

T HE CORE IDEA THAT WE SHOULD DESIGN BUILDINGS TO HAVE A SMALLER ecological footprint had great power. It fit right into the sustainability ethos that increasingly gained supporters in the early 1990s. But how would we know if a building was green? What were the criteria? Who would decide?

The answers had appeared first in 1991 in the United Kingdom. At a national laboratory, scientists and engineers created the first-ever scoring system for green buildings, called BREEAM, the Building Research Establishment Environmental Assessment Method. BREEAM considered many issues, including energy savings, water conservation, building materials, human health, and land use. The scoring system was arbitrary, but it made enough sense that practical people accepted it. In the late 1990s, the rating system migrated to the U.S., where the U.S. Green Building Council (USGBC) adapted it for American use.

Keeping score played well with the competitive nature of professionals. Americans all like to know the score, who's winning, who's losing. Tennis players often say, "If you're not keeping score, it's only practice."

In 1993, so the story goes, three guys met at a Washington, DC, bar and created the USGBC. After struggling for the first five years, a story told by one founder, David Gottfried, in his "kiss-and-tell" book, by 1998 the USGBC had attracted attention from architects, the U.S. Department of Energy, and some visionary developers in New York City. The first green high-rise, *Four Times Square*, completed in 2000, attracted widespread attention, even during design, for its novel approach to greening a large commercial office development and for putting a solar-powered billboard atop the building, right in the center of the known universe: Times Square, Manhattan.

Interest in the movement grew. Except for a few visionary leaders like Steve at Glumac, however, engineers lagged architects in accepting and using green design. In 1998, USGBC created a pilot (test) version of its Leadership in Energy and Environmental Design (LEED) rating system to rate and certify the "greenness" of buildings. From 1998 to 2003, under the leadership of its CEO Christine Ervin, a former Clinton Administration energy official, the USGBC became the fastest growing nonprofit in the United States, eventually growing to 15,000 corporate members and accrediting more than 175,000 building professionals.

Watching the green building movement grow was like watching a plane take off. For the first third of the takeoff run, the slow roll, not much appears to be happening—it's easy to believe, *this will never get off the ground*. During the next third, the plane is clearly moving faster, and you believe—*maybe now there's a chance*. As it accelerates toward the end of the runway, it lifts off quickly. The number of new commercial building projects registering their intention to pursue a LEED rating increased from 45 in 2000 to 1,236 in 2005, reflecting the efforts of hundreds, later thousands of building industry supporters.

Clearly the time was ripe to combat the emerging threat of climate change caused by global warming. More importantly, *the green building movement grew out of expertise*. Unlike Earth Day, a student-led movement enthusiastically supported by the public, green building represented from its inception a movement of practicing architects and engineers, building contractors and developers: experienced professionals who saw the need for environmentally benign buildings and who organized conferences and events to build a knowledge base for the movement.

Unlike students and ordinary citizens who followed up Earth Day with social and political action, these experts implemented green building primarily through their work: designing and constructing buildings.

Most architects in Portland had attended the University of Oregon, where environmentally conscious design had been at the heart of the architecture curriculum for more than twenty years. Portland became an epicenter for the movement. Because I lived there, I came upon green building when and where it first took root. Taking part in this movement almost from the inception gave me a life-affirming way to return to my environmentalist roots.

Jessica went with me to several green building events and met many local leaders and practitioners. She later reflected, "What impressed me was how much affection and respect people had for each another."

I hadn't seen this level of personal commitment among professionals since the early environmental movement. It showed me green building went beyond narrow business interests. Only a strong movement could have taken competitive, career-oriented professionals in design, construction, and development and converted them into a tribe, not of hippies, but of "hope-ies," people who saw the potential for crafting their daily work as a life-saving activity for the planet.

I quickly saw how the phrase *green building* nicely summarized my interests and passion for renewable energy and environmental protection dating back to the first Earth Day. Reflecting on my work twenty years earlier with SolarCal and OAT, I knew I *had* to do this work. It was like manna from heaven, a divine intervention showing me the right path for the next phase of my life.

Using information from the early pilot projects, USGBC revised LEED and released a second version in 2000 for use in assessing commercial and government buildings. Most architects still found it a hard sell to their clients, building owners and developers. But its time was coming. By the end of 2005, more than 2,300 projects had registered for certification, a fifty-fold increase in five years.

In 1999, I attended USGBC's second annual member summit, held in Virginia's Blue Ridge Mountains. In the first half-day, about 150 attendees introduced themselves and shared briefly how they promoted green building. Even with a one-minute limit, it took nearly three hours for each person to describe what they were doing in green building. *I was as excited, personally and professionally, as I had ever been*; I had tapped into a powerful movement at an auspicious time.

I met amazing people there: Kath Williams, a self-described "cowgirl from Montana" with a PhD and a passion to build a new green building at Montana State University where she served as assistant to the director of research; Bob Berkebile, a bearded, wise Yoda-like elder, a prominent architect from Kansas City and one of the founders of the national architects' (AIA) Committee on the Environment; Bill Browning, an MIT master's grad who five years earlier had written the first book on green property development; Stu Simpson, an architect working for Washington State's General Services department who had taken the initiative to bring green building ideas into his state government; and Rob Watson, a senior scientist with the Natural Resources Defense Council who chaired the LEED committee, reminding everyone that any credible green building rating system had to address key environmental issues. The list went on: people with strong credentials, outsized personalities, and deep social and environmental concerns.

After I came home from the member summit, I told Steve, "We've got to join the USGBC and get on this bandwagon. It's going to be big."

His response: "Go for it. We'll write the check." Steve reoriented the company's engineering practice to emphasize green building design. The next year, Glumac helped design the first LEED-certified public office building in Portland.

In 2000, the next annual member summit took place at the Salishan resort at the central Oregon coast, one of the first resorts on the West Coast designed to blend in with nature. Attendance doubled again from the previous year. More than 300 people came from all over the country. It took the entire first day for all of us to share our activities, even with the one-minute limit. After 2000, USGBC shelved the practice of having people describe their work at the annual meeting; the movement had already become too large.

But Glumac's owners were still skeptical. Although we knew our clients wanted more energy-efficient buildings with good day-lighting and other sustainable features, many engineers at the firm preferred to stick with standard design approaches. Engineers are temperamentally conservative and don't accept the latest ideas without a lot of vetting. After a building is constructed, whether you call it *green* or *brown*, engineers are responsible for the per-formance of what they designed—the mechanical and electrical systems—and they have to work.

Trying to push architects into green building, in 1998 and 1999, I organized two seminars in Portland, with Glumac joining the local electric utility, Portland General Electric (PGE) in highlighting engineering designs responsive to LEED criteria. They attracted a lot of clients, every marketer's dream, so Steve and I decided to replicate the seminar at Glumac's head office in San Francisco.

In the spring of 2000, we invited our local clients to a breakfast seminar in the Embarcadero Center, the country's largest office development, for which Glumac provided the original engineering design in the 1970s and 1980s. We got a decent turnout, about 40 people. As he introduced the seminar, the firm's president Dick Glumac, almost seventy, minimized our efforts, illustrating the challenges we faced inside the firm. Almost dismissively, he said, "This is something our marketing department dreamed up."

That pissed me off, but I didn't show it. I knew Dick and the rest of the old guard at the firm wouldn't easily embrace innovative ideas in energy-efficient building design, but I knew these ideas represented our future. Although I figuratively could have stran-gled Dick right there, I listened impassively as Steve presented innovative design methods embodied in our Portland projects.

It's easy to imagine dramatic "road to Damascus" conversions with green building, but it usually didn't happen that way. In building design and construction, change happens slowly, incre-mentally, with thought leaders chipping away at ossified ideas, demonstrating the technical and financial superiority of innova-tive approaches as they completed projects and put design ideas to the test.

GREEN BUILDING SERVICES

IN THE SUMMER OF 2000, my friend Nathan Good, an architect working at PGE, took me to lunch. Over the previous four years Nathan had worked hard to convince PGE to become more active in green building. He and I first met at some early sustainability and green building events; later, we worked together to put on Glumac's two green-engineering seminars.

In his early forties, Nathan was fully bearded, always smiling, calm-spoken. He was both a licensed architect and certified interior designer, a rare combination. Nathan had one particularly endearing quality: he laughed at my occasional witticisms, calling them "Yudel-isms." He was straightforward, no artifice about him, genuinely a good person. I respected his dedication to making sustainability happen within a large bureaucratic organization like PGE. Now he had something new in mind.

After some small talk, he threw his pitch, "How would you like to work with me to create a green-building consulting group inside PGE?"

I paused with my fork in the air, a bit of salad dangling above the plate, not sure what to make of this overture. After I finished listening, I put down the fork.

"What do you mean?"

"We've already registered a name. We're going to call it Green Building Services (GBS). PGE has set aside a million-dollars to support GBS, but we need someone like you, someone with marketing savvy and solid ties to local architects, engineers, developers, and contractors."

I asked, "Where does the money come from?"

"It's unregulated money, from shareholders not ratepayers. That gives us a lot more freedom to spend it. We'll make you a co-director along with me, and you could work full time to promote green building," he offered.

Nathan had brought his supervisor to lunch. Jim explained how GBS fit in with PGE's state-mandated energy-efficiency goals.

I demurred. "No, I'm not interested. I like what I'm doing at Glumac. I'm not sure I want to be a consultant again. I'd rather stay on the design side."

I didn't like the idea of going back to work for a large institution, whether state government or a utility company. I preferred the flexibility and fast-paced action in a design engineering firm, although I didn't enjoy the resistance to green building that I still faced from some skeptical partners at Glumac.

At the same time, I was aware that my position there was getting tenuous because of my insistence on pushing the firm into green building, but I didn't see right away how joining PGE offered a way to support the green building revolution.

After I came home that day, Jessica and I discussed the situation. She mostly listened while I went through the pros and cons of changing jobs after three years at Glumac. As we talked, I warmed to the idea. I'm a verbal person, and do some of my best thinking while talking, something that's always puzzled me; but that's how my mind works. Some people make visual sketches to envision new possibilities; I did the same, but with word pictures. I could see how joining a large utility company would give better support and more credibility to my efforts, and I wouldn't have to fight daily to get senior engineers at Glumac to buy into the green idea.

A few days later, I called Nathan back.

"I've changed my mind. I'm interested. If you can match what I'm making at Glumac, I'll do it. Let's have lunch again and go through the details."

"That's great news! I'll tell Jim. Let's meet again to go over details, then we'll get HR to put together the paperwork for a formal offer. If you have questions about benefits, they can answer them."

After I got PGE's offer, I told Steve I was leaving. He wasn't pleased; we had a good working relationship. If I left, he'd need to find someone else to do the marketing. But he also didn't try hard to keep me by offering a raise or a promotion, so I went ahead. Every job has its own natural duration; Steve and I had taken our green-building collaboration a long way. We parted on good terms.

What a contrast: I went from a loosely structured, project-oriented design firm with forty employees to a hundred-year-old corporation with entrenched bureaucratic procedures and 2,500 employees. As a state-regulated electric utility, PGE was conservative, rigid, bound by a variety of rules, regulations, and norms. You had to ask permission to do anything out of the ordinary, even to remove partitions between offices to allow people to work more easily as a group.

No one challenged the status quo. After all, this was an electric utility. So long as the lights stayed on for customers, life was good. If you tried to change anything, it had to go through a long approval process. If you were moderately bold, saying, "I'd rather ask forgiveness than permission," people looked at you as if you were the Antichrist. This insular culture was one reason that PGE had lost its independence in 1996, taken over by Enron, a leading energy company of the roaring 1990s.

During my first week, I learned more about PGE's unusual (to me) corporate practices. On Thursday, we had a team-building exercise involving all forty people from the energy-efficiency team. That morning we boarded a bus outside the headquarters and traveled sixty miles east along I-84 through the Columbia River Gorge to Hood River, a small town world-renowned for wind surfing. We got off the bus and took a small tourist train a few miles upslope toward Mount Hood, where we arrived at a park with a large grassy picnic area. Before lunch, we played various team-building games like hacky-sack and Frisbee.

After sharing a catered picnic lunch, we took the train back downslope to Hood River to wander through the town, have a coffee, or go shopping. We got back into the bus at 3:00, aiming to arrive at the headquarters building at 4:01 pm, because if we got back after four o'clock, PGE's rules allowed us to go straight home and not report back to our offices. We duly recorded this day as "team building" on our timesheets; but fundamentally, we were goofing off.

Despite chafing at the hide-bound culture, I recognized that corporate ownership had a positive aspect: they gave us money to hire staff without expecting us to make a profit right away. Encouraged by Enron's entrepreneurial focus, PGE set aside a million-dollar investment in the new green building business, and we could chart our course without focusing on immediate profitability. After I came on board, I developed a marketing plan that front-loaded educational efforts with architects, engineers, developers, and contractors. We hoped this approach would pay off later in consulting work to help them with their LEED paperwork. In 2000, *paperwork* meant real paper: printed forms, accompanied by project details and product data sheets, stuffed into large three-inch thick, three-ring binders and shipped off to USGBC (in six copies) for review.

The four of us at Green Building Services (three architects—Alan Scott, Ralph DiNola, and Nathan—and me, the lone engineer) went out to look for consulting work and generally aimed to avoid PGE's stifling bureaucracy. But we still worked inside PGE's high-rise headquarters, separated into individual cubicles with 66-inch-high partitions, not our idea of a green or healthy working environment. We put up with it because the green building cause was more important than our individual comfort or preferences.

After a year, PGE moved the energy efficiency team into a suburban office building. Instead of walking to most appointments with architects, we had to drive everywhere to see them. This was not sustainable, in our view, but we accepted the inconvenience in favor of the mission. At the new office, we crafted a way around the detested tall partitions and individual cubicles. Before we moved, Nathan used his insider knowledge of PGE's facility management practices to situate our group in a back corner of the new building. We arranged our desks at four corners of a square with a conference table in the middle, without any partitions between us. With this setup, we could quickly swivel our chairs around and have a meeting at the center table or overhear someone's phone call and offer helpful advice on the spot.

We soon got a plum consulting assignment, providing certification for the first LEED project west of the Mississippi, a small three-story office building in Lake Oswego, called Viridian Place. We later certified a major renovation project in Portland, the Jean Vollum Natural Capital Center, a hundred-year-old brick warehouse in a mixed-use neighborhood a few blocks north of downtown. Funded by a local philanthropist, the renovation aimed to show how older buildings could be re-purposed and made super-green. This project appealed especially to Ralph, who had an undergrad degree in historic preservation architecture.

This project's green highlights included the first green roof in Portland, water-free (no flush) urinals, and the first *bioswale* in the city, a vegetated ditch that collected runoff from the parking lot, held it briefly to settle the silt and remove contaminants, and then discharged it into the storm sewer. The Vollum building became a commercial success, with Hot Lips Pizza (which recycled heat from their pizza ovens to make hot water), a coffee shop, a holistic pharmacy, and a Patagonia store all on the first floor, and city government offices on the second floor.

In December 2001, the GBS team got it certified as the first LEED Gold-certified (one step below Platinum) historical renovation and only the second Gold project of any kind in the country. The project showed how green building concepts could find practical use, even in complex historic renovation projects like this one.

We had other firsts as consultants, including the first LEED-certified school, Clackamas High School, and the first new corporate office to be Gold-certified, for Honda's American headquarters in Gresham, Oregon. Excited by how many building types LEED could potentially certify, I enthusiastically promoted the green building and environmental agenda to Portland's leading architects and developers.

Not all architects welcomed the new push for green building, especially more experienced practitioners. Like most professions, architecture is self-referential, i.e., most architects believe only licensed architects (and maybe a few well-educated journalists) had the authority to comment on architectural matters. When GBS visited architecture firms to promote green building, they didn't always receive us with open arms. Sometimes, we encountered overt hostility, much like 19th-century European missionaries sent to convert heathens in Africa. I'm sure at times we sounded like religious zealots.

At one firm where Alan Scott had worked previously, he and I gave a late-afternoon introduction to the LEED system. During our presentation, the firm's owner, a highly regarded, award-winning architect, peppered us with questions, asking things like, "Why should we pay attention to green things when our projects already win lots of awards?"

It was clear to us that, in his opinion, architectural merit should trump any overblown concerns about environmental impact. He added, "Anyway, who are you to tell architects how to design our buildings?"

Alan coolly responded, "Your designs may win awards, but they don't incorporate environmental values, which are equally important. That's why we need to work together to make them greener and to have lower operating costs, something your clients will like."

We pointed out deficiencies in their current approach, measured not against what had come before, but against environmental concerns becoming more important with each passing year. In sessions like this, my meditation practice came to the forefront: I was willing to listen, take time to understand their viewpoints, and yet respond firmly. This proved to be the best way to win people over.

GBS soon got a reputation as Oregon's go-to consultants for green building and as a national leader in the field. As the consulting business grew, we added staff, including several more architects and two interior designers. Nathan and Alan became certified as LEED "accredited professionals," among the first ten in the world. I made it into the first 100.

If necessity is the mother of invention, *passion is the catalyst for achievement*. After joining Green Building Services, I could put my passion for green buildings to greater use. In 2001, Alan and I became two of the first ten LEED system trainers in the country. Several times a year, we flew to various cities, team-teaching all-day seminars.

Whenever I gave a seminar, I knew that I had made my own small contribution to making green building the "go-to" option for people in design and construction. I communicated the passion I had for sustainable design and the LEED system, and I could see how my enthusiasm helped convince skeptical architects and engineers that they could learn this approach and apply it to their projects. We were successful: in the first six years, the LEED faculty trained 45,000 industry professionals.

At GBS, we were on a roll, but life intervened, scarcely a year later, from an unexpected source. Our corporate parent, Enron, once a high-flying public company in the late 1990s, declared bankruptcy toward the end of 2001, becoming a national symbol for corporate greed and a victim of its own improbable hype. Several top executives eventually went to jail for various financial crimes related to the company's failure. With PGE's corporate ownership and financial future suddenly in doubt, I thought they might close our still unprofitable operation.

Long past the age when I would blithely quit a job without knowing where I might land next, I thought about what I wanted to do, how I could put my passion for green building to work in a productive way, and how to do it while still living in Portland. After ten years, we had many good friends and had sunk deep roots into the community: Jessica as an acting teacher and speech coach, and me as a green building advocate. As I was considering my options, I got a call from Omid Nabipoor, the new president of Interface Engineering, a local consulting firm. He wanted to meet for lunch.

GREENING AN ENGINEERING FIRM

O MID THOUGHT I WAS THE RIGHT PERSON TO LEAD INTERFACE'S SUSTAIN-
ability practice and direct the marketing team. In this role, I could help him and a new group of partners take a conventional engineering firm and reorient it toward green building and sustainable design.

I accepted the challenge and left GBS in a few weeks. The firm's partners envisioned a serious commitment to green engineering to grow the company, as Glumac and other local competitors had already proven their credibility in this field. By upgrading our work in sustainable design, we hoped to gain leading-edge architects as clients. We looked for a few good projects where we could demonstrate our "green cred."

One partner, Andy Frichtl, a talented and articulate mechanical engineer, was firmly committed to sustainability and had built a strong track record in energy-efficient building design. Another partner, Jon Gray, a former commercial plumber turned plumbing-systems designer, pioneered innovative approaches to greywater reuse in large buildings.

In 2003, Jon directed Interface's first landmark project. We worked with Seattle's Mithun architects to design a rainwater-harvesting project for a new building: a six-story dorm at Portland State University, with classrooms and offices on the first floor using, in a Portland first, recycled rainwater to flush toilets. Jon assured local building officials that recycled rainwater collected from the dorm's rooftop wouldn't cause any health problems (e.g., from aerosol formation caused by toilet flushing), after passing through an elaborate filtration and ultraviolet disinfection system he designed.

The architect wanted to make rainwater collection and reuse an integral part of the project, but Portland's building department wasn't convinced about the health issue. They required us to post signs above the toilets saying in large letters, *Recycled Rainwater. Do Not Drink*. Now, who would drink water from the bowl of a public toilet, except for creatures like dogs and cats who can't read? We all laughed at the absurdity, but signs are cheap, and we did what the city wanted.

As a result of our commitment to sustainability and green building, a year later we landed another landmark project, a large contract for the engineering design of a new $150 million, 400,000-square-foot healthcare building in Portland, which aimed to achieve LEED's highest rating, Platinum. Andy led the project for Interface, designing several innovative features into the project, including the largest building-integrated solar photovoltaic system in the country.

To harvest Portland's less-than-ideal sunshine, solar panels would sit atop sunshades over the south-facing windows of the 16-story building, providing sixty kilowatts of electric power and cutting the demand for air-conditioning in summer through keeping direct sunlight out of the building. By reducing the need for cooling, the project could install a smaller (and cheaper) air-conditioning system, a great example of *integrated design*, "doing more with less."

In December 2004, a week before Christmas, I went around town distributing small business gifts to our good clients, including the architecture firm leading this project. When I got there, the partner in charge of this project invited me into his office, closed the door, and read me the riot act.

"We've got big problems with your guys. They aren't good at keeping in touch. We need to know what they're doing on this project at least once a week. If your team can't get its act together, we'll have to hire another firm to finish the job. This project is too important for us to mess around with our engineers."

Thirty years into a meditation practice, I didn't react. I listened calmly, accepted his comments, took mental notes, and thanked him for his candor.

"I appreciate the feedback. I'll take it back to Andy; I'm sure he'll fix things in a hurry."

True to my promise, Andy quickly made regular communication with the architects his top priority, got our efforts back on track, and eventually completed the design on time, saving $4 million of the original construction budget for engineering systems.

This project had an unexpected benefit: it kicked off my writing career. In the fall of 2005, I produced a 48-page, full-color book showing Interface's design work for this project. For the first time, this publication explained in depth the sustainable engineering features of a large, high-performance green building. Interface sent it for free to more than 12,000 people worldwide over the next few years.

But spreading the message of green building to one engineer or architect or contractor at a time wasn't going to create a revolution in the building industry. We still had to demonstrate green building could be a profitable business, by getting product manufacturers and building owners more heavily involved. Showing that would take something more: a national trade show.

THE WORLD'S LARGEST GREEN BUILDING SHOW

I LOVE TRADE SHOWS. I love the intensity, the activity, the chance to meet people from around the country and abroad, the sheer size and scope of what's presented in a large national exhibition, the art of squeezing everything I need to see into a three-day window. But the green building industry didn't have its own show. Each separate profession—architects, engineers, contractors—had their own event.

In 2000, the USGBC Board decided to sponsor a national conference and show and scheduled it for the fall of 2002. The City of Austin, Texas offered to host it. This event would establish USGBC's position as the leader of the U.S. green building movement. At the 2001 annual member summit in Tucson, the CEO Christine Ervin appointed me and another Board member, Ross Spiegel, to lead a committee to develop the conference and create a trade show to accompany it.

Ross had served as president of a large national architectural association. We were the only board members who knew anything about organizing big conferences and trade shows, something I had done sporadically during the 1980s. This next phase for the green building movement meant taking what we had to offer, moving it beyond an audience of a few hundred enthusiasts, and offering it to the larger building industry.

We set to work creating the first national green building conference and trade show, with hours of conference calls and days of in-person planning meetings. We had no idea what to expect, how architects and engineers would receive it, and whether product manufacturers would buy exhibit space to display products at this new event. We only had fifteen months to make it happen, an unheard-of tight timeframe for producing a new national trade show.

We expected perhaps five hundred to a thousand people, a gradual increase from attendance at USGBC's four previous member summits. During the months before the conference, Ross and I watched with growing surprise as registration numbers grew much larger. As October 2002 arrived, more than 2,500 people registered for the conference. Two hundred manufacturers wanted to exhibit. We ran out of booth space in the main hall and placed some exhibit booths in hallways. Green building had become a commercial phenomenon overnight, moving beyond a vanguard wearing Birkenstocks and Patagonia fleece vests into the coat-and-tie corporate world.

After landing at the Austin airport, as I descended the escalator to baggage claim, I saw a huge sign draped across the balcony above: "Welcome to the First International Green Building Conference and Expo." I was thrilled; I could sense green building had arrived on the national stage.

The renowned Canadian environmentalist David Suzuki delivered a passionate keynote address. For many attendees, this conference and his speech became a time when green building merged their business activity with their personal passion. An environmentalist spirit animated the conference, sparked by Suzuki's speech.

Amazed and excited that we had an enormous success on our hands, as I went around the Austin show I recognized fewer than a hundred people I had met at three earlier member summits. But now more than *two thousand* new people had come out for green building, almost all of them with projects underway. I could sense the green building movement was ready to take off in a big way. By the next year in Pittsburgh, the number of attendees and exhibitors doubled again and the event, now called *Greenbuild*, became an annual fixture for the green building movement.

After the 2003 event, Ross stepped back from an active role. I chaired the steering committee for Greenbuild for the next six years, working with Paul Shahriari, a younger green construction expert from Florida. With USGBC staff doing the heavy lifting, Paul and I helped steer it into a "must attend" event for the world-wide green building industry. Greenbuild became the largest green building program and fastest growing professional and business event in the United States, attracting 10,000 people to the fourth show in Atlanta in 2005.

In many ways, green building represented a *paradigm shift* for building developers, owners, designers, and contractors. Now people would judge their work not only by economic viability or architectural merit, but also by the LEED score: how green it was. Paradigm shifts are like kinks in the fabric of space-time, permanently shifting perceptions and leading to dramatic new discoveries. Such shifts happen regularly in science, but in professional fields such as architecture and engineering, perspectives and practices had seldom changed so dramatically within a few years.

By 2005, China was the world's second-largest global source of carbon dioxide emissions, behind only the United States. If the green building revolution was going to change the environmental impact of building operations worldwide, it had to take root quickly in China. But we knew little about Chinese building practices and their perspective on green building. I soon learned first-hand how differently China approached building design and construction.

THE GREAT (GREEN) WALL: CHINA

IN A FEW YEARS, LEED had gained the high ground as the main green building system in the U.S. In 2006, an article in the *Harvard Business Review* confirmed this. Noted real estate expert Charles Lockwood wrote,

> "Today, the term [green building] suggests lower overhead costs, greater employee productivity, less absenteeism, and stronger employee attraction and retention ... owners of standard buildings face massive obsolescence."

His article clinched the argument for me: green buildings made good environmental sense and good business sense. Who wouldn't want to build green?

What about the rest of the world? Some projects used green rating systems outside the U.S., in the UK, Australia, Canada, Japan, Spain, Hong Kong, Taiwan, and several other countries. But we still missed the bigger targets: China, India, Brazil, fast-growing economies of Asia and Latin America, and most of Europe outside the UK. With the massive amount of construction happening there, China needed to adopt green building standards.

U.S. green building leaders saw China as a new market opportunity for sustainable building. At the Greenbuild conference in Portland in 2004, USGBC invited China's national vice-minister of housing and urban-rural development, Dr. Qiu Baoxing, to speak about green building.

Many prominent Chinese leaders at both local and national levels have backgrounds in economics and engineering, unlike most U.S. politicians, who tend to come from law and business.

For example, the current head of the People's Republic of China, Xi Jinping, studied engineering at the most prestigious technical school, Tsinghua University in Beijing, "China's MIT." Minister Qiu had PhDs in both economics and urban planning.

What did the Chinese want to learn about the American approach to green building? I found out a few months later.

In March 2005, USGBC sponsored a trade mission, sending leading green building professionals to China to create more buzz around green building. I joined the group, taking along my colleague from Interface Engineering, Zhonghu Li, a native Mandarin speaker and former Chinese academic. While on the faculty at Tsinghua University in the 1980s, Li wrote the first textbooks in China on using computers in architectural design. In 1989, he moved to the United States with his family. At Interface, he was a lighting designer. This was his first trip back.

Li clued me in right away to one key aspect of our visits with top-level people in China. He knew I had a master's degree in engineering from Harvard. It was the only university in the U.S. known to everyone in Chinese academia, professions, and government. Li familiarized me with how Chinese regarded credentials.

"When I introduce you, I'll mention you have an engineering degree from Harvard. That will make a favorable impression."

Later, he shortened the introduction to, "He has a master's from Harvard," and most people assumed he meant a Harvard Business School MBA. I didn't correct him—people would have considered it impolite—but I smiled inwardly at the irony: my graduate work at Harvard, which I had turned my back on almost forty years earlier, now returned to support me in China.

We traveled first to Beijing and met with leaders at the leading national construction and design ministries. I learned right away that green building was mostly unknown in China. The way design and construction happened there presented major obstacles. The building boom in China was so frenzied that contractors often poured concrete footings for large buildings *before* developers hired architects to design them. The prevailing ethos was: Ready, fire, aim!

One day, Li and his wife hired a cab to drive us to the Badaling section of the Great Wall, only 50 miles from Beijing. The best pre-served and most representative section, it is the section that visitors to Beijing usually want to see. The Great Wall is not visible to the naked eye from space, as urban legend insists, but it's impressive nonetheless for its sheer massiveness and great length. On one side I saw many narrow openings in stone ramparts, where archers would stand to shoot arrows against Mongol invaders from the north.

Modern civilization's enemies are not as visible or clearly defined. They're not all concentrated in one place like Mongolia. In 2010, for example, more than *one billion* motor vehicles in the world polluted the atmosphere each year with *billions of pounds* of carbon dioxide, carbon monoxide, unburned hydrocarbons, nitrous oxides, and particulates.

A famous *Pogo* cartoon from the time of the first Earth Day remarked on modern society's penchant for environmental de-struction: "We have met the enemy and he is us." We were now in a race to prevent a climate catastrophe; we were all in it together. We were all both sinners and (potentially) saints.

Before visiting China, I had made an important personal com-mitment. In January 2005, Gurumayi offered a contemplation exercise for her students. Each day we could reflect on a specific attribute of supreme consciousness, a word posted on the Siddha Yoga website. I decided to take on this challenge and write one poem daily using that day's attribute.

In Beijing, after Li and I met with three architects at the coun-try's largest design agency, I wrote this reflection on the *purifying* power of the divine energy, that day's posted attribute.

The Purifying Power

The purifying power gives rise to generosity and clean speech.
We celebrate the success of others and want to uplift them where
    we can.
Pure thoughts about the Master and the path
send the spirit soaring, allow me to see the purity in others,
even when they may not see it themselves.

In the meeting today, I sense a shift. I see the three Chinese
    architects
as a panel of sages, transmitting the ancient wisdom of their
    craft.
I see a radiant glow around the meeting, transforming our
    conversation.
We see them later at a reception; already there is a friendlier
    attitude.

Seeing the "other" as wise and benevolent purifies our own
    vision,
allows the light of the Self to manifest.
As this vision of light illuminates the entire room, outlooks
    soften,
for the Self is the fount of relaxation and prosperity for all.

When the Purifying Power is active within,
there is no place that I cannot visit, no person I can't meet,
no one disturbing, no perception strange.

I am amazed at how I see so little difference between us—
Attitudes, behaviors, intentions, outcomes—the same.
This outlook stems from the grace of the Master, who has
    gifted me
her own purifying power through initiation and instruction.
I hold this power close to my heart, as my heart.
I offer it freely to others, finding the right form to support
    my intention.

The purifying power harmonizes opposites,
balances twin forces of Yin and Yang,
drives perception toward wholeness, fulfillment, balance,
    harmony.
The Painter uses the purifying power to compose and complete
    the work,
as the Sculptor locates the place of pure tension within the
    stone.

After meeting with several Chinese architects, quickly under-standing how little they knew of green building, I became concerned. Would green building get a foothold in China soon enough to reduce environmental impacts from its massive con-struction boom? After several days in Beijing, Li and I went to Shanghai, China's commercial center, to check out the situation. We paid $800 for the U.S. Consulate's *Gold Key* service. A commer-cial attaché arranged meetings with large property developers. Much like speed dating, each hour another developer came to our table.

I had one question: "Why would you want to build a green building?"

As a native Mandarin speaker who'd trained as an architect and now worked on commercial building projects, Li was invalu-able. He knew the terminology on both sides.

Developers answered consistently:

"We don't want to spend any extra money to build a green building, at least not to LEED standards, but we do want to get multinational companies as tenants for our office buildings. If they tell us they want it green, then we'll learn how to build it green and get it certified."

Why? Foreign companies represented better long-term tenants than Chinese companies, more likely to pay their monthly rent on time, less likely to skip out on a lease, in which case they'd have to collect payments in a Chinese court. As preferred tenants, if they wanted it green, we'd do it. Otherwise, we'd do it the cheapest, fastest way we can. Their attitude was clear. Green building was purely a business decision.

After meetings in Shanghai, I spent Saturday morning as the sole Westerner walking along Nanjing Road, the pedestrian-only, mile-long commercial street in Shanghai's center. Watching the multitudes, I wrote another poem, this day contemplating the *universal* power of the divine energy:

The Universal Power

Universal power animates the human flow along Nanjing Road.
Saturday shopping energy.
Touts and hustlers are out, people eat ice cream on sticks.
A young girl squats to pee near a construction fence.
Unconcerned with hundreds of onlookers, she finishes,
pulls up her pants, runs to rejoin her family.

China in all its power and contradictions:
People everywhere trying to get rich,
using "guanxi," connections, more important here
than justice, fairness (impotent Western concept!),
even performance or talent.
Corruption and petty theft are everywhere.
Yet behind this façade there is family,
friends catching up after
a decade and a half apart, easily resuming familiar patterns,
face gained by hosting banquets.
An endless cycle of favors and obligations
circles this world like the moon, captive yet distant.

Within and among all this human activity,
she waits for us along the dark alley
visible from the crowded street.
Beneath the hanging laundry, above the
noodle shop, the universal power
casts the I Ching and changes forever
how we view the world.

The ink pot, ink stick, brush, and paper,
merging with universal power, give rise to
beautiful writing and 3,000 years of mind
merging with heart, hand with intellect,
emotion with frailty, inscribing this message
to loved ones from a lonely border post:
Remember me to one who lives there;
She is still in my heart; the dark smoky room
where we last met keeps haunting my mind.

Below the surface awareness, I can encounter joy
or loneliness and make the choice between them.
Amid surging Saturday crowds, in a land so unlike my own,
once again, I choose universal joy
over happiness itself.

SOUTH BY SOUTHWEST

I N 2000, Jessica's doctors diagnosed her with a potentially fatal, but not contagious mycobacterial disease, a fast-moving lung infection, 95 percent curable with a combination of three strong antibiotics for a year. The side effects wiped her out physically; she had to stop after nine months. The treatment worked, but she had recurrences of lung infections twice over the next two years. We knew things weren't going to get better, that her lung problems and frequent doctor visits were going to be a permanent part of our life. Her doctors told her she'd be better off leaving Portland's cool wet climate. Life changes circumstances quickly, makes our careful plans the casual plaything of destiny, as a cat plays with a captured mouse. We needed to put her health first and move to a warmer climate.

But where?

In 2000, I attended a meditation retreat at the ashram in Oakland, where I shared a room with three other men. A real estate agent from Tucson occupied one bed. He shared how much he loved the city and the surrounding Sonoran Desert. From this "chance" meeting (nothing occurring in an ashram happens by chance, I'd learned), we decided to investigate Tucson.

During the next five years in Portland we made a half-dozen trips to Tucson to check it out. Jessica stayed there for six months one winter, living in a condo at a new ecologically designed development at the far eastern edge of town. Before deciding to move there, we wanted to experience each season, something we hadn't done before moving to Portland.

In the Sonoran Desert, the most dramatic season is the summer monsoon, which runs from mid-June to early September, featuring wild downpours of drenching rainfall, coupled with surprisingly high humidity and widely fluctuating daily temperatures. One July, we flew from Portland, arriving late in the afternoon, rented a car, and drove to the historical Westward Look Resort, a former dude ranch nestled against the Catalina foothills on the northwest side of town. Along the way, a driving rain erupted, water pouring out as if a giant knife had slit the belly of a large raincloud; visibility plummeted nearly to zero. I slowed, driving cautiously on the I-10 freeway through blinding sheets of rain compounded by water splashed by other cars and trucks. A few minutes later, as suddenly as rain had appeared out of nowhere, skies cleared, dark clouds vanished, and the sun shone. The air was clear, clean, sparkling. In the eastern sky, we saw a full rainbow, radiant against the sky.

We arrived at the resort at sunset. While still in the parking lot, I stood mesmerized, gazing at the cloudy western sky. Over a few minutes I saw colors change from a spectacular bright orange to the glowing red embers of a campfire, as the dying light of day coagulated into a rapidly blackening evening sky. Soon the remaining clouds parted, and I could see Venus shining brightly. I watched the evening darken, the stars and planets brilliant in clear skies, enchanted. Here was the desert of my dreams, the landscape Elle and I searched for thirty years earlier in our trips to Santa Fe and to Hopi and Navajo lands in Arizona.

Framed north and south by nine-thousand-foot mountain ranges creating and embracing its stark isolation from the rest of the West, Tucson is a unique place, a "desert sea" surrounded by "sky islands," punctuated everywhere by thousands of iconic saguaro cacti, pleading arms stretching skyward toward a distant salvation.

Delighted by what we saw and experienced during several visits, we decided to move there. In the summer of 2005, we put our Portland home on the market. We sold it quickly and moved into a LEED-certified, green, high-rise apartment building in the Pearl district for six months, preparing to move the following spring.

We'd been in Portland fifteen years, but it was time to leave.

After helping Interface with developing a sustainability reputation for the past four years while also leading its marketing efforts, I wanted to focus solely on green building and sustainability. The idea of moving didn't bother us; we had joy in our lives, a loving marriage, and a beloved five-year-old Scottie, Madhu, whom we got as a puppy the year after Mukti and Lady died at an old age. We could be happy anywhere.

In the middle of April 2006, we packed a few suitcases and drove out of Portland, with the moving truck set to follow a few days later. The day we left, Portland's high was 48 degrees, rain was one-third inch, nearly identical to the cool, wet weather I'd encountered years earlier on my first trip. Because it was raining and cold in Portland, as we drove south, we encountered heavy snowfall along Interstate 5 while crossing over seven 2000-foot passes in southern Oregon. After driving through the snowstorm for several hours we arrived at the California border. By the time we hit Sacramento, five hundred miles into our journey, the rain had stopped, and the days became sunny and warm.

Three days later, after driving 1,500 miles from Portland, we arrived during a heat wave. It was 95, about ten degrees above average and nearly fifty degrees warmer than Portland. Always cold in Portland, Jessica loved Tucson's heat. For Madhu and me, it took longer to adjust; I loved the cool weather of Portland and he was a Scottie, bred for rain and coolness, well accustomed to it after living in Portland his entire life.

On the day we arrived, the Tucson City Council voted to create a sustainability office, an auspicious sign. Over the next few years we found ourselves in a place that supported green building and sustainability. To our dismay, Jessica got another lung infection (that her doctors were able to cure) but which diminished her lung function. Still, we continued living the way we wanted, traveling to many places on our bucket list, living with the realization that these often fatal infections could return any time.

THE GREEN BUILDING REVOLUTION

THE GREEN BUILDING REVOLUTION TOOK OFF LIKE A ROCKET IN THE EARLY-to-mid 2000s. By the end of 2006, cumulative LEED-registered projects totaled 3,156, an increase of 7,700% from 2000. Nothing in the building industry had ever changed this fast. Could it last? Could we approach the USGBC's stated goal of encouraging 25 percent of the building industry to use the LEED standard?

In a way, our success in accelerating the green building movement from 2000 to 2006 resembled what the first environmental movement achieved from 1970 to 1976, creating benefits we still enjoy fifty years later.

In less than ten years, a relatively small group of committed green building zealots had persuaded one of the largest and most conservative industries—building design and construction—to adopt a much greener way of doing business. We had done a lot, but we knew there was even more work ahead.

In Arizona, I became a missionary for green building, resuming the role I had in Portland. I would talk to anyone to convince them to build green. One day, two young employees from a large Phoenix developer came to a talk I gave at Arizona State University. I spoke about how green building represented commercial development's future, specifically how it was going to be important for people's careers to get on board now with this trend. A few weeks later they invited me to talk to the company's owners.

One sunny fall morning in 2007 I found myself in the company's boardroom in a new and decidedly upscale office building on Camelback Road in Phoenix. Six skeptical "suits," the partners in the firm, sat across the table. I wasn't intimidated; I had given these presentations for several years and, like them, I had gray hair, so I didn't look like a young revolutionary or someone at his first rodeo.

I enjoyed these encounters. I had a convert's enthusiasm, but I could talk like a businessman. With as much meditation as I had done for thirty years, I found it easy to handle their skepticism. I saw other people, even those who questioned or doubted what I was saying, as playing roles assigned to them, as I was. I could sense the same intelligence working within me was also in them. That bred respect, Baba's essential teaching for dealing with people, which they could sense and appreciate.

With facts and examples, I explained to these executives the business case for green building, as Charles Lockwood had presented it in the *Harvard Business Review* article. Higher rents + faster occupancy + higher resale value = greater profits: facts, facts, and more facts.

I threw in everything I thought would appeal to developers making multi-million-dollar business decisions. They listened, posed some questions, and thanked me for coming. I accepted this role, feeling like those two young men in white shirts and dark pants—Mormon missionaries—you see pedaling bicycles around cities and suburbs, explaining their religion to nonbelievers. I found joy in making the *right effort*, not in getting immediate results, seeing it all as spiritual work.

A year later, I received a call from the developer. They had a shopping center under construction in Oro Valley, ten miles north of Tucson, and wanted me to help get it LEED-certified, so they could acquire some "green cred" with local officials and pave the way for approvals of future developments in the area. They'd already designed the main building. Construction was ready to begin, usually the worst (and most costly) time to introduce green building measures into a project. I accepted the assignment and met with the building team to explain LEED's requirements.

Over the course of several meetings we found enough low-cost design changes that met LEED criteria to get the building certified. When construction finished, I submitted the documentation package to USGBC. We received a Silver (second-level) certification, Arizona's first green retail building. My missionary work paid off. The hard-nosed developers had come to our green church (at least for one Sunday.)

From many similar experiences, *I knew the green building revolution had arrived in the United States*. I wanted now to take the message—the business case—around the world. I thought writing books was the best way to do this, so I plunged ahead. I found publishers for each book idea, got contracts, and committed to deadlines. As I got more comfortable with writing, I got more adventurous with the topics I chose. I wanted to move outside my comfort zone, so in 2008 I sold an environmental publisher, Island Press, on the concept of a book profiling European green building practices.

To write that book, I had to go to Europe and learn how architects and engineers designed green buildings in a very different economic and cultural context. My first trip was to Germany, which had had a long history of environmental design dating back to the Bauhaus movement in the 1920s.

DÜSSELDORF DREAMS

MY CELL PHONE RANG. I saw it was a number from the +49-country code: Germany. It was a Monday morning in the spring of 2008. I'd arrived barely an hour ago on American's overnight flight from DFW to Frankfurt. I answered while sitting on the toilet in a public restroom on a concourse leading from the airport to the train station.

"Hello?"

"Herr Yudelson?"

"Yes?" Still red-eyed and tired from the nine-hour time change and lack of sleep, I wasn't sure who was calling. The setting was not conducive to a lengthy conversation.

"It's Dagmar from Ingenhoven's office. You sent an email Friday asking to meet with Christoph."

Now it registered. "Yes, I did. Of course. Thank you for calling. *Wie geht's?*"

Last week, I'd fired off several last-minute emails to leading architects in Germany, asking to interview them for my new book on green building trends in Europe. I had searched diligently through online news stories and magazines to identify architects doing leading-edge sustainable design. Three days ago, I'd come across Ingenhoven's name, got the email address for the firm, and sent off a request for a meeting, a shot in the dark, with an email addressed impersonally to "info@."

She asked, "Where are you now?"

"In Frankfurt airport, on my way to Bielefeld to visit with Schüco," a leading manufacturer of energy-efficient façades for commercial buildings. I thought it sounded more impressive than telling her I was sitting on a toilet, still waking up.

"No problem. We're in Düsseldorf, it's on the way. Christoph can meet with you before lunch today. Would that be convenient? You can take the train here and go on later to Bielefeld. I'll meet you when you arrive."

"That will work. I can be there later this morning. Thank you— *Vielen Dank!*"

I was more hopeful now that this trip was going to work out better than I expected. Most of my meetings after Schüco were still tentative. The only thing on the schedule for sure was a meeting in three days with Behnisch Architekten in Stuttgart, leading green designers with some super-green U.S. projects. I was hoping to get referrals from them so I could parlay one meeting into another and have a successful trip.

This was only my second time in Germany since my fellowship year in Aachen forty years before. As a student, my German was fluent. Back then, I'd used a simple method for learning languages: I had a girlfriend who spoke no English. When I was with her, I spoke only German, learning romantic words like *Schätzchen*, "darling," and a few others unsuitable for publishing in a family newspaper. She helped me get comfortable with the language, and I stopped speaking English. During my last six months there, I dreamt only in German. Sometimes I still did.

The previous fall, Schüco invited me to speak at a green building conference in Frankfurt, and I found my German-speaking ability gradually returning. From my student days, I still remembered basic grammar, but my vocabulary had largely vanished. The average adult uses 20,000 words in daily speech, and if I wanted to speak German again, I'd have to relearn many of them, plus add the professional vocabulary used by architects and engineers I'd meet. There was no way to learn without stumbling, like a baby learning to walk.

As a student, I liked Germany and Germans. Students in Aachen were generally pro-American, except for the Vietnam War, which they considered a colossal blunder. I lived my last six months there in a traditional, politically conservative German fraternity house, a *Burschenschaft*. Surprisingly, during the Arab-Israeli Six-Day War in June 1967, I remember vividly my German student friends cheering each radio news report of Israeli advances. Maybe they admired the Israelis as good fighters or maybe they were rooting for the underdog, symbolically atoning for persecution of Jews by their parents' generation during the Nazi era.

I loved the language, the local craft beers, their friendliness to Americans, the diversity of the landscape, and the two-thousand-year history. Under their chief, Hermann, Germans had defeated the imperial Roman Army in Teutoburg forest in 9 AD, keeping Rome out of the Teutonic heartland. Aachen became the capital city for Charlemagne, crowned Holy Roman Emperor there in 800 AD, with his tomb, Aachen's cathedral, completed in 813 AD. Relatively undamaged in World War II, the original Romanesque cathedral connects to a large Gothic addition. It's as integral to the cultural landscape there as the far more famous Cologne cathedral forty miles east.

Ingenhoven studied architecture at the university in Aachen. At age 25, he opened his own office, something unheard of in Germany. He was smart, innovative, and bold. Over the intervening twenty years, he'd won major competitions that helped grow the firm, which now had forty employees. He had an impressive track record in sustainable buildings, designing the first green high-rise office in Germany, a headquarters for the utility company RWE, completed a dozen years earlier in nearby Essen.

I bought a ticket for the trip to Dusseldorf at the airport's *Fernbahnhof*, the long-distance train station five minutes' walk from the airport terminal. Boarding a quarter before ten, I arrived there shortly after eleven. The train was fast, clean, and comfortable. Dagmar saw me outside the station and waved. I wasn't hard to spot, with a large roller bag, rumpled overcoat, and slightly haggard look.

"Herr Yudelson? I'm Dagmar. *Sehr angenehm*—nice to meet you." She reminded me of Angela, Stewart's wife in Santa Cruz, speaking with the same British-accented English that Germans learn in school and polish during vacations in London.

Fifteen minutes later, we arrived at the *Plange Mühle*, a converted flour mill with Ingenhoven's office on the fifth floor, commanding a sweeping view of the Rhine harbor. Three dozen architects were working on computers, facing each other across a single long table with only a low divider between them, far different from the individual workstations I'd seen in architectural offices back home.

Christoph welcomed me: tall, blue-eyed, smiling, movie-star-handsome, graying slightly at the temples. Sitting in his office, sipping an espresso, I explained the book I was writing, *Green Building Trends: Europe*, scheduled for publication the next year. I told him I'd interested the publisher in a three-book series, with two more books to follow on green building trends in Asia and in Australia. Christoph became even more attentive because he was designing his first project in Australia.

As we sat in Ingenhoven's office, he explained in first-rate English his philosophy of green building and how the firm implemented it. I was impressed; I hadn't heard a better exposition of the *hows* and *whys* of green building from an American architect.

Twice an employee wandered in with a problem. Ingenhoven instantly switched roles, moving from the pleasant interviewee to the *Meister Architekt*, berating them loudly for one mistake or another. There was no doubt who was in charge. My German wasn't good enough to get most of the conversation, but the tone of the message was clear. When he finished, the person left, chastened. We resumed our pleasant, high-level conversation, as if nothing had happened, much like the famous bar scene on the planet Tatooine in the first *Star Wars* movie.

After taking copious notes and drinking two more cups of espresso to stay awake during the hour-long meeting, I took a cab back to the train station. After a short wait, I boarded the next train for the 120-mile trip to Bielefeld.

Six months later, to do more research for the book, I returned to see some of Ingenhoven's projects in Germany and Luxembourg and to visit with several other leading German architects and engineers I'd contacted. This time Dagmar met me at the Frankfurt airport; we took a shuttle bus to visit one of Ingenhoven's highlight projects: a recently completed world headquarters for Lufthansa on the airport grounds. It was impressive, unique, huge; a seven-story, 1.3 million-square-foot, "horizontal skyscraper" sprawling over several hundred yards, with seven winter (indoor) gardens, one for each large wing, collectively representing different continents or places to which Lufthansa flies. In one garden, I saw a beach volleyball court, whimsically reflecting twice-daily flights between Frankfurt and Los Angeles.

On our way back to the airport parking lot, I learned an indelible lesson in cultural differences. To get back to the shuttle bus pickup, Dagmar and I had to cross a wide street. The light was red, but traffic was light during the mid-morning hour, with no cars in sight. I took a step into the intersection, clearly intending to cross the street. Dagmar grabbed my arm.

"You can't cross now; the light is red."

"But there are no cars," I replied, ever the practical American.

"We can't go—it would set a bad example for the children."

"But there are no children here," once again stating the obvious. It was no use; she wouldn't step off the curb until the light turned green.

From this incident and others like it—once I met someone who got a ticket for jaywalking across a narrow street in Stuttgart at two in the morning—I got insight into how Germans (and many Europeans) think, and why Americans tend to be more creative in business and technology. In Europe, after a thousand years of rule from above, if the government doesn't expressly *permit* something, it's generally not done. In America, whose unruly people barely tolerate any government, who are skeptical of all rules and regulations, if the government doesn't expressly *forbid* something, we feel free to do it. Sometimes we'll do it even if (or simply because) it's forbidden. During Prohibition, making alcohol was illegal but widely practiced; until recently, smoking marijuana was illegal, but millions did.

When Ingenhoven went out on his own at an early age, he violated one of the culture's implicit norms: you must first serve a long apprenticeship under another Meister before you strike out on your own. He thought differently and was willing to take more risks while still young. I'm sure that's why he was open to promoting green building and sustainable construction, well ahead of the pack. In Europe, there's often a big penalty for failure: you might be branded a *loser* for life because of a youthful indiscretion such as setting up your own practice too early (and failing), whereas in America we mostly view early failure as a learning opportunity, something to help you become more successful later on.

Of all my books, *Green Building Trends: Europe* stretched me the most: tackling a difficult subject, opening myself to vastly diverse cultural approaches to green building, and learning new ways to achieve our common goals of energy-efficient, sustainable construction. Writing this book, leaving my comfort zone to do the research, kickstarted my career as a keynote speaker, leading to speaking roles later that year at major real estate industry conferences and events in München (Munich) and Frankfurt, which gave me further credibility as a global green-building expert. In turn, this growing reputation led to invitations to keynote events in Singapore, the Middle East, and Australia, as well as other places in Europe.

The lesson I learned from this and similar experiences: never, ever give up. Keep doing what you know is right. The power behind your benevolent intention will usually reward you for making the right effort.

So many amazing things came from that first blind email to Ingenhoven and from the phone call that I had the good sense to answer while sitting on a toilet in the Frankfurt airport, pants around my ankles, groggy and sleep-deprived.

A VOLCANO UNSETTLES A GREEN BUILDING CONFERENCE

THROUGH SPEAKING AT DOZENS OF CONFERENCES AND MEETINGS IN OTHER countries, I spread the green building gospel, once dodging fallout from a volcanic eruption. The Global Financial Crisis in 2008 and 2009 reduced worldwide construction dramatically, but green building certifications continued to grow. In early 2010, I received an invitation to give a keynote speech in Budapest for *Build Green - Central and Eastern Europe*, the first green building conference of central and eastern European countries. In April, the day before I arrived in Hungary to prepare for the conference, the Icelandic volcano *Eyjafjallajökull* erupted, its ash cloud pushed toward Europe by prevailing westerly winds.

The UK and Scandinavian countries soon grounded flights to avoid engine damage from the massive ash plume, expected to cover central Europe in a few days. When the conference opened Thursday morning, many visitors worried they wouldn't get home Friday evening after the conference. As the opening speaker at the event, I had already planned to leave right after my talk.

Nearly one hundred delegates had crowded into an ornately decorated nineteenth-century conference room, a relic from Hapsburg days when Budapest and Vienna served as the Empire's twin capitals. People came from all over Europe, but mainly from Poland, Romania, Hungary, and other former Soviet Bloc countries.

In my opening keynote I told them,

"Today I am going to give you some good economic and business reasons why governments, NGOs and businesses worldwide are adopting green building. Even during the worst economic times in memory, green building use still grew in 2009 by 70 percent on a cumulative basis. Think about it: while commercial construction in the U.S. declined 30 percent, and even more worldwide, green building was growing and gaining market share."

I wanted to convince the audience that green building represents good business and good economics, something many still questioned.

"No matter what type of building you have, whether it is a commercial office building, a corporate headquarters, a school, a public building, the economic and business benefits of green buildings are significant for all building types."

Some architects had convinced builders and developers in their countries to adopt green building approaches, but many had not. Conferences like this encouraged them to carry the green building message to their clients and to share best practices with each other. I reinforced the core rationale for green building.

"Green buildings are about people. We shouldn't see buildings only as consuming energy and generating carbon emissions that we must reduce. Buildings are there for people to live, work, play, and study in. They should aim to make people healthy and productive. That's where we can create real and lasting benefits."

I shared with them what I thought would be an encouraging example.

"In 2006, we saw a real change in the Zeitgeist, the spirit of the times. Everybody started saying we should be doing green building, especially in commercial buildings. In one case, at a large biotech company in Boston with 900 employees, the main benefit of daylighting and natural ventilation measures in their LEED Platinum-rated building was a five percent annual reduction in voluntary employee turnover. Forget energy use, forget water savings, forget anything else—for this corporate headquarters, reducing employee turnover each year had significant monetary value, about twice the building's annual energy expenses."

Usually commercial office buildings adopted green practices first, because they catered to multinational tenants, as I discovered five years earlier in China. Businesses from Western Europe already wanted green-certified office space for their workforce because their employees demanded it. Green building made even more sense in central and eastern Europe, in places like Budapest, Warsaw, Belgrade, and Bucharest with heavy air pollution. By banning smoking and adding extra ventilation, green building created far better air quality inside offices.

Why was this important?

"Tenant or employee demand, increased productivity, and superior environmental performance are three major factors pushing green buildings into the mainstream."

I gave this same message wherever I could find an audience. The green building revolution in each country usually began with one leading-edge project, followed by another, and another, each representing a single step in the thousand-mile journey to a sustainable future. I encouraged these leaders to begin the journey:

"It doesn't matter how little information you have or what other people think. If you're a leader, you act before all the data are available, before it's obvious to everyone this is the right thing. As a leader, you benefit the most."

As I keynoted the opening program, I was the only speaker who had direct experience working with design firms on real projects. Could I show them why it made business sense? How would architects, engineers and builders, many trained during the socialist period, respond to my "the private market knows best" pitch?

During the discussion period after my talk, one architect commented, "I would like to thank you for a really inspiring presentation." The founder of the Romanian green building council later wrote, "We remember and appreciate your extra effort to support us in Budapest."

Responses like this made the effort all worthwhile. I saw my keynoter role as presenting useful information, changing perspectives, motivating people to green their next project, and inspiring them to take that next step. I wanted to convince them this was important work, that their combined efforts made a significant difference.

I concluded by urging them to do more.

"Absolute energy performance leading to massive reductions in carbon emissions from buildings is the only thing that counts in the long run. We can fool ourselves into thinking we are making progress by cutting carbon emissions a little, but we can't fool Mother Nature."

At ten that morning, right after my talk, I left the conference and hustled into a waiting taxi. I had barely two hours to get to the airport and onto a noon flight to Paris. I had to give another keynote the next day at a green building conference in Houston, traveling there via Paris and Atlanta. My biggest travel concern? The ash cloud was now descending from the north toward western Europe. Could I get through Paris before Charles de Gaulle airport closed?

At the conference, my friends from Spain and Germany had already canceled their return flights and booked trains to get back to Madrid and Stuttgart the next day. After a short cab ride, I got to the airport in time to board the plane.

When I left Budapest, more European airports had closed. While I might have worried that I wouldn't depart from Paris in time to get to Houston, I found my inner state calm. After years of travel, after decades of meditation, I found it easy to let things happen according to their own destiny.

I arrived in Paris at two in the afternoon. Two hours later, I boarded another plane for Atlanta. At ten o'clock, six hours after

I left Paris, all western and central European airports closed for almost a week. My American colleagues were stuck in Budapest for the week at the Four Seasons Hotel, but I made it to Houston without trouble, got a good night's sleep at the conference hotel (courtesy of the seven-hour time change from Budapest), and the next day gave a lunchtime keynote presentation to 150 architects at *Gulf Coast Green*.

It was a nice twist: in the same way I had gone to Budapest to share new American perspectives in green building, in Houston I could share innovative European approaches with American architects.

My environmentalist passion focused on spreading the message of green and sustainable building. I knew the urgency: each year carbon dioxide in the atmosphere increased by a few parts per million. By 2010, with CO_2 concentrations already forty percent higher than pre-industrial levels and growing annually, each year global warming increased perceptibly. Buildings—a third of global carbon emissions—had to be an important part of the solution.

THE GREEN BUILDING REVOLUTION PLATEAUS

I N 2012, SOMETHING HAPPENED THAT I'D NEVER FORESEEN. After ten years of dramatic double- and triple-digit increases, green building *growth* in the U.S. stopped, even as the commercial building industry grew, recovering from the Great Recession. Interest in LEED had peaked. Each year, slightly fewer projects registered for certification. The system had become too expensive, the certification process too cumbersome, the wait for a decision too long. It lost its PR value, since it was no longer possible to be the "first" green-certified project anywhere of any building type. For the last project I certified as a consultant, a large corporate headquarters in Tucson, the certification process took more than a year after we submitted the required data, far too long for most clients. They wanted the PR value from certification when the building opened, not long afterward.

Architects and developers still used LEED criteria to design their projects, but many no longer bothered with certification. Green building claims sometimes crossed the threshold into *green-washing*, with projects projecting huge energy savings to get certified, but never measuring actual use after operations began.

After 2012, I became openly critical of USGBC's role in the green building movement. Movement leaders had become complacent, forgoing needed innovations in LEED, making only incremental changes in an unnecessarily complex and overly costly system. USGBC seemed content to give LEED certifications to those projects willing to jump through the right hoops, mostly new commercial and government projects, ignoring millions of existing buildings contributing most of the energy use and carbon emissions from that sector.

This situation should have created a dilemma for the environmental movement. If we want to preserve this beautiful planet from the ravages of global climate change, environmentalists must insist that every solution, each eco-label offered by well-meaning organizations, conducts real-world, independent testing of outcomes. Otherwise, we will fool ourselves into believing we're making progress. The global green building movement never insisted on such testing, the mainstream U.S. environmental movement had other priorities, and nothing changed.

After more than twenty years of LEED ratings of thousands of buildings, shouldn't environmentalists insist on proof of their claimed effectiveness, or else withdraw their support? It's human nature to not want to upset the apple cart but in this case, I knew we had to reinvent the green building movement to take it farther.

Without engaging the owners of existing buildings, the green building movement will never achieve the full scope of energy reductions essential to reducing carbon emissions. Each year only about one existing building in ten thousand (0.01%) in the United States, LEED's major market, receives certification.

After devoting twenty years to promoting the green building movement, in 2017 I decided to step back from green building and focus on the larger issue of climate change, doing what I could, along with thousands of experts and activists, to address the overriding environmental issue of this century. This remains my "outer" work, but along the way, the inner work shone with its own beauty, urgency, and importance.

VIII
THE ROAD TO ENLIGHTENMENT

IN A DEEP MEDITATION at one of Baba's meditation Intensives, I experienced a past life. In a flash, I saw my death as a soldier at Dunkirk in 1940, the site in France of the epic battle and rescue of more than 300,000 British soldiers trapped on the beaches. Thousands died there, including my previous self. I experienced the noise, smoke, and confusion of combat and the awful moment my body became lifeless, hit by strafing aircraft.

That I was born a few years later to this present life proves nothing, of course, but neither can I deny the intense meditation experience. In 2017, I went to see the movie, Dunkirk. *Tears flowed during the opening battle sequence. Once more, I was there, alone and vulnerable in that terrible last moment.*

Wisdom traditions around the world describe each soul as moving from life to life, given each time an important task to complete. When the soul develops a strong yearning for liberation, meeting a great master provides the means for accomplishing the final task: becoming free from this never-ending cycle.

Once in 1974, Baba gave a public program in Aspen. Someone asked him to explain "dispassion," one of the key practices on the path, letting go of illusions and delusions. Baba expressed delight. I recall him saying, "I've been in America almost six months and that's the first time anyone asked this question." Practicing dispassion demands vigilance every moment. Vigilance paves the road to enlightenment.

I needed constant reminders to incorporate these practices into daily life. Gurumayi's generosity proved indispensable. She took every spiritual practice and broke it down into digestible bits. Over time, I engaged fully with the primary task of a seeker: becoming whole again, dispassionate, fully present in each moment.

SPIRIT IN DAILY LIFE

HOW DID I PRACTICE CONNECTING WITH THE INNER SPIRIT EACH DAY, each moment? That was a great challenge; I didn't journal regularly, but occasionally when I went through a time of memorable inner experiences, I recorded them daily. As a meditator I relished ecstatic experiences, but I wanted most to experience inner transformation, no matter how long it took. The contemporary Polish poet Adam Zagajewski wrote:

> "We live in ecstatic moments, but epic pauses stretch between them. At times, we think nothing will ever happen, the sadness will never end. But we're usually mistaken ... we live, by necessity, in two registers, not just in one: we live both in the moment and in duration."

During a time of intensive journaling in 2000 and 2001, several experiences stood out, showing me the way to inner peace, guiding me to experience joy, develop purity of intention, and focus on my highest purpose. I also had one startling revelation about the power of my thoughts to create the world I lived in.

INNER PEACE

Today after lunch I left my office in the World Trade Center in Portland to run an errand. I walked out into a beautiful sunny winter day, seen through a glass-enclosed open walkway between two towers. I walked over to the elevators leading to the basement parking garage but paused before pressing the button. I turned around and looked behind me, taking in the entire scene. Everything became still for a moment: I experienced a conscious awareness of grace, gratitude, and contentment. The scene became crystal-clear. My mind was quiet. Each moment could be peaceful and clear like this. Yesterday I taught a meditation course with another teacher. Today I experienced the fruits of offering such service: total stillness inside, in this moment and during the entire day. My day was so easy—magical—much activity, but amid all, stillness. This is what yoga calls *inaction in action*.

A MOMENT OF JOY

This morning I stopped at the post office on my way to work. Over the past several years I've gotten to know a clerk named Joy. She's always smiling and when she waits on me, I like to share with her something uplifting. She exemplifies her name; her heart is always open.

Today she greeted me with, "I really love waiting on you."

What a wonderful recognition of the pure love we can share with each other, even in brief encounters. How many other people feel their lives brighten, even for a few moments, because we don't hesitate to share our love? Years ago, Gurumayi gave her students a resolution to contemplate, one I had adopted as my own: *I will no longer hide my pure love from the world*. I learned to look at each encounter, with strangers or friends, as a chance to share what I have received in full, overflowing measure from her, nothing but God's own pure love. In each person, I can see God expressing exactly as that person. I can turn each encounter into a conversation with God and I can hold this awareness of God's presence wherever I go.

THE LESSON OF THE COCONUT

In spiritual life, the coconut is a symbol of the ego, its hard outer shell hiding the sweet meat of the soul inside. Working for a few days one summer in the ashram kitchen in New York, I got a new perspective on the humble coconut. I was cracking the outer shell, removing the meat and chopping it into pieces for the next day's meal. From experienced cooks I learned it's critical to remove all the impurities from each piece of coconut meat before chopping it and storing it. Otherwise, rot sets in quickly for the entire batch.

Some impurities are obvious, while others require careful inspection.

This lesson clearly applied to spiritual life. Living a pure life is the best means for pursuing *sadhana*, the spiritual path. Purity does not necessarily mean puritanical, denying all of life's pleasures, but it does require a little discipline. It means if I'm a meditator I must attend to all aspects of my life, root out any tendencies toward laziness in work or speech, stop indulging in habits wasting time or energy, stop entertaining thoughts —

Entertaining—what a great word! "Please come in and have a seat in the living room of my mind. Make yourself comfortable. You're such a lovely thought. Won't you stay for a while? Would you like a cup of tea? Lemon or milk?"—which don't lead to higher awareness, stop hanging out with people who don't share my goals, eliminate mental habits like dwelling on problems. I remember Gurumayi once saying in a talk that *clear intention leads to clear attainment*. If I want all she has to offer, I have to stay connected to the Shakti, to the energy of the inward-turning path. The best means for doing this is to consciously remove impurities from my life.

SPHERE

In the 1998 movie *Sphere* (based on the eponymous novel by Michael Crichton), a team of scientists investigates a mysterious 400-year-old spaceship lying on the ocean bottom. Inside is a golden sphere. As each person approaches it and sees their perfect reflection on the surface of the sphere, they acquire the power to manifest their thoughts. Whatever they think and dream becomes manifested as a physical reality.

As they do this, the three main characters encounter their worst fears and, by doing so, create havoc for the others. Each has the power to dream delightful things, but each chooses (without realizing it) to create the world they fear most. What would our world be like if we could create our own reality through our thoughts or dreams? Would we focus enough on our goals to manifest only the highest, purest thoughts? But isn't this exactly what we do? As every master teaches, we create our experience of the world through our mind. Life does imitate art after all!

At the movie's end, the scientists all agree to forget what they have seen. We don't have this option to forget so easily. But forgetfulness of our own greatness, willful ignorance of how we manifest our life experiences with our thoughts, does seem to represent the entire conundrum of spiritual life. Yet, no matter how often we forget, still we press on, aiming to enter the cave of the heart where the unstruck sound continually resounds. In the movie, after many disasters, it dawns on the scientists how much mental power they have.

How many disasters have we created for ourselves and for others through this same unconsciousness? When will we wake up to our true power to create a world full of happiness and good fortune for ourselves and for those we encounter? My spiritual practices help me maintain an awakened life. Only constant awareness of my thoughts and vigilant self-control work to move me toward the goal.

THE FINAL GONG

We visited Gurumayi's ashram in New York one summer for a spiritual retreat, arriving in the early evening. Before unpacking, we went to the temple for prayer and meditation. This evening, as I settled into meditation, sitting cross-legged on the soft carpet, a gong rang three times, soft but resonant and firm, signaling the temple was about to close. A peaceful downy blanket of stillness enveloped me, but thought ripples remained, forming small waves on a vast calm ocean of awareness.

Not yet ready to leave, I sank back into a reverie. Again, the gong rang three times, this time louder. I had to leave. In the same way the temple closed for the evening, reopening the next morning, one day this brief life will end. We will quietly "expire" with the last breath. Perhaps in another life the temple will stay open longer, but for this life we know with certainty one day the last gong will sound. Will I have completed my meditation on the Self by then? Will I have finished my spiritual journey, before that time comes?

One day this dream-life must end; can I use the power of the grace I've received to leave this world of appearances and enter the heart, living solely in the present moment, before the final gong softly sounds and the sweet breath, *prana,* the vital energy of life, becomes, once again, simply air?

GOD'S BODY—THE DIVINE POWER WITHIN

WHAT WOULD IT BE LIKE TO CONTEMPLATE GOD'S INTRINSIC NATURE every day, to look regularly for the hand of the divine in ordinary events? As I mentioned, in 2005 Gurumayi invited her students to contemplate a different attribute of the divine, the inner power of conscious awareness, each day for the entire year.

Studying each attribute became a way to envision one aspect of "God's Body," not as something abstract or remote, but as my own body, my own experience.

Each evening I wrote one poem incorporating the day's events along with perceptions I'd had, relating them to the daily attribute. I contemplated or envisioned a specific aspect of the inner divine power operating behind the day's mundane activities. Through these poems, I grasped that we all possess these divine qualities in some measure. Because we do, we can recognize them operating in outer events and inherent in other people, in nature, in the rhythm of life.

In 2006, Gurumayi extended the same invitation again. Over those two years, writing one poem each day, I wrote more than seven hundred, all incorporating some aspect of this *twofold consciousness*: the outside world cresting as a wave on the inner shore. I crafted a new relationship to my spiritual practices: I had to look for inspiration both within myself and in the world around me. This daily practice opened my eyes to a new way of seeing reality as pulsating with hidden meanings, stories, dreams, ancestors, and teachings. What a rich, intricate life I found!

During those two years, I was outwardly busy. I traveled to China for the green building trade mission. We sold our home in suburban Portland and moved to an apartment for six months. We bought a home in Tucson and remodeled it into a green home. I left my job at Interface Engineering in Portland, opened my own consulting firm in Tucson, and completed my first three green building books. With this much going on, I found it challenging to maintain the discipline of contemplating my experiences each day, but I did. This practice revolutionized how I approached writing—and living. For the first time, I forced myself to *see* and to *reflect* on what happened in my life each day.

I set myself the task of dealing directly with the day's events and how they affected my inner state, but as a poem it also had to *sound* right. Poetry aims squarely for the ears. Every poem should be spoken or sung, not merely read. A song might have printed lyrics, but they tell you little about how to sing it; it's even truer for poetry. You can't read a poem on a printed page and know how the poet would say it or sing it: the pauses, the intonation, the importance of each word.

I added one further requirement: each poem could only be one page long. I wanted the poem to represent, in a tight and powerful burst, the energy I'd found in contemplating the daily attribute, a perspective I learned years earlier from studying the poet Charles Olson's work.

Olson's celebrated 1950 essay, "Projective Verse," pushed poetry toward expressing only a moment's energy and away from relying on rhyme and meter. I found I could take bits and pieces from the day's activities and observations, working like an archaeologist carefully sifting through ancient rubble to extract shards of pottery, reassembling chips of memory and pieces of events into a graceful urn displaying an artistic contemplation for the day.

Olson maintained that the breath, and the pauses between breaths, should underlie each poem, more so than the words. I tested each poem by reading it aloud and revising it until I could be sure it contained the pure energy of the day's contemplation and rang true to events. In reading it, I wanted to make sure it conjured a place of inner stillness, joy, and wonderment.

Here are two poems from my daily practice. With their focus

both on the rhythms of everyday life and on my spiritual contemplations, I wrote these poems to integrate what I experienced within and what I observed in the world outside.

The Unaffected Power

She wears a veil in church,
hides her face out of modesty,
gives no offense to anyone,
offers her help to all.

Unaffected by life's changes,
mountains, rivers and gullies
guiding our passage,
she remains calm no matter what.
Yet she is not inert.
She makes all changes her own,
sees them as secret rays emanating from her own blissful Self.

Look for her standing behind the counter
at every shop in town.
She is modest, dynamic and eternal.
You only notice her when you too are unaffected
by life's inevitable ups and downs.

Try this exercise:
Take something that really bothers you.
Look at it from all sides, like a many-faceted diamond.
Find the dazzling blessing flashing through your discomfort.
Ask yourself: How can I turn my difficulties into nectar?

In this way you'll find the secret cave
of the unaffected power within,
the space within the heart that holds all pairs of opposites,
the still place between coming and going, entering and leaving.
Let that be your church.

The Forgiving Power

Struck by an assassin's bullet,
Gandhi reaches out to him,
his mantra *Sri Ram, Sri Ram*,
mingling with his last breath,
offering in that terrible moment
complete forgiveness and grace.

Yellow buds ready to break out
into blossoms this season
forgive the winter:
Its harsh winds,
unrelenting cold
and slyly false February warming spell,
tempting less experienced trees to bud
only to have returning cold and ice
shrivel their swelling.

Without forgiving the winter,
a tree remains stunted,
afraid to burst out into full-throated
splendiferous song, holding
the memory of winter's abuse
like a damaged child
unable to become emotionally mature.
Without forgiveness and
the forgetting that must go with it,
shoulders always hunch
waiting for an expected blow,
a fighter ready to defend, or attack.

The forgiving power within
leads us to a spring path of forgetting,
opens our arms wide to the warming sun
teaches us that glorious summer,

still a distant memory,
will once again ripen our springtime budding.

Forgiveness flows from a glad heart.
Seeing all that has come together to make this moment,
this ecstatic moment,
gives thanks for the dream—
and for its end.

IX
THE GODFATHER OF GREEN

I LOOKED OUT THE WINDOW OF MY HOTEL ROOM EARLY IN THE MORNING, ten stories above the hot, dry sands of Abu Dhabi. I was a green building missionary, spreading the green gospel to people still struggling to understand their roles in the green-building revolution. By 2012, my long engagement with green building had taken me to a pinnacle of recognition, expertise, and full immersion in this world. I'd spoken in Australia, Singapore, Eastern and Western Europe, Turkey, the Emirates, South Africa.

A few hours later, I gave the keynote talk, outlining the business case for green building to an audience of sheiks in traditional Arab attire, the men dressed in white thawab robes with a red checkered keffiyeh on their heads, the most important people lounging on plush chairs in the front row. Weary with jet lag, I'd neglected to bring a paper copy of my presentation deck with me, relying on the monitor in front of me.

I began my talk. After a few slides, the ancient projector on a tall stand in the back of the room overheated and quit. I had to wing it. As I spoke, I could see hotel technicians frantically waving a sheaf of manila file folders behind the projector, creating an improvised fan and bringing it back to life. I began again. A few slides later, the projector overheated once more and then quit for good. Luckily, I'd given the talk so many times, I could deliver it from memory.

Over several years, I accumulated hundreds of thousands of frequent flyer miles, preaching the green-building gospel to skeptics and converts alike. Gradually, the global green building movement took hold; green building projects arose everywhere, in more than 150 countries. But would it be enough to reduce the massive contribution that buildings made to carbon emissions, fast enough to have a measurable effect on global warming?

FINISHING THE JOURNEY

MY ENVIRONMENTAL ODYSSEY ACCELERATED. After moving to Tucson, I moved from cruising speed into the fast lane. Though I had already turned 62, for the next decade, I was highly productive. Freed from limiting constraints of working for other companies, I created the consulting business I had always wanted: one dedicated exclusively to green building and sustainability. A consultant off and on for almost forty years, my new focus fit the mood of the times. People wanted to get a handle on sustainability; I could offer a decade of insights and experience.

Years of meditation practice gave me the ability to dive deeply into whatever I was doing and be productive. I could sit on my living room couch for six weeks and write a 65,000-word draft of a book on green building. Stephen King's book, *On Writing: A Memoir of the Craft*, inspired me. King wrote that anyone who could write 2,000 words a day (which I could do on a good day) could write a novel in 90 days (180,000 words.) Simple math! While I couldn't write like him, I followed his recommendation to write productively almost every day.

I became a prolific author, producing two or three books a year during the first four years in Tucson. At a time in life when most professionals slowed down, I sped up. I wanted to share all that I had learned and inspire others to push the green-building revolution forward.

With writing books in addition to supervising a consulting practice, I was busy most of the time, the way I liked it. But Jessica reasonably expected I'd be more available to her in her sixties, not less. In Tucson, by starting a business, giving keynote talks (first around the country and later around the world), and writing books, one after another for seven years, I didn't often take time off, working a lot of weekends and evenings. I had to admit that staying busy was a way of life. I didn't see relaxation and recreation as "productive." Meditation and studying Gurumayi's books were enough downtime for me.

The hardest thing for Jessica was giving up teaching, especially weekly improv classes she held for non-actors in our Portland home, something she loved and at which she was intuitive and brilliant, integrating mindfulness work with acting exercises. But recruiting students in Tucson was hard; our home was on the outskirts of town, at least a half-hour's drive from where most potential students lived, so she couldn't hold classes there.

After I hired people to work in the consulting business, four or five occupied a large office at the front of the house, sometimes spilling out into the living room, working with their laptops at a dining table or in a chair. Phone conversations often echoed throughout the front of the house. When she made a late breakfast, Jessica had to navigate past people making coffee in the kitchen five mornings a week and stashing their lunches in "her" refrigerator. It was uncomfortable for everyone, but we put up with it because I wanted to keep the business in the home: it made more financial sense. After the Great Recession, I had to downsize the business; that solved the problem.

In 2008, our beloved Scottie Madhu got sick. He was only eight. One day he collapsed on the living room floor, right at my feet. We rushed him to emergency; he survived that episode, but it was the beginning of a series of health setbacks brought on by a rare cancer. We tried everything to save him.

On a Saturday in November 2008, I gave a talk in Hawaii to a national contractors' meeting. On the return trip, I flew into Las Vegas to change planes, planning to fly to Houston and on to Dubai to give a talk. I called Jessica to check in.

As we were talking, she suddenly cried, "I think he just died."

Madhu had collapsed again, right at her feet. We both knew intuitively that he'd gone, but she hung up and rushed him to the closest emergency vet, only five minutes away. It was no use. Jessica sat with him for an hour afterward. I needed to honor my commitment in Dubai but disliked leaving her alone to deal with his death and the aftermath. I offered a silent prayer for Madhu, asked Gurumayi to help him cross the rainbow bridge, and stayed in constant touch with Jessica while away.

Jessica left our dear Madhu with the vet for cremation. Several months later, we drove up the Catalina Highway toward beautiful Mount Lemmon and scattered his ashes in a forest grove at 7,000-foot elevation, where he could rest in peace.

HOW I BECAME THE "GODFATHER OF GREEN"

In 2011, I unexpectedly acquired the moniker, "The Godfather of Green." A writer for the leading popular technology magazine, *Wired,* called one day in June to interview me about green homes. My answers appeared in the September issue. In the interview, I presciently predicted the rise of *net-zero-energy* homes with 2-3 kW of solar photovoltaics on the roof, a renewed focus on water conservation in home design including both plumbing fixtures and landscaping choices, and the rise of smart home thermostats (which came onto the market a couple years later as the Nest.). *Wired*'s illustrator created a caricature from a headshot and the magazine appended the headline, *Godfather of Green.* Right away, I knew *Wired* had given me a great gift. Although I acquired this appellation by accident, I've used it ever since. The funny part was, many people seemed comfortable (even pleased) knowing someone who was the "Godfather" of anything, almost as if they knew a real celebrity. After the article appeared, whenever I gave talks, especially in other countries, they introduced me as *The Godfather of Green.*

THE GREEN BUILDING INITIATIVE MAKES WAVES

In the middle of the *Greenbuild* exhibit hall in New Orleans in October 2014, I was surrounded by a half-dozen ideologues of various persuasions plus several self-styled green building experts, debating whether I had abandoned the green building movement by advocating for Green Globes, the leading U.S. competitor for LEED. What had happened?

In the fall of 2013, I saw a job posting for president of the Green Building Initiative (GBI), a small nonprofit with a rival green building certification that had become LEED's main U.S. competitor. I was intrigued; would it be possible to take my growing misgivings about LEED's effectiveness and help grow the green building movement with an alternative rating system that got the same results, but was simpler, faster, and cheaper? After I interviewed with GBI's board, I got more interested in what I could do with this opportunity.

Earlier in 2013, the U.S. General Services Administration, the country's largest landlord, approved Green Globes as equivalent to LEED for assessing federal building projects, an endorsement which gave me confidence in its perceived value. A dozen projects already had both certifications; each system certified them at the same level of "greenness." To my mind, that made the two standards equivalent.

For years, LEED partisans claimed GBI was a tool for the chemical and forest products industries, with weaker certification requirements. After checking out these claims, I decided these critics essentially nit-picked minor details to satisfy their ideological preferences. In December 2013, when GBI's board offered me the job, I accepted.

I had some concerns, which I discussed with Jessica at length. No matter how anyone looked at it, green building activists would consider me an apostate, competing with a LEED system I had supported and advocated for during the past fifteen years. In some jaundiced eyes, I would be a green Darth Vader, going over to the dark side of the force. At this point, I wanted most to advance the green-building cause by pushing for a better approach. Green Globes had one major selling point over LEED. It was officially an "American national standard," adopted through a formal, years-long and rigorous consensus process, something LEED had never attempted.

My decision created a stir in the insular green building world.

Activists of all stripes love to have "enemies," people they consider less pure, less devoted to "the cause." They saw Green Globes as the enemy, challenging LEED's hegemony.

The resulting brouhaha reminded me of a statement I read years ago, perhaps dating from Puritan New England: "There's no one pure in this world except Thee and me … and I'm not so sure about Thee."

Some green building insiders claimed I had betrayed the cause. I didn't care what others thought; I thought of the little boy in "The Emperor's New Clothes," pointing out the obvious: the emperor is naked and the "new clothes" he wears are thin air. At the time, USGBC's leadership had turned green building into a wide-ranging social movement, in the process losing touch, I thought, with its primary purpose: transforming the building industry into a more environmentally responsible business. If we wanted to halt global warming, a goal that USGBC had strongly endorsed as "Job One" since 2006, we had to get serious about having all buildings meet low-carbon goals, especially those certified as green.

After I took the job at GBI, many colleagues privately told me they liked Green Globes, considered it as LEED's equal, but wouldn't say so publicly and buck the consensus among their peers: whatever its faults, LEED was still the best system we had—we had to stick with it. Once I began working at GBI, I created a wide-ranging promotional plan to raise awareness of Green Globes and worked to put GBI on a sounder financial footing.

In October of 2014, I went to the annual Greenbuild conference, as I had done every year since I helped create it, for the first time as president of GBI. After I took the job, some activists began sniping at me. At Greenbuild, I'd decided to confront them head-on. As I learned thirty-five years earlier working with Tom Hayden at SolarCal, most activists don't like it if you question their goals and methods, even if you're "right," but they do appreciate dialog even when they disagree with you.

I'd been engaged for months in an email and phone discussion with a self-styled "forest advocate" who was adamant that the only legitimate certification for wood products was from the Forest

Stewardship Council. Green Globes also recognized other certifications, including SFI: the Sustainable Forestry Initiative, the largest
in the country. I had a practical approach: I'd rather give credit to
any legitimate forest certification program than argue about which
was the better, FSC or SFI, SFI or FSC, take your pick. Anything
with independent inspectors and legitimate industry standards
was okay in my book.

Forests aside, I thought green-building certification should
mainly focus on reducing carbon emissions; the rest was important
and useful, but ultimately only window dressing if we didn't cut
carbon. In green-building certification, I was for pragmatism and
against ideological purity, a stance that put me at odds with many
activists and some influential industry publications.

The editors at *Environmental Building News* (EBN), the leading
monthly newsletter for the industry and a frequent GBI critic, invited me to sit in their exhibit booth for an hour and answer
questions from anyone who wanted to pose them. I gladly accepted
the invitation; it's one thing to criticize someone in the press or
on social media, yet another to have a conversation face to face.
EBN publicized the upcoming event widely to draw a crowd.

A dozen people were waiting when I arrive at the booth. I sat
on a stool surrounded by a skeptical audience. We plunged into
an animated discussion, people firing questions from all directions.
Most had never heard Green Globes explained; they were sure it
was "bad" because its board consisted mostly of people from business. I told them why Green Globes has a better approach to
certification, that Green Globes is faster, cheaper, and more effective, both for building projects and the environment. At the
end of an hour, we finished the discussion and I left the booth,
satisfied with what I had achieved: a respectful dialog about our
differences.

I'm not sure I changed anyone's opinion about GBI or Green
Globes, but afterward the sniping abated. This experience showed
me once again the wisdom of not putting off even unpleasant
things "for later," something I had first learned while presenting
that gift to Gurumayi nearly thirty years earlier.

Still, results are results. In the end, LEED's established market presence proved powerful and durable. We couldn't appreciably increase market share for Green Globes, and I left GBI during my second year as president. In 2016, I wrote my final professional book, *Reinventing Green Building: Why Certification Systems Aren't Working and What We Can Do About It*, to present lessons learned and offer a prescription for creating a more vibrant future for green building.

HOMEWARD BOUND

FOR ALMOST FIFTY YEARS, I participated in three major environmental movements: Earth Day and its aftermath, solar and wind power, and green building, each time working to make a difference by applying passion, knowledge, and a strong environmental conscience. In this work, my spiritual practices guided, informed, and nourished me. They are indispensable to understanding who I have become.

There are now hundreds of green-building rating systems used worldwide. I am confident the work we did to promote green building globally in the formative 2000s decade will continue to grow worldwide well into the 2020s. In the green building revolution's beginning stages, we planted a seedling, but it's only now, in 2020, that it's grown tall and spread worldwide. Its fruits may not ripen for yet another decade.

What has satisfied me the most?

First, I gave to this work everything I learned over a fifty-year career working with politicians, businesspeople, solar power experts, wind power developers, mechanical engineers, architects, property developers, academics, and government officials.

Baba once wrote, "If we do not use our knowledge, it becomes a burden. Whatever knowledge we have, we must put it to use in our daily life."

I understood Baba referred to spiritual knowledge you hear about and profess, but don't implement in your life, but I also applied his admonition to my environmental work, to using whatever I had learned to implement changes I thought beneficial.

Second, over the past fifteen years, I've touched tens of thousands of people with my books, lectures, and keynotes. Hundreds of people sent me emails or thanked me personally for something they had read in a book or heard in a talk. One mid-career professional recently wrote to me on LinkedIn, "Your true gift to green building is the impact and legacy you left on the industry. In a sense you are the master teacher of all of us." Testimonies like this one made me optimistic that my work had served to advance and enhance the green-building revolution.

I had given what I had to offer—insights, energy and expertise—to improving the world we live in. I contributed what I learned from my spiritual efforts to uplift people I met. My work, such as it is, is nearly done. The outward-bound journey must one day conclude, but the inward-turning journey never ends. The wheel turns, the cycle renews, the gyre spins, there's no direction home; instead, home is a state of being, not a place. Home is everywhere I feel and express love.

I've learned one truth: love is the only story worth telling. My story of love is upbeat: love of joyful inner work, love for nature, love for the teacher and the path, love for God who dwells within me as my true Self, love for animals, love for the work I've done, and especially love for Jessica and the people I've worked with.

Love alone endures. Love alone—in its many perversions, penances, pauses, persuasions, and perturbations—is the sole reason for living and undergirds our entire existence. For my life's dear companion, Jessica, our love shines with a special dimension after more than thirty-three years. Sometimes a simple thing like sharing a meal shows love best.

Love After Seventy

I've seen you at breakfast ten thousand times,
 and it never gets old.
Last night, you showed me sunset photos—your eye
 has such beauty, joy, intense feeling.
Your heart melts with kindness for animals
 and softens mine as well.
There is wisdom in age,
 but only when we walk together,
Sharing a silent glance, the joy
 of looking at each other once more.
Now it's breakfast time again;
 As usual, you have only one question:
"Do you want oatmeal?"

A FINAL BLESSING

Gurumayi once recorded a *qawwali*, a devotional song written by a Sufi mystic. Toward the end of this song, he sings,
 "The world instructs me: become this, become that;
 become this, become that; become this, become that" ...
 (But) "by becoming no one, I have found my Self in ALL."
With exuberance and joy, this stanza summarizes the paradox of spiritual practice: *To find your (great) Self, you first must lose your (small) self.*

 Should a memoir end with a paean to invisibility? Why not? Isn't the ultimate goal of inner work to grasp that our life, each individual life, a life we cherish and protect, is only an infinitesimal element, a small node in the great web of life, a miniscule speck in a limitless, joyfully expanding universe where energy and matter are interchangeable, and your sense of self downright malleable, depending on time, space, and circumstance? As Gurumayi's student for more than thirty-five years, I've seen my life enriched beyond measure by her grace, teachings, and beautifully expressed compassion for the Earth and its creatures. Each day I live is a blessing, an opportunity to connect with life's beauty.

⌒

The clock reads 10:03. The neighbors' noisy A/C unit, only thirty feet from our open bedroom window, mercifully cycles off. In the warm humid August night I hear only late evening's wind whispers and crickets' chirping sounds. Nights are getting longer now, as the steep slope of the solar sine curve dips toward the equinox three weeks distant. In the Kindle's soft glow, I see Bodhi the Scottie sprawled across the foot of the bed in a long black lump, safely beyond reach of our feet. Jessica wears an eye mask: even the Kindle is too bright for her. Lovingly, I stroke her head, the once abundant silky hair now thinning. Still sitting, I gaze over this tableau, displayed like something you might see in an eighteenth-century English painting, "After the Hunt"—two springer spaniels asleep at his feet, the hunter reclining in an easy chair before the fire—and feel a visceral sense of contentment, of well-being after eating a full meal of more than six decades of life. Isn't this inner peace the fruit of my spiritual quest, the goal, to arrive at the place, as Eliot wrote a hundred years ago, "where we began and to know the place for the first time"? I have a delicious sense of inner and outer silence, primal and ineffable, pervading my life. I click off the Kindle, consigning what I've been reading, Mary Karr's *The Art of Memoir*, to pixelated oblivion. I lie down next to my sleeping wife and, as I do lately, hold her hand as I, too, slip into sleep.

At journey's end there is only silence,
    sweet silence,
        sweet vibrant silence.

X

EPILOGUE: CLIMATE CRISIS

IN OCTOBER 2016 I VISITED PARIS DURING A EUROPEAN VACATION, *the last over-seas trip Jessica would take because of her declining health. One afternoon, I decided to visit Shakespeare & Company, the iconic bookstore on the Left Bank. I browsed through the store but didn't find anything I wanted to buy.*

As I was leaving, I spotted a book at the checkout stand with an intriguing title: The Great Derangement, *by the Bengali novelist Amitav Ghosh. In three essays, Ghosh indicts our cultural unwillingness to deal directly with climate change's onrushing challenges. By turning our backs on humanity's accumulated wisdom about the aliveness of the natural world and the current scientific consensus about anthropogenic climate change, he argues modern society has become* deranged.

In his condemnation, Ghosh includes not only politicians and businesspeople, the usual suspects, but also artists and writers focused primarily on the "moral adventures'" of the individual, intent on expressing outrage at the personal abuse they've suffered, while ignoring climate change, the greatest abuser of all. After reading The Great Derangement, *I focused my attention on the climate crisis.*

Near the end of my career, I wanted only to deal with what mattered most, to bring what I had learned from my spiritual path to this work. I didn't want to waste time condemning bad actors, however satisfying that might be. We're all in this together: our modern lifestyle created the crisis. Only young people have the energy, openness, and resolve to deal with our current stasis. What could I tell them?

LETTER TO A YOUNG CLIMATE STRIKER

EARTH DAY 2020

Last year, I had to clean up my language. For several years, I talked about climate change as if it were only some new kind of pollution. *I'm through with that now. We're in a genuine, full-blown climate crisis, a climate emergency that will define the rest of this century.* You and your friends are inheriting the greatest challenge since my generation faced the prospect of mass annihilation from nuclear war in the 1950s and 1960s. We've managed to dodge that bullet (so far), but the climate crisis is real, it's immediate, and it will surely worsen over the next several decades.

Seven months ago, on September 20, 2019, inspired by the example of a modern Cassandra, the Swedish teenager Greta Thunberg, millions of students staged peaceful school strikes, climate walkouts, and demonstrations in more than 150 countries, demanding the world's governments take immediate and effective actions to deal with climate change. You made an incredible statement: students can—and must—force climate action onto a slow-changing world.

What can I possibly tell you to help with this fight? As students in the 1960s, we saw the world much as you see it today. We sang protest songs like Bob Dylan's "The times they are a-changin'." We worked through the crises of the Sixties: the Vietnam War, racial conflict, and rampant pollution. The same spirit of protest is again in the air, and none too soon. What I can tell you is this: I have your back, your elders have your back, but what else can I share about lessons I learned as an environmentalist, as an activist, realizations you might use today?

My environmental journey began during tumultuous and clouded times of street protests, civil unrest, political conflict, epidemic pollution, and personal confusion. Gradually, these clouds parted, as they always do. When I could see more clearly what I needed to do, how I could live and serve in a more holistic way, I began to move toward a lifetime of environmental action.

I hope the story of my eco-spiritual odyssey will inspire you to work on saving the earth, while listening closely to your own heart, growing in your capacity to offer love and service to all. I hope you liked this story. Over many years and through many personal trials, I worked in causes like environmental protection, renewable energy, and green building.

Change does happen, but sometimes it takes a lot longer than we expect. Along the way, we have to guard against backsliding. So, my first lesson is this: Ask for everything you need—no, ask for what you know you should get, but always ask for *more* (because the climate emergency is so all-encompassing.) Be prepared to stay on top of politicians, government agencies, corporations, and others who will promise anything to get you off their backs, then proceed to ignore their commitments, as they surely will.

When students created the first Earth Day in the spring of 1970, we wanted to change people's minds and their hearts. Earth Day was the biggest mass demonstration in American history. More than 2,000 colleges and 10,000 secondary schools participated in celebrations and teach-ins; twenty million people attended, nearly ten percent of the U.S. population.

While we demonstrated for a clean environment in the early 70s, millions of others engaged in an inner search they called "consciousness-raising." This movement touched something deeper. During the next few years, I investigated it, but held back, fearing too much change. After some time, I had the astonishing good fortune to meet a celebrated Indian spiritual Master, Baba Muktananda.

One experience made me into a real environmentalist, not just a smooth talker. During a meditation retreat with Baba, I walked out into a redwood forest in northern California, relishing the aftermath of an ecstatic meditation experience, feeling the same vibrant consciousness in the forest as within myself. The world outside sparkled with freshness. I saw everything—every rock, every tree—as alive with conscious energy. I connected with the essence of the forest around me, sensing I was one with all creation, one with a redwood tree in front of me, which I wrapped my arms around. Tree-hugging didn't fit into my self-image as a political activist or my intellectual commitment to environmental protection, but there it was: an experience I couldn't deny.

Through Baba's teachings, I learned a new way to look at environmental activism, my second big life lesson. I could do this work, but I could view it differently: as selfless service to humanity and the planet, offered from a place of love and respect. I found this approach profoundly uplifting.

The most effective political movements of the 20th century came from this same place of nonviolence and love, exemplified by leaders such as Mahatma Gandhi in India, the Reverend Martin Luther King Jr., in the United States, and Nelson Mandela in South Africa. They moved mountains and overcame opponents through the power of love, offering selfless service, guided by a fierce determination to make a better world. You can cultivate these same qualities, if you have the courage and wisdom to make them yours.

Here's my advice: take the time to work on yourself. Do the inner work along with the outer work. We all have a spiritual nature. At first, I had no clue how to access it, how to make it work as part of my larger social concerns. You're going to need all the strength you can muster to fight against climate breakdown.

There are many ways to do this. Take time to be in nature. Right now, I live in southern California two miles from the Pacific Ocean. A short trip to the beach or a longer trip to the mountains for "forest bathing" provides a tonic for anyone.

There's a third lesson I'd like to share. Over time, the first environmental movement made a place for everyone; not only activists and politicians, but also scientists and engineers, poets and philosophers. Some people function well as activists, but most don't. We all can show up to demonstrate, but there's also a role for highly educated scientists and engineers in designing new technologies, for businesspeople in figuring out how to deploy solutions such as carbon capture and storage, for writers and artists in opening people's hearts to the importance of climate action. To grow this movement, make a place for everyone!

I hope you'll take this advice into your work, tackling this massive challenge threatening everyone, especially the poorest among us. I know the earth and life itself will bless you for doing this work.

Your friend and best well-wisher,
Jerry

ACKNOWLEDGEMENTS

With supreme gratitude, I want to thank my wife Jessica for multiple reviews of the manuscript, recollections of events we shared, numerous helpful comments, and *many* pointed questions. I thank writing coaches Margaret Bendet and Gali Kronenberg for their helpful comments on early drafts.

Thanks also to my peers and colleagues, Victoria Betancourt, Robert Cassidy, Nathan Good, Gene Hakanson, Guenter Hauber-Davidson, Renie Kelly, Kelsey Mullen, Wayne Parker, Sonja Persram, Devin Saylor, and David Schaller, who reviewed various stages of the manuscript and offered friendly, concise, and insightful feedback.

I owe special thanks to my high-school friend, Bill Gibson, for sharing his recollections about life in Van Nuys in the 1950s and early 1960s, and to my Earth Day partner at Caltech, Paul Wegener, for generously sharing his recollections of that seminal event.

Thanks to my agent, Maryann Karinch of The Rudy Agency, who saw the potential in this book and encouraged me every step of the way. Thanks also to Nancy Cleary at Wyatt-MacKenzie, who responded so favorably to the book proposal that I *had* to give it to her for publication, confident she'd meet the desired release date: Earth Day 2020.

ENDNOTES

EPIGRAPH

Javier Marías, *Thus Bad Begins*, translated by Margaret Jull Costa, New York: Vintage International, 2016, p. 442.

CHAPTER 1 – THE ODYSSEY BEGINS

Page 8 Philip Roth, video interview, https://www.nytimes.com/video/obituaries/100000000708582/the-last-word-philip-roth.html, accessed May 23, 2018, at 0:57.

Page 9 Julian Barnes, *The Noise of Time*, New York: Knopf, 2016, p. 135.
"What could be put up against the noise of time? Only that music which is inside us—the music of our being—which is transformed by some into real music. Which, over the decades, if it is strong and true and pure enough to drown out the noise of time, is transformed [as art] into the whisper of history."

Page 9 Carlo Rovelli, *The Order of Time*, New York: Riverhead Books, 2018, pp. 97-98.

CHAPTER 2 – EARTH DAY

Page 16 For growth of the San Fernando Valley suburb of Los Angeles: https://publicpolicy.pepperdine.edu/davenport-institute/content/reports/changing-face.pdf.

For role of restrictive covenants in causing housing discrimination: https://www.kcet.org/shows/city-rising/how-prop-14-shaped-californias-racial-covenants.

Page 29 Patrick J. Buchanan, "With Nixon in '68," *Wall Street Journal*, April 7-8, 2018, p. C1.

Page 42 Paul Wegener, "Caltech's Ecoweek," *Engineering & Science*, May 1970, p. 21.

Page 43 Adam Rome, *The Genius of Earth Day: How a 1970 Teach-In Unexpectedly Made the First Green Generation*, New York: Hill and Wang, 2013, p. 273.

Page 45 Amor Towles, *Rules of Civility*, New York: Penguin, 2011, p. 324.

Page 54 Robert Bly, *The Kabir Book*, Boston: Beacon Press, 1977, p. 23.

Page 55 "This period of depression ..." I found some validation for this viewpoint from a short passage in one of Vincent van Gogh's letters to his brother Theo:

> "What molting is to birds, the time when they change their feathers, that's adversity or misfortune, hard times, for us human beings. One may remain in this period of molting, one may also come out of it renewed, but it's not to be done in public, however; it's scarcely entertaining, it's not cheerful, so it's a matter of making oneself scarce ... instead of giving way to despair, I took the way of active melancholy as long as I had strength for activity, or in other words, I preferred the melancholy that hopes and aspires and searches to the one that despairs, mournful and stagnant."

Quoted in *Brain Pickings* newsletter, https://mail.google. com/mail/u/0/?zx=gt9skf66swvt#inbox/FMfcgxwDqnkwcfkXWdNFcHFHb-GRwvMQW, accessed August 21, 2019.

Page 58 "The truth of John Muir's understanding ..." https://vault.sierraclub.org/john_muir_exhibit/writings/misquotes.aspx, accessed August 16, 2019.

Page 69 "In the early 1970s the mindset of most public officials ..." The report, "Desolation Row: The Proposed Lighthouse Point Convention Center," is available at the Santa Cruz Public Library, accessed January 19, 2019. https://catalog.santacruzpl.org/polaris/search/title.aspx?ctx=1.1033.0.0.1&pos=1

Page 69 "Within a month we gathered 4,000 signatures..." "Convention Center Stirs Debate," *Santa Cruz Sentinel*, 14 June 1972, p. 13, https://cdnc.ucr.edu/?a=d&d=SCS19720614.1.13&srpos=4&e=———-en—20—1—txt-txIN-yudelson+santa+cruz+1971———-1, accessed January 30, 2019.

CHAPTER 4 – SUN DAY

Page 114 "After considering Sim's pitch for an office devoted ..." California Congressman George E. Brown Jr. read Governor Brown's Executive Order into the *Congressional Record*. I had personally invited Congressman Brown to be the keynote speaker at Caltech on *Earth Day* in 1970, so in a way this made a connection from Earth Day to the founding of OAT.

Page 114 "In early May 1976 Governor Brown created ..." https://www.library.ca.gov/Content/pdf/GovernmentPublications/executive-order-proclamation/9714-9716.pdf, accessed 19-Jan-2019.

Page 122 "Beyond solar enthusiasts ..." The year 1974 was the historical peak of the nuclear industry's growth. Many nuclear power plants built in the 1960s and 1970s to make cheap electricity are being retired today, and very few nuclear plants have opened in the US in the last forty-five years.

Page 122 "Many activists regarded nuclear power ..." The events at Three-Mile Island in 1979, Chernobyl in 1986 and Fukushima in 2011 later gave credence to that fear.

Page 122 "Brown thought Hayden might run against him ..." As another self-proclaimed socialist, Senator Bernie Sanders, ran in the primaries to the left of Hillary Clinton in 2016, contributing to her defeat in the ensuing Presidential election.

Page 122 "For the first time, instead of putting a red light ..." I owe the "red light/green light" formulation to a 2017 article by Daniel C. Esty, "Red Lights To Green Lights: From 20th Century Environmental Regulation To 21st Century Sustainability," 2017, *Environmental Law,* 47.1, 1-80, https://law.lclark.edu/live/files/23903-47-1estypdf, accessed October 27, 2018.

Page 123 "The largest tax credit ever..." Over the next eight years, before they ended in 1985, the solar tax credits cost the Federal government more than $1 billion (1985 dollars). As public policy, it failed, as it never established an industry that could prosper after the initial incentives disappeared. http://www.nytimes.com/1985/12/30/us/solar-power-s-future-unclear-as-tax-credit-faces-end.html?pagewanted=all, accessed September 15, 2017.

Page 123 "People relate to Gaia, the earth goddess ..." Even now, forty years later, when we see the long-term potential and the absolute necessity for moving to 100% renewable energy, it's still hard to get the public emotionally excited about solar power.

Page 123 "Carter later showed his commitment to solar power ..." https://www.scientificamerican.com/article/carter-white-house-solar-panel-array/, accessed January 21, 2019. In 1986, Carter's successor, Ronald Reagan, had them removed.

Page 128 "Bottom line: homebuyers weren't demanding solar ..."

Understanding customer demand is a slippery thing, often a "chicken-and-egg" situation. Henry Ford once said, "If I had asked people at the beginning what they wanted, they'd have said, 'a faster horse.'" Residential solar PV eventually took off in California around 2010 when a few pioneering homebuilders made it standard equipment. In 2018, the California Energy Commission mandated solar for all new homes starting in 2020. This time, the homebuilding industry supported the move.

Page 128 "The plan offered a detailed program for developing ..." I recently bought a pristine copy of the *SolarCal Plan* on Amazon.com. I found it amazing that a state government report was still available after 40 years!

Page 130 "We flew to Albuquerque to attend ..." J. Douglas Balcomb, "Passive Solar in the United States, 1976-1986," https://www.nrel.gov/docs/legosti/old/3059.pdf, accessed April 22, 2019.

Page 143 "Dehlsen was a no-nonsense business owner ..." Today, Jim Dehlsen is known as *The Father of American Wind Power*.

CHAPTER 5 – A NEW LIFE

Page 152 *Carmel Postcard* (poem). I first read this phrase in the poems of Howard McCord in the early 1970s. It stuck with me for its description of the inner journey, venturing along the shore of the ocean of consciousness, probing our deepest self as far as we dare and coming back to our everyday world with an expanded awareness.

Page 175 "The novelist Javier Marías wrote ..." Javier Marías, *Thus Bad Begins*, p. 172.

Page 188 "I learned, as William Blake wrote ..." https://www.poetryfoundation.org/poems/43650/auguries-of-innocence.

CHAPTER 6 – POLITICS

Page 197 "I had to learn new skills: fundraising, speaking ..."
A phrase first popularized by President Theodore Roosevelt
in 1910, http://www.theodore-roosevelt.com /trsor-
bonnespeech.html, accessed August 2, 2018.

Page 201 "One day I went to the Democratic Congressional
Campaign Committee ..." Rahm Emanuel has had a long career
in politics, serving as a Congressman from Illinois, as President
Obama's first chief of staff and as Chicago's Mayor from 2011
to 2019.

Page 204 "The Dalai Lama once wrote ..." http://highexist-
ence.com/rules-for-living/, accessed October 2, 2017.

CHAPTER 7 – GREEN BUILDING

Page 218 "After struggling for the first five years ..." David
Gottfried and Paul Hawken, *Greed to Green: The Transformation of
an Industry and a Life*, San Francisco: Worldbuild Publishing, 2004.

Page 219 "The number of projects registering their intention ..."
Yudelson, Jerry, *Marketing Green Building Services*, New York: Rout-
ledge, 2007, p. 32. LEED stands for Leadership in Energy and
Environmental Design and is the USGBC's "eco-label."

Page 229 "In six years, the LEED faculty trained ..." Yudelson,
ibid., p. 29.

Page 231 "through keeping direct sunlight out of the building ..."
https://www.portlandoregon.gov/bps/article/437418, accessed
June 24, 2018.

Page 236 "Noted real estate expert Charles Lockwood wrote ..."
Charles Lockwood, "Building the Green Way," *Harvard Business
Journal*, June 2006, https://hbr.org/2006/06/building-the-green-
way, accessed February 1, 2018.

Page 237 "Minister Qiu Baoxing had PhDs in both economics …" The last U.S. president with a technical background was Jimmy Carter with an engineering degree from the U.S. Naval Academy. Before that, Herbert Hoover, elected in 1928, had a career as a mining engineer.

Page 255 "Most visitors worried they wouldn't get home …" Eventually airlines canceled flights for 10 million European travelers.

Page 255 "In my opening keynote …" The entire talk is viewable on YouTube: https://www.youtube.com/watch?v=4136oX0QaV0&t=28s.

CHAPTER 8 – THE ROAD TO ENLIGHTENMENT
Page 265 "The contemporary Polish poet …' Adam Zagajewski, *Slight Exaggeration*, translated by Clare Cavanaugh, New York: Farrar, Straus and Giroux, 2017, p. 205.

Page 271 "Olson's celebrated 1950 essay …" https://www.poetry-foundation.org/articles/69406/projective-verse, accessed September 30, 2017.

Page 271 "Olson maintained that the breath …" William V. Spanos, "Charles Olson and Negative Capability: A Phenomenological Interpretation," *Contemporary Literature*, Winter 1980, page 70, www.jstor.org/stable/1207863, accessed January 17, 2018.

CHAPTER 9 – THE GODFATHER OF GREEN
Page 284 "Baba once wrote, 'If we do not use …'" *Darshan* magazine, (South Fallsburg, NY: SYDA Foundation), 1991, *87*, p. 36, "In the Company of the Guru."

Page 285 "My work such as it is, is nearly done …" See Gary Snyder, "Waiting for a Ride," 2001, https://www.poetryfoundation.org/poems/47752/waiting-for-a-ride, accessed April 14, 2018.

Page 286 "Gurumayi once recorded a qawwali ..." *Jangal, Jangal Phir Divane*, Recording and translation by Gurumayi Chidvilasananda, South Fallsburg, NY: SYDA Foundation, 2002.

CHAPTER 10 – EPILOGUE – CLIMATE CRISIS

Page 289 "... while ignoring climate change, the greatest abuser..." Amitav Ghosh, *The Great Derangement: Climate Change and The Unthinkable*, Chicago: The University of Chicago Press, 2016, p. 127.

ABOUT THE AUTHOR

Known worldwide as "The Godfather of Green," Jerry Yudelson is the author of 12 previous business and professional books on green building, sustainable development, water conservation, green homes, building performance, and green marketing. For the past 20 years, Jerry has been a key player in the U.S. and global green building movements, training thousands of professionals and keynoting events in more than 20 countries. Jerry has been a student of Siddha Yoga meditation since 1974; he lives in Southern California with his wife and Scottish terrier.

@jerryyudelson   Jerry_Yudelson   jerry.yudelson

www.jerryyudelson.net